THE EARLY ABBASID CALIPHATE

The Early Abbasid Caliphate

A POLITICAL HISTORY

HUGH KENNEDY

CROOM HELM LONDON

BARNES & NOBLE BOOKS
TOTOWA, NEW JERSEY

© 1981 Hugh Kennedy
Croom Helm Ltd, 2-10 St John's Road, London SW11

British Library Cataloguing in Publication Data

Kennedy, Hugh
   The early Abbasid caliphate.
   1. Abbasids
   2. Islamic Empire — Politics and government
   I. Title
   909'.09'767101   DS38.6
ISBN 0-7099-0092-9

First published in the USA 1981 by
BARNES & NOBLE BOOKS
81 ADAMS DRIVE
TOTOWA, NEW JERSEY, 07512

ISBN 0-389-20018-2

Reproduced from copy supplied
printed and bound in Great Britain
by Billing and Sons Limited
Guildford, London, Oxford, Worcester

CONTENTS

To my parents
In love and gratitude

ACKNOWLEDGEMENTS

I would like to take this opportunity to express my gratitude to a number of people who have helped in the preparation of this work and without whom it would never have been completed. I would like to acknowledge my debt to my teachers at Cambridge, especially Martin Hinds, M.A. Shaban, Malcolm Lyons and Jean Scammell; many of their ideas and approaches may be found in the present work but it goes without saying that all the errors are my own. I also owe a great debt to the Department of Mediaeval History in the University of St Andrews. Few, if any, other history departments in the country have been prepared to appoint a specialist Islamic historian and I must express my gratitude to colleagues who have been prepared to tolerate such eccentricity. I would also like to take this opportunity to thank my friend Salah al-Haideri and all his family in Basra and Irbil for making it possible for me to visit the homeland of the Abbasid Caliphs and welcoming me so warmly into their homes.

I must also thank the Arts and Divinity Research Fund of the University of St Andrews for financial aid to cover the expenses of preparing the typescript. I am most grateful to Professor Holt and the School of Oriental and African Studies, in London, for offering me academic hospitality during the summer of 1979 and to Mr and Mrs Kenneth Wybar for making my stay in London possible. I would also like to say 'thank you' to Mrs Annabel Egremont and Mrs Dorothy Patrick for the care and trouble they took over typing a complex manuscript. My thanks must also be extended to Mr Peter Sowden of Croom Helm for his help in publishing this work. Richard Kimber of the Department of Arabic in the University of St Andrews has read the typescript and I am most grateful to him for many valuable suggestions. I owe a special debt of gratitude to Helen and Robert Irwin, not only for reading and commenting on the manuscript, but also for encouragement and hospitality over many years. Finally I must thank my wife, Hilary, for so much love and moral support throughout.

A NOTE ON REFERENCES

In the notes at the end of each chapter, works are referred to by the author's name and short title. The full references can be found under the author's name in the bibliography on pages 224-30.

ABBREVIATIONS

The following abbreviations are used in the notes:

EI (1)   is *Encyclopaedia of Islam* (Old Edition)
EI (2)   is *Encyclopaedia of Islam* (New Edition)
RSO   is *Rivista degli Studi Orientali*
RANL   is *Rendiconti dell Accademia Nazionale dei Lincei, Classe di Scienze Morali, Storiche e Filologiche*

A NOTE ON DIACRITICALS

Diacriticals are not used in the main body of the text but are given in full in the bibliography and index.

GLOSSARY OF ARABIC TERMS

Technical terms have been kept to a minimum but the use of some Arabic words for which there is no English equivalent, has been inevitable. The most common of these, with approximate definitions, are listed below.

abna'	soldiers of Khurasani origin settled in Baghdad
aman	safe-conduct or pardon
badu	Arab nomad, beduin
barid	official post and information service
da'wa	religio-political propaganda organisation
dinar	standard gold coin
dirham	standard silver coin. The exchange rate varied but in the Abbasid period there were between ten and twenty *dirham*s to the *dinar*
diwan	list of those entitled to government salaries
dehqan	eastern Iranian prince or noble
farsakh	Iranian distance measurement of approximately six kilometres
ghuta	irrigated gardens and orchards around Damascus
hajib	chamberlain
hajj	the annual Muslim pilgrimage to Makka
jund	soldiers
khutba	address given in the mosque at Friday prayer in which the ruler's name is mentioned
katib pl.*kuttab*	secretary or administrator
mawla pl.*mawali*	(usually) freed slave employed in government service
qadi	Muslim judge
qanat	underground water channel in Iran
sahib al-haras	commander of the Caliph's guard
sahib al-shurta	chief of police
sa'ifa	annual summer raid against the Byzantine Empire
sharif pl.*ashraf*	noble, rich man
suq	market
wazir pl.*wuzara'*	vizier, chief minister

Table I: The Abbasid Caliphs

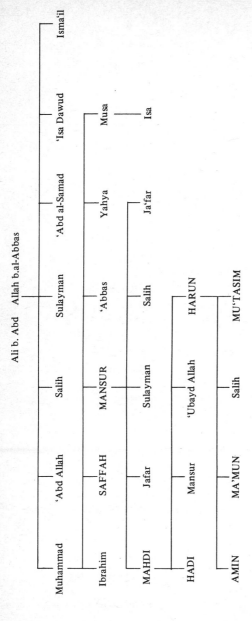

Names in capital letters are those of reigning caliphs.

Table II: The Main Branches of the House of 'Ali

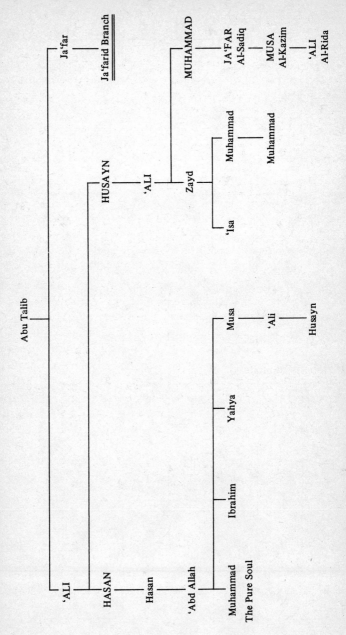

Names in capitals are those members of the family who came to be considered as *imams* by the main body of 'Twelver' Shi'is.

The Western Caliphate

The Eastern Caliphate

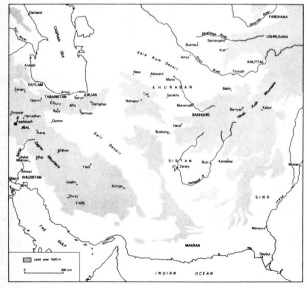

Central Iraq in the Early Abbasid Period

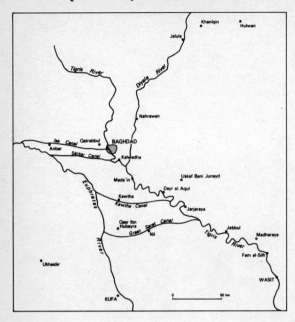

Baghdad in the Early Abbasid Period

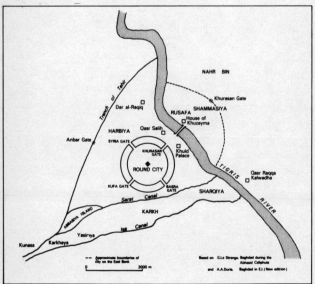

INTRODUCTION

> The career of the revolutionary leader is fantastic and unreal if told
> without some indication of the composition of the faction he led, of
> the personality, actions and influence of the principal among his
> partisans. In all ages, whatever the form and name of government, be
> it monarchy, republic or democracy, an oligarchy lurks behind the
> facade.
>
> Sir Ronald Syme, *The Roman Revolution* (Oxford, 1952), p. 7

The subject of this book is the political history of the early Abbasid
caliphate. Political history can be defined, for the purposes of this
study, as the way in which the leading groups and individuals in the state
related to each other and determined their status. To understand these
processes fully, it is necessary to go beyond the narrow confines of the
ruling élite to examine why such figures were powerful and what
support they could command. Different societies develop different
ways of expressing these rivalries and deciding their outcome. In modern
western European democracies, for example, the main political processes
are the election and the industrial dispute, and it is around these that
the different parties take up positions and try to demonstrate their
strength. In the early Abbasid period, political differences were worked
out in succession disputes and provincial rebellions.

Neither of these processes was as simple as it might appear at first
sight. There was no clearly accepted formula for determining the
succession in the Abbasid caliphate; the rights of the dynasty were
challenged by a succession of Alid pretenders, while there were intense
rivalries within the ruling house itself. During the reign of a caliph, two
or three of his sons or other relatives would emerge as possible successors.
Each of these would attract a party within the governing class who
would link their fortunes to his and try to secure the throne for their
candidate. When the reigning caliph died, or soon after, there would be
a trial of strength between the parties concerned and the party which
proved the strongest and most forceful could expect to enjoy the
favour of the caliph they had helped to put on the throne. The succession
dispute was much more than a rivalry between two brothers or a family
quarrel; it was the way in which the composition and character of the
government was decided: the main disputes, Mansur against 'Abd Allah
b. 'Ali, Mahdi against 'Isa b.Musa, Harun against Hadi and Ma'mun

15

against Amin were the decisive turning points in the history of the state.

The provincial rebellion is a characteristic feature of the period. It was the mechanism by which those who were outside the ruling class and who felt they had no spokesman or representative in that class expressed their discontent. Sometimes, like Sunbadh's rebellion in Iran, or the Khariji revolts in Ifriqiya, these movements adopted a rival ideology; in other cases, like the Coptic revolts in Egypt, they seem to be the product of inarticulate despair. As with the succession dispute, first impressions can be misleading. The Arab sources maintain the fiction that all areas within the frontiers of the caliphate were under government control and so the attempts by people of remote and mountainous areas, Ustadhsis or Babak, for example, to resist the incursions of the Arabs and preserve their traditional independence, are treated as rebellions. Paradoxically, such disturbances are not necessarily a sign of government weakness; they may mean that the government is extending its authority over areas it has not ruled before. Frequently, too, such rebellions were ended as much by compromise as by repression and what appears in the chronicles as an Abbasid 'victory' may simply be the establishment of a new *modus vivendi* between government and the local population.

The 'early Abbasid' period discussed in this book extends from the Abbasid Revolution to the restoration of Ma'mun's authority, after the end of the great civil war. Dividing history into periods is rarely a very satisfying exercise, but the Abbasid Revolution marked a real break with the Umayyad past and both contemporaries and later writers saw it as a new beginning. A suitable terminal date is less obvious; the state which emerged after the revolution effectively destroyed itself in the civil war, and the reign of Ma'mun which followed was a period of transition, out of which a new order, based on Mu'tasim's new army and his new capital at Samarra, was to emerge. It is, therefore, at the reign of Ma'mun that this survey will end.

The period of the early Abbasid caliphs was of great significance for the history of Islamic society. The caliphs ruled a vast area and their government had an impact on the subsequent history of all the areas between Tunisia and Turkestan. The eighty years covered by this work were also formative in the development of Muslim culture. The four great doctors of Islamic law, Abu Hanifa, Malik b.Anas, Shafi'i and Ahmad b.Hanbal, all practised during this time and it seems that it was in the years after the revolution that Ja'far al-Sadiq and his circle elaborated the doctrine of the imamate which has been the basis of Shi'i religious thought ever since. It was a time, too, when the history of the early Muslim community was described in detail in the works of Ibn Ishaq, Ibn Saʿd, Abu Mikhnaf, Madaʾini and others and the period saw the beginnings of the translation of Greek philosophy, medicine and science into Arabic. Imaginative prose in Arabic was developed at the hands of Ibn al-Muqaffaʿ and Jahiz, while the poets of the period, like Abuʾl-ʿAtahiya and Abu Nuwas, are still enjoyed today.

But early Abbasid history is more than just the backdrop to an age of cultural efflorescence. For the student of politics and political science it is fascinating to see how so many diverse peoples and countries were brought under the control of a single régime. The early Abbasid system also represented a sustained attempt to reconcile the ideals of Islam with the demands and constraints of secular government. The problems faced by the early Abbasid caliphs in this respect are very similar to those faced by some Islamic governments today.

This book does not pretend to be a general history of the period. Much basic research remains to be done and many problems remain to be solved before it will be possible to produce a 'standard work'. The purpose of this work is twofold; to introduce the period to the student, both historian and Arabist, and to suggest some new problems and approaches to the expert. No doubt both these groups will find much to criticise and disagree with, but I hope they may also derive some interest or enjoyment from this account.

Hugh Kennedy
St Andrews

1   THE GEOGRAPHICAL BACKGROUND

The early Abbasid caliphs ruled a vast area;[1] 6,500 kilometres as the crow flies, from their eastern frontier on the banks of the Indus to the western borders in Tunisia, and 3,000 from the Yamani capital at San'a' to the capital of Arab Armenia at Bardha'a, near the Caucasus. This area was marked, then as now, by great contrasts of climate, physical geography and population. The usual image of the Middle East is of an area of hot, sandy deserts and palm-fringed oases and such places do exist. But there are also fertile river valleys, grain-growing prairies, upland meadows and the mountains on which the snow never melts. There were areas of dense population and teeming urban life but these were often separated by vast areas of sparsely inhabited desert or difficult mountain passes. This geographical pattern had a profound affect on the workings of government and political life. It was very difficult for the caliphs to exercise real authority over the deserts and mountains, where population was too scattered and communications too difficult to allow their representatives to control the situation. The picture was further complicated by the fact that Arab settlement and the spread of Islam was very uneven. There were areas like Iraq, Syria and parts of Khurasan, which had been heavily settled, others like Egypt and most of western Iran, where the Arabs and Muslims were still a small ruling élite, and others still, like Armenia, Tabaristan and much of Transoxania, where local leaders continued to exercise their traditional powers, paying little more than nominal allegiance to the caliphs. This government was very patchy; the densely populated areas of large towns and settled agriculture were the centres of Abbasid power; the limits of the caliphate were the foothills of the mountains and the last villages before the desert began.

Iraq was the centre of the caliphate and, even before Baghdad was founded, it was the Sawad which provided much of the wealth on which Abbasid power was based.[2] The Sawad, or Black Land, was the name given to the vast area of irrigated land, stretching south from Baghdad to the sea, which is watered by the Tigris and Euphrates and their tributaries and canals. Here the wealth came from the harvests of wheat, barley, dates and other fruits which could be produced in

18

abundance by the warm climate and careful husbandry. The key to this prosperity lay in the irrigation system. This was based on canals radiating from the rivers. It is one of the fortunate peculiarities of the area that the Euphrates is a few metres higher than the Tigris at an equivalent point. This meant that canals could be led from one river to the other, distributing water to the fields which bordered them. The waters of the two great rivers are heavy with silt, which, as the current becomes slower towards the sea, settles on the bed of the stream, so that, in time, the river or canal becomes higher than the surrounding countryside. In many ways this is beneficial; it means that no pumps are needed to bring the water from canal to field, since it can be done by gravity. But, at the same time, this can be a menace; if the banks are not properly maintained or the spring floods too violent, then the banks will burst, causing widespread inundations. The system is not a static one which can be left to look after itself. It changes constantly; canals become silted up and new ones have to be built to replace them and, if water is left to evaporate in pools beside the watercourses, it will leave deposits of salt which will, in time, render the land infertile. The irrigation of the land needs constant, dedicated labour. In turn, this needs organisation and security. From the kings of Sumer and Akkad on, rulers of the area co-ordinated the efforts of their subjects to develop and maintain this system. Insecurity was fatal, since the system needed long-term planning and investment; if the government were in chaos or the landowner felt no long-term commitment to the land, then decay would inevitably set in. It did not need a Mongol invasion to destroy the prosperity of the area; lack of active maintenance and repair would do that just as effectively.

Umayyad and early Abbasid rulers continued the traditions of their great predecessors in this endeavour. Members of both ruling houses and their favoured subjects spent large sums in restoring and extending canal systems and bringing land into cultivation.[3] It was expensive, but it was a worthwhile investment and could bring vast profits to their fortunate owners. The period of the civil war after the death of Harun, on the other hand, must have been one of destruction and decay and it is possible that it saw the beginning of the decline of the prosperity of the area, which is so marked in the succeeding centuries. The decline of the agricultural system also meant the decline of the caliphate based on its resources.

At the time of the Abbasid Revolution, the Sawad supported three major cities. The most important of these was Basra. The wealth of the city was derived as much from commerce with the Gulf regions and

Sind as from the agricultural hinterland. Though founded as an Arab garrison town, it had rapidly acquired an economic *raison d'être,* in addition to its military role, and had taken over the commerce of previous ports on the site.[4] The position of the second great city, Kufa, was less healthy. This had been founded on the western border of the cultivated area and, while communications with the Arabian peninsula were of prime importance, its position was a good one. However, the site had none of the commercial possibilities of Basra. Such evidence as there is suggests that it was much the less prosperous of the two in the years following the revolution, a fact which may account for the constant discontent in the city, and the foundation of Baghdad as an alternative centre in the area effectively sealed its fate. The third city, Wasit, had been founded as a Syrian garrison town to control Iraq. Naturally, it lost this role after the revolution but it still remained a town of some size.

On its western borders, the Sawad is met immediately by the desert; the trees stop and the sand and stones of the wilderness begin abruptly. In the east, however, the land rises slowly to the foothills of the Zagros and, in two areas, the mountains give rise to rivers which irrigate fertile plains. In the south is Khuzistan, the ancient kingdom of Elam. Here the warm winter climate and the water from the mountains mean that intensive agriculture has always been possible. In early Islamic times, the area was also famous for its textiles. The largest city and political capital was at Suq al-Ahwaz, usually known simply as Ahwaz. Arab settlement seems to have been limited in this area and, despite its evident prosperity, its people played little part in political events.

The other fringe area was the Diyala valley. Here, again, a river from the mountains provides irrigation for the plains between the Tigris and the beginning of the hills. From earliest times, the Diyala valley was an outpost of Mesopotamian civilisation, and in early Abbasid times this importance was increased by its position on the all-important main road from Baghdad to Khurasan. The area was too close to Baghdad to develop a major urban centre of its own; the towns of the district, Nahrawan, on the great canal of that name, and Hulwan, in a strategic position at the entrance to the first of the Zagros passes, were never more than local market centres and there was no provincial capital.

The traveller going north or west from Baghdad had two choices of route. He could either go due north along the Tigris or in a more westerly direction by the banks of the Euphrates. Whichever way he chose, he would soon notice a change in landscape and patterns of settlement. The flatness and fertility of the Sawad and its criss-cross of water courses are replaced by a barren, stony area where the desert approaches the river banks. Here the settlements were small and sparse (at least before the foundation of Samarra) and the irrigated land beside the rivers too small to support a large community. Yet, further up the Tigris, the traveller would find the land changing again. The barren, rocky hills would be replaced by rolling, soil-covered plains. If he were lucky enough to be travelling in spring he would find the land covered with grass, flowers and the green shoots of the crops (much less advanced than in the Sawad) and he would see in the distance the gleam of the snow on the mountains of Kurdistan. He would probably be heading for Mosul, the largest city of the area. Mosul was a comparatively new town but, as Baghdad was the successor to Babylon and Cteisphon, so Mosul was the successor of Nineveh and Nimrud. Before the coming of Islam, there had been a small settlement here but, after the Muslim conquest, when Jazira ceased to be a frontier area and became instead a great grain-producing district, the fortunes of Mosul improved dramatically and it replaced Irbil and Nisibin as the main centre. The city was a centre of Arab settlement and both a market town for the agricultural area which surrounded it and a trading city with connections in many parts of the Islamic world.

The agriculture in the plains of Assyria around Mosul was quite different from that of the Sawad,[5] as it was largely dry farming, relying on rainfall rather than irrigation for the water supply. This meant that the land was less intensively farmed and less potentially wealthy but the system was more resilient. The highly developed agriculture of the Sawad needed constant maintenance and investment, the rainfall agriculture of the plains of Mosul, Jazira and northern Syria did not and, as a consequence, was less vulnerable to political disturbances and upset. Not all the farming here was grain-growing; there were fruit trees in favoured irrigated areas or near banks of rivers, like the Zab, and there was sheep-raising on the fringes of the desert and the foothills of the mountains. It was a country of small villages, many of them Christian, and monastic life was still thriving, especially in the mountains of the Tur Abdin, which bordered the plains to the north. There were also Arabs leading a nomadic or semi-nomadic life, who often preferred living as Kharijite brigands, existing off protection money paid by the villages and small towns of the plains, to paying taxes and accepting the authority of the government.

The traveller leaving Mosul for the northeast soon found himself in a very different landscape. The open plains of Assyria are replaced by forbidding mountains, communications are difficult and the settlements often very isolated in remote upland valleys. This was the homeland of the Kurds[6] and, although we hear very little of them in the early Abbasid period, we can be certain that they were, then as now, determined to retain their traditional customs and independence and there is no record of the Abbasids attempting to exercise real control over the area.

Northwest from Mosul, the traveller could follow the course of the Tigris, by Balad and Nisibin, to Amid (Diyarbakr). From Amid he could reach the remote Muslim outposts on the Armenian frontier, Shimshat, Akhlat and Qaliqala (Erzerum). Despite Arab forays, however, these uplands were essentially under the control of the Armenian princes, with whom the Arab governors had to establish a working relationship if they were to be successful. The country was comparatively poor and remote, the mountains bleak and the climate very severe. In the whole area, from Lake Van north to the Black Sea, there was scarcely an Arab settlement.

There was a choice of route for the traveller setting out from Baghdad to Syria. The most direct was the Euphrates road through Anbar and Hit to Raqqa but, probably because supplies were easier, the longer route through Mosul and across the plains of the northern Jazira was often preferred, especially by armies. Whichever way he chose, he was likely to pass through Raqqa, on the Euphrates, an important political and military centre under the early Abbasids as well as an *entrepôt* for the grain of Jazira. From Raqqa west by Balis, the Euphrates valley was more fertile and the road led from the westernmost point on the river to Manbij and Aleppo. There was another important route from Raqqa, the one taken by troops heading for the Byzantine frontier, which led north, through Saruj, Harran or Ruha (Urfa, Edessa) to the strategic crossing place on the Euphrates, at Sumaysat (Samosata). From here, the main frontier outposts of Malatya, Hadath and Mar'ash were easily accessible.

Aleppo was the cross-roads for northern Syria in the way that Mosul was for northern Iraq. This had not always been so. In the Umayyad period, the main centre in the area was at the old Roman city of Chalcis, now called Qinnasrin, but, in the early Abbasid period, this was gradually superseded. Like Mosul, the town was surrounded by rich agricultural land with enough rainfall to make it good grain-growing country and the area was famous, then as now, for its pistachio nuts. From Aleppo, a road led west to Antioch, a town much reduced in size and importance since its days of glory under the Roman Empire. Continuing northwest, over the Amanus mountains, the traveller would reach the hot coastal plain of Cilicia. Protected by the Taurus from northerly winds and watered by the twin Sayhan and Jayhan rivers, this area had been fertile and well-populated under the Byzantines, but it was now frontier territory and remained a no-man's-land through most of the Umayyad period. The early Abbasids began a policy of advancing settlement and Muslim garrison towns were established at Massissa, Adhana and Tarsus. North of Tarsus lay the narrow defile of the Cilician Gates, one of the main crossing points into Byzantine territory.

Syria and Palestine is an area of widely differing landscapes and patterns of settlement, lacking the geographical unity of Egypt or the Sawad. The fertile plains around Ramla, the hills of Jerusalem and Tiberias, the rugged and impenetrable mountains of the Lebanon and the steppe-lands of the Syrian desert were all inhabited by different communities with different customs, and the spread of Islam had been very uneven.

The complex physical geography and differing climatic zones meant that there was very little unity between the different cities and provinces of Syria and Palestine. The cities of the coast had declined rapidly in importance since classical times. We hear little of Beirut, Tyre, Sidon or Caesarea; Mediterranean commerce was negligible and the sea was the scene of constant struggles between Arab and Byzantine. Without commerce to bring prosperity, such towns had only a limited role as centres for naval activity. Inland, however, the situation was different. The largest and most prosperous cities of the area, in the early Abbasid period, lay along the fringes of the desert. Going south from Aleppo, the traveller would cross fertile country, dotted with villages and small towns, until he reached the Orontes at Hama. Here he could turn off east to Salamiya, favoured and developed by the Syrian branch of the Abbasid family, or he could go on south to Hims, one of the most important cities of the area. Nothing has survived of early mediaeval Hims, but frequent mention in chronicles makes it clear that it was a busy and often turbulent centre, its citizens often opposed to the Abbasid regime. South from Hims, the road skirted the edge of the desert to reach Damascus. Like all the most successful cities of the area, Damascus was both a commercial centre and the capital of a fertile agricultural district. The waters of the Barada emerging from the anti-Lebanon mountains are meticulously divided, first among the quarters of the city, then among the gardens and orchards of the *ghuta,* stretching away to the east. In Damascus, much of the old city remains and we can still feel the contrast which would be apparent to the early Abbasid traveller, between the noisy heat and animation of the *suq*s and the magnificent tranquillity and spaciousness of the Umayyad mosque in their midst. But Damascus in this period was in eclipse politically and we hear more about the men of Hims than we do of its citizens. Of the mountainous areas of the Lebanon the sources tell us next to nothing. We can only presume that the local Christian inhabitants kept themselves to themselves in their mountain villages and had little contact with the outside world. The modern area of Palestine and Jordan was divided into two provinces. Urdunn, or Jordan, to the north, was based on Tiberias and stretched from Acre, on the sea coast, to Jarash, on the east bank of the river. Further south was the province of Palestine, with its capital at the Umayyad foundation of Ramla but also including the city of Jerusalem. Jerusalem was of little importance as a political centre but, as ever, of great significance in religious terms. Like the Umayyads before them, the Abbasids embellished the monuments of the city, especially Mahdi, who began the building of the Aqsa mosque. Despite this attention, however, Palestine seems to have suffered more than any other area from the transference of the capital to Iraq. The Umayyads had built extensively in the area but the Abbasids did not. We hear little about it in the chronicles and the archaeological evidence suggests that villages and towns were abandoned during this period.[7] Northern Syria, on the contrary, seems to have maintained its population and prosperity much better; it was from the north that the Abbasids recruited their Syrian followers and in the north that the Syrian branch of the ruling dynasty established itself. It is worth remembering, as well, that, although Syria was valuable for its manpower and of great strategic importance, it was comparatively poor. Tax yields from the province were much smaller than from Egypt or Iraq. In historical terms, Umayyad rule from Syria was something of an aberration; in the ultimate analysis, the country was not populous enough, united enough or wealthy enough to sustain a vast empire. Under the Abbasids, it became again a valuable and important province of a larger state.

To the south of Palestine stretched the deserts of Sinai, and travellers seem to have kept to the coast road, going by Gaza and 'Arish until they reached Farama, the most easterly of the cities of the Nile Delta. Throughout history, the population of Egypt has been dependent on the river for its livelihood and the Arab conquest had little effect on the basic facts of Egyptian existence. The agricultural system of the country remained largely unaltered. Like the Sawad, this was irrigation, not rainfall, agriculture but here the irrigation was mostly natural. The annual flooding of the cultivated areas by the rising waters of the Nile was not so dependent on human effort as the elaborate canal systems of the Sawad, and was correspondingly less likely to be damaged by war and maladministration. The agricultural wealth of the country, along with the thriving textile industry of the Delta, meant that Egypt was, after the Sawad, the largest contributor to the budget of the caliphate. But this financial importance was not reflected in its political status.

Arab settlement here had been small and was mostly confined to the cities of Fustat and Alexandria, and, like other areas where Arab settlement was slight (Fars and Isfahan for example), Egypt remained politically fairly unimportant. The caliphs seem to have left the running of the country in the hands of local Arab families and were only seriously concerned when tax yields began to fall. The most important change which followed the arrival of the Arabs was the transfer of the capital from the coastal city of Alexandria to the inland site of Fustat, at the head of the Delta, and, throughout the early Islamic period, Fustat remained the centre of government and of political life. The decline of Alexandria mirrored the decline of the coastal cities of the eastern Mediterranean; the sea was now a war zone, not a way for commerce, and the grain exports of Egypt, which had fed the imperial capital of Constantinople, were now diverted to the newly important cities of the Hijaz. Abbasid authority stretched as far south as Aswan, on the borders of Nubia. The vast majority of the people remained Coptic Christians and, apart from the influence exerted from time to time by their patriarch, still resident in Alexandria, they played little part in political life.

The most westerly province of the Abbasid caliphate was Ifriqiya, which comprised modern Tunisia and parts of eastern Algeria. There were three distinct geographical zones in the country: the coastal plain and the low hills which border it to the east, well cultivated and populous in classical and early Islamic times; then the mountains, the Aurès to the east and the Jabal Nafusa to the south of Tripoli, which were strongholds of Berber tribes; finally, to the south, there was the desert. Before the Arab conquest, the area had been ,ruled by the Byzantines from their capital at Carthage. In addition to the Byzantine ruling class, which seems to have disappeared with the arrival of the Arabs, the country was inhabited by people known as the Ufariqa, who seem to have been the Romanised natives of the coastal plain and who remained numerous, especially in the south around Gabès on the coast.[8] These played little part in the political life of the period and seem to have been content to accept Arab rule. The Berbers were quite a different proposition. They inhabited the remoter areas, both the mountains and the fringes of the deserts, in a bewildering number of tribes and tribal groups. While they had no towns and the tribe, rather than the principality or the province, was the usual political unit, they resisted Arab rule with fierce determination. As elsewhere around the Mediterranean, the arrival of the Arabs meant that the centres of urban life moved from the coast inland. Qayrawan, in the central plain, replaced Carthage as the capital. In the north, Tunis, more protected from sea-borne raids, was founded and Carthage abandoned. In the southeast of the province, Tripoli remained an important centre. To the west of Ifriqiya proper lay the province known as the Zab. Here the rivers which rise in the Aurès mountains are used to create a series of oases on the fringes of the desert. In the early Abbasid period, this was a somewhat isolated outpost of Arab rule, often threatened by the neighbouring Berbers, but the capital Tubna (about forty miles northeast of modern Biskra) was a strong and well-fortified city, which usually managed to hold out. Further to the west, lay areas over which the Abbasids never exercised control: the Kharijite principalities of Tahert and Tlemcen, the trading city of Sijilmassa, in southern Morocco, and Fes, which became the centre of the first independent Alid state during this period.

If a traveller from Baghdad decided to visit the eastern half of the empire, he would take the Khurasan road, the most important highway in the Abbasid State, from the city, through the fertile lands of the Diyala basin to the foothills of the mountain range often known as the Zagros, but called by the Arabs simply 'Al-Jibal' (the mountains). The Zagros is not a single range but rather a whole series of parallel ranges, separated by enclosed and often fertile plains. The Khurasan road ascends from Hulwan, the strategically placed town at the foot of the mountains, through a series of passes. Some of these, like the defile above Hulwan, are steep and narrow and the road reaches its summit at the pass of Asadabadh, 2,000 metres high and frequently closed by snow in the winter. The intervening plains supported small towns and villages, of which the now vanished city of Dinawar, slightly to the north of the main road, was the most important. South of the road lay Nihavand, where the Arabs had inflicted a crushing defeat on the Sassanians, and, to the east of that, towards Isfahan, was Karaj, centre of the *ighar* or tax-free area of the Arab leader, Abu Dulaf al-'Ijli, and his followers. The only alternative to this long and mountainous road between Iraq and Iran is further to the south, where it is possible to ascend from Ahwaz, through Arrajan to Shiraz, but this was too out of the way to be of great significance.

Having surmounted the last great obstacle at Asadabadh, our traveller would now find himself on the Iranian plateau. The word 'plateau' should not be taken to mean that the land was either flat or uniform. The centre is taken up with the Great Salt Desert, which divides east from west and renders the middle of the country uninhabitable. Round the fringes of this desert are found the cultivated areas and the great cities. The first of these to greet the traveller would be Hamadhan. Early Islamic Hamadhan has disappeared as completely as the Ecbatana of the Achaemenids which preceded it, but we know that it was a town of some size, an important stage on the road and a centre for the largely Kurdish peoples of the surrounding mountain areas. Like most of the towns of western Iran, it was, as far as we can tell, largely unaffected by Arab settlement and its people play only a passive role in the politics of the period.

At Hamadhan the road divided. The south-bound traveller would soon leave the comparatively cool and well-watered mountain areas and skirt along the western fringes of the great desert. Here, there were still mountains but they were dry and waterless, divided by hot, arid plains, and settlement was confined to oases. Often these were artificial, with the great underground water channels, the *qanat*s, leading water from the foot of the mountains far out into the plains to water small, miraculously green gardens, enclosed and protected by mud-brick walls. The greatest of these oases was, like Damascus, formed by a river, running from the rain-gathering western mountains. The Zayandarud created Isfahan in the same way as the Barada created the Syrian capital. Though all the great monuments for which Isfahan is now famous date from after this period, there is no doubt that the city was an important provincial centre in the period.

From Isfahan the traveller south would pass on the fringes of the desert to Fars. In the early Abbasid period, he would first have reached the city of Istakhr, entirely deserted today but the centre of the area in pre-Islamic times. Perhaps because it was a centre of Iranian and Zoroastrian custom, the Arabs chose a new capital at Shiraz and the foundations of the existing old mosque in the city date from the period when it was the provincial capital of Fars under the caliphs. The plains of Fars were better watered than the arid lands bordering on the great desert and, apart from the Iranian inhabitants, this was a centre of the Kurds in early Islamic times. Despite the mosque in Shiraz, there is no evidence that here, among the Achaemenid ruins of Persepolis and the abandoned palaces of the Sassanian rulers, Islam had made any great progress, and Arab settlement was, again, very slight. The modern traveller can go on from Shiraz to the coasts of the Gulf and the

Indian ocean but neither of these routes was much used before the emergence of Siraf as a great port during the period from the fourth (tenth) century.

If he wished to go further east, the modern traveller could go from Isfahan or Shiraz to Yazd, long a stronghold of Zoroastrian beliefs. Further south and east the road leads through many miles of desolate desert country to the oasis of Kirman. Here the sources are disappointingly silent on the place's history. We know that Kirman was a separate province but we are rarely told who governed it or what problems they faced. From Kirman it was possible to travel on, through Bam, Jiruft and Makran, to Sind but historical evidence suggests that people preferred to go by ship from Basra, rather than endure the long overland journey.

If the traveller from Hamadhan had decided to take a more northerly route he would have passed through less barren and difficult country. The main road led towards the foot of the mountains of Tabaristan. Here, rainfall on the hills provided water to irrigate a whole series of settlements. The traveller could turn to the northwest and travel up through Qazvin, a city fortified and garrisoned to contain the incursions of the wild men of Daylam to the north, and then to Zanjan and Azerbayjan. Here were high plains and steppe-lands, more suitable for grazing than for crops, which is why the Mongol Il-Khans favoured the area, five hundred years later. Throughout the early Abbasid period, Arabs, mostly from the Mosul area, continued to move in and settle the area, attracted, at least in part, by its mineral wealth. As always, they favoured the plains and they developed cities at Ardabil, Tabriz, Marand and Maragha.[9] The high mountain areas of Azerbayjan were virtually unaffected by the Arab conquest until the great Muslim campaign against the so-called 'rebellion' of Babak in the reigns of Ma'mun and Mu'tasim, when the armies of the caliph made a real attempt to subdue the people of the hills.

North from Azerbayjan, the traveller would reach the fertile plains of the Araxes River, the centre of the Muslim province of Armenia. The provincial capital was normally at Bardha'a and the authority of the governor reached to Tiflis, Darband and Dabil (Dvin). To the north and west lay the independent principalities of Georgia and Armenia while, beyond the Caucasus mountains, the Khazars, a people of Turkish origin, roamed the steppes of southern Russia and made occasional raids into Muslim areas.

If he were heading for Khurasan, however, the traveller would skirt the northern fringe of the great desert and there, at a crucial position between the mountains to the north and the desert to the south, he would reach the ancient city of Rayy. Despite its strategic position, Rayy does not seem to have attracted much Muslim settlement until the period when Mahdi was working as his father's deputy in the east. He made Rayy his capital and began a large-scale development, which made the town into an important centre.[10] Rayy was the gateway to Khurasan but it was also, with Qazvin, a point of access to the mountainous country which lies to the north. Even in a land of violent contrasts, there can be few more dramatic than that experienced by the traveller who goes from Rayy to the Caspian. Almost as soon as he leaves the city, the road begins to climb and soon the torrid plain is replaced by high mountains, a land of open grassy valleys and rushing streams. As he reaches the summit of the pass, perhaps by the great snow-capped cone of Mount Damavand, he begins to descend through a landscape of increasingly luxuriant forest until, when he reaches the hot, humid plains by the Caspian, the climate and vegetation are almost tropical.

As might be expected, the mountains were the strongholds of traditional culture and society and the most famous of the local princes, the *ispahbadh*s of Tabaristan, consciously maintained the old Iranian traditions. On the plains by the Caspian, on the other hand, there was some Muslim settlement, especially at the towns of Sariya and Amul (the birthplace of the historian Tabari). At this time, these Muslim settlements were always in some danger from attack by the peoples of the hills. Further west, along the coast, in the small district of Ruyan and Daylam, Muslim influence and Abbasid government were almost non-existent.

East of Rayy, the traveller skirts the southern fringes of the mountains, where there were a series of communities strung out along the road and drawing their water from *qanat*s from the mountains, notably Semnan and Damghan (which preserves the only surviving early Abbasid mosque in Iran). After many days' journey he finally reaches the great city of Nishapur, the cross-roads of Khurasan and one of the great cities of the province. Nishapur was a large but fairly compact city, dependent like the others on *qanat*s from the neighbouring hills[11] and it became a major political centre after the civil war, when the Tahirids transferred the capital of Khurasan from Marw. From Nishapur, our traveller could take the northerly route to Jurjan. The mountains, so high and forbidding further west, have now become wooded hills which gradually level out towards the north. This was the edge of the Islamic world. To the north stretched the vast, flat plains which border the eastern margin of the Caspian sea. It was possible for merchants to reach the Khazar capital at Khamlij from here, and it was to Jurjan that the Rus merchants brought their furs and swords, after the long journey down the Volga and across the sea. Thence, they took them by camel to Baghdad and the great markets of the East. But the frontier situation often brought danger as well as profit, for the steppe-lands were the home of nomadic Turks, who would seize any opportunity to pillage the settled communities.

East of Nishapur, the traveller would approach Eastern Khurasan and Transoxania, the cradle of the Abbasid movement.[12] Since Sassanian times, the oasis city of Marw had been the centre of government for this area. The geography of the area is very complex and is treated in more detail in a latter chapter, but it can best be understood as a series of river basins, somewhat similar to the *ghuta* of Damascus or the oasis of Isfahan, separated by high mountains or vast tracts of waterless desert. As elsewhere in the Islamic world, it was the cities Marw, Bukhara, Harat, Balkh and Samarqand and their surrounding areas which were the centres of government, while the peoples of the mountains and deserts retained their old customs and were only gradually incorporated into the Islamic world.

South of Khurasan lay Sistan, a typical central Asian oasis settlement. This fertile area was watered by the rivers Farah and Helmand, bringing water from the mountains of central Afghanistan. Zaranj was the capital but Abbasid authority rarely extended far beyond the city and its immediate surroundings, the rest being in the hands of Kharijites and brigands of both Iranian and Arab extraction. Further east, along the Helmand river, was Bust, which seems to have been the most easterly point of Arab settlement and an area where the governors made sporadic attempts to assert their authority. Beyond that lay Kandahar, which recent excavations show to have been a thriving Buddhist centre at this time, and distant Kabul, over which ambitious governors of Khurasan sometimes claimed to exercise sovereignty.

The southeastern extremity of the caliphate was the province of Sind.[13] The sources for the history and geography of this area, in the early Islamic period, are very scanty indeed; we have the names of many of the governors but very little information as to whom they ruled and the extent of their authority. It seems that the area should really be regarded as a series of trading outposts. Sometimes the Arabs were able to demand tribute from the local people, at others they were virtually confined within their city walls. The port of Daybul, on the south coast, seems to have been the earliest Arab centre and some 4,000 Arabs were settled there. In late Umayyad times, a new capital was founded on the Indus at Mansura, and the Arabs sometimes controlled the city of Multan as well. But there is no record of any Arab settlement outside the towns and no mention of any large-scale immigration. The colony was an important stopping place on the way to Ceylon and China and it is interesting that the great Muhallabi family of Basra, with its close links with the trading community, took a keen interest in the area from the time of the conquest.

It is, perhaps, one of history's ironies that the Arabian peninsula was one of the first areas to escape from the rule of the caliphs, but it should not surprise us; before the advent of the aeroplane and the motorcar there was no effective way in which governments could contain or control the movements of nomads over the vast spaces of Arabia. As always, Abbasid control centred on the towns. Makka and Madina were under the control of the government, except during times of Alid rebellion. Makka, in its narrow rocky valleys, was never an important centre of government, and Madina, a much more open oasis city, was the administrative centre. The city was something of a pleasure and retirement resort. It was famous as a centre for musicians and singers and social life was dominated by the descendants of the early heroes of Islam, who lived in dignified but powerless obscurity, far from the centres of political life. The Abbasids also appointed governors of San'a', in the Yaman, but it is difficult to know whether they exercised any authority beyond the walls of their city. On the Gulf coast, the situation was much the same. There was a governor of Yamama, a country of small villages without any real urban centre, but, beyond that, Abbasid power seems to have been non-existent. The government was little concerned with the interior, except in so far as it was important to safeguard the pilgrimage route. Here the water supply seems to have been more of a problem than the *badu*, to judge from contemporary accounts, and a whole string of cisterns, some of them still extant, were built to help the pilgrim from Iraq. Apart from that, the nomads of central Arabia went about their own business, occasionally providing refuge for a rebel but rarely interfering in the life of the settled communities.

In the far south, 'Uman was effectively independent under its Ibadi rulers. The Abbasids launched occasional punitive expeditions, but made no real attempt to exert their authority, and the Hadramawt and most of rural Yaman were unvisited by government agents. This did not necessarily reflect the weakness of the caliphate: the vast expense and difficulty in mounting military operations in these areas far outweighed any possible benefits in terms of increased taxation. As long as they did not challenge essential Abbasid interests, like the organisation of the *hajj,* it was much more sensible to allow these people to manage their own affairs.

Such diversity of country and enormous distances meant that communications were always a problem and journeys from one part of the caliphate to another could take weeks and even months. This was a particular problem for the caliphs, since decisions about provincial affairs could easily be out of date by the time they were made and revolts could gather momentum before the caliph could take action. To deal with this problem, rulers from the time of 'Abd al-Malik had made use of the *barid,* or official information service. The officers of the *barid,* who were usually *mawali,* were stationed in each province and were required to send detailed reports to the caliph. Under Mansur, according to one, probably exaggerated, source, the agent of the *barid* was required to write twice a day on affairs in his province. The decisions of the governor and the *qadi* were recorded and special attention was paid to the price of basic commodities, presumably so that action could be taken to avoid large increases and the consequent unrest.[14] The *barid* was thus crucially important for decision making. When Ma'mun cut off contact with the *barid* in Khurasan from his brother Amin, at the beginning of the civil war, it left the latter at a great disadvantage.[15] Correspondingly, when Tahir failed to mention the caliph's name in the *khutba* in 207 (822), this was swiftly reported to Baghdad by the *sahib al-barid* and the rebellion, if such it was, was nipped in the bud.[16]

The *barid* maintained a series of post stations on the main roads, where official messengers could pick up new mounts, and these are listed by some of the early geographers. According to Ibn Khurdadhbih,[17] there were twenty-two stages from Baghdad to Aleppo, twenty-eight from Baghdad to Damascus and forty-seven from Baghdad to Fustat. From Fustat to Qayrawan was another fifty-eight. Going east from the capital, there were nineteen stages to Hamadhan, thirty-two to Rayy and sixty-six to Marw. The stages were usually between four and six *farsakh*s (24 to 36 kilometres) and this probably represented a day's journey for ordinary travellers (a camel can be expected to travel between 24 and 32 kilometres per day).[18] Government messengers, able to get fresh horses and working in relays, could carry messages much faster. When Mansur died in 158 (775), near Makka, the news reached Baghdad, a distance of about 1,500 kilometres, in ten days; that is, an average speed of about 150 kilometres per day.[19] In 169 (785), Mahdi died near Baghdad, while his son and heir Hadi was campaigning in Jurjan. Hadi immediately returned to Baghdad, using the *barid* with a small entourage. The journey, again about 1,500 kilometres, took him twenty days.[20] When Harun died, in 193 (809), the *sahib al-barid,* who was with the court, sent a message to his subordinate in Baghdad, who then told Amin that he was now caliph. This was probably done by relays of messengers, but at the same time Raja' al-Khadim was sent with the news from Tus to Baghdad and took only eleven or twelve days for a journey of 1,900 kilometres, which, again, gives 150 or more kilometres per day.[21] Even higher speeds were recorded; the news of Tahir's victory at Rayy, in 195 (811), took just three days to reach Marw, some 1,150 kilometres away.[22] This gives an astonishing 400 kilometres per day, but even this very high speed is not without parallel. The Mamluk sultan, Baybars, is recorded to have ridden the 800 kilometres from Cairo to Damascus in only three days, while a week was the usual time taken by the Mamluk *barid,* again giving us about 120 kilometres per day.[23] Impressive though these figures are, they still mean that fifteen days was the effective minimum period for a letter from Baghdad to the Khurasani capital at Marw and, no doubt, there were frequent delays, due to adverse weather conditions and general inefficiency; when Ma'mun announced the appointment of 'Ali al-Rida as his heir, in 201 (817), it took no less than three months for the news to travel from Marw to Baghdad.[24] Distance was a major obstacle to the unity and government of the empire. One can only wonder that the problems it caused were so successfully overcome.

Notes

1. This description is based on the accounts of the early Arab geographers, on modern descriptions and on the author's own travel notes. For the geographers, see Miquel, *Geographie Humaine* (Paris, 1967), *Djughrafiya* in EI (2); G. Le Strange, *Palestine under the Moslems* (London, 1890) and *Lands of the Eastern Caliphate* (Cambridge, 1930). See also X.de Planhol, *Les Fondaments Geographiques de l'Histoire de l'Islam* (Paris, 1968) and articles on all the major cities and provinces in EI (both editions).

2. For the Sawad, see R.McC. Adams, *The Land Behind Baghdad* (Chicago, 1965) and D. Waines, 'The Internal Crisis of the Abbasids' in *Journal of the Economic and Social History of the Orient,* vol. 20 (1977).

3. Qudamah, *Kharaj* p. 241; E. Ashtor, *Social and Economic History of the Near East* (London, 1976), pp. 46-7.

4. C. Pellat, *Le Milieu Basrien et la Formation de Djahiz* (Paris, 1953), pp. 46-7.

5. For useful comments on the historical geography of this area, see D. Oates, *Studies in the Ancient History of Northern Iraq* (Oxford, 1968), pp. 1-18.

6. For the Kurds in this period, see Kurds in EI (1) and I.C. Vanly, 'Le Déplacement du Pays Kurde vers l'Ouest' in RSO, vol. 50 (1976).

7. Ashtor, *Near East,* pp. 52-8.

8. Ibn Khurdadhbih, *Masalik,* p. 86; Ya'qubi, *Buldan* p. 350.

9. Ya'qubi, *Ta'rikh*, vol. 2, p. 446.

10. Baladhuri, *Futuh*, p. 392.

11. R. Bulliet, *The Patricians of Nishapur* (Cambridge, Mass., 1972), pp. 3-19.

12. For the historical geography of this area, see V. Barthold, *Turkestan down to the Mongol Invasion* (London, 1928), pp. 64-179.

13. For Sind, see Y. Friedmann, 'A Contribution to the Early History of Islam in India' in *Studies in Memory of Gaston Wiet*, ed. M. Rosen-Ayalon (Jerusalem, 1977).

14. Tabari, *Ta'rikh*, vol. 3, p. 435.

15. See below, p. 137.

16. Tabari, *Ta'rikh*, vol. 3, p. 1065.

17. Ibn Khurdadhbih, *Masalik*, pp. 18-87.

18. R. Bulliet, *The Camel and the Wheel* (Cambridge, Mass., 1975), p. 24.

19. Tabari, *Ta'rikh*, vol. 3, pp. 389, 456.

20. Ibid., vol. 3, pp. 547-8.

21. Ibid., vol. 3, p. 764.

22. Ibid., vol. 3, p. 802.

23. J. Sauvaget, *La Poste aux Chevaux dans l'Empire des Mamelouks* (Paris, 1941), pp. 35-6.

24. See below, pp. 157-9.

2 THE ORIGINS OF THE ABBASID REVOLUTION

The Abbasid came to power as the result of a revolution. It was no *coup d'état* or palace intrigue but a massive social and political upheaval whose objectives went beyond the setting up of a new dynasty to the reforming and purifying of society according to the laws of Islam. The new order was formed by this revolution and by the attempts of the caliphs to harness and organise it to found a stable and lasting state. To understand the Abbasids, it is necessary first to have some idea of the forces which brought them to power.

Early Islam had suggested a society where the old distinctions based on tribal status and wealth would disappear and be replaced by one where the leadership would be chosen from among those who had joined the movement early and shown themselves to be good Muslims. Religious excellence was to be more important than secular power. But the old structure of tribal loyalties and tribal chiefs would not simply wither and die; men and families who had been powerful before the coming of Islam clung on obstinately to their old status, even though their conversion had been late and half-hearted. There were figures like Ash'ath b.Qays al-Kindi, last of the pre-Islamic kings of Kinda, who remained a major power in Iraq, despite the fact that he had joined the *ridda,* or apostasy, after the Prophet's death. Even more offensive to many believers was the position acquired by the Umayyad family. Abu Sufyan, father of the first of the Umayyad caliphs, had been the leader of the Makkan opponents of the Prophet, yet his son, himself a late convert, had challenged the Prophet's cousin and son-in-law, 'Ali, and siezed the caliphate for himself.

Not only did the old leadership remain powerful but the conquests produced a new élite from those who had made fortunes out of the expansion of the Muslim empire. In theory, the conquered lands were to be used to provide an income for all the Muslims but, in fact, much of the land found its way into private hands, and men like 'Abd al-Rahman b.'Awf, an early convert and associate of Muhammad, made themselves enormously wealthy. For the poor Arab and the non-Arab convert, the ideal of a community based on Islam, justice and the equality of all believers was a very long way off.

Discontent appeared in many quarters but, above all, in Iraq. Large numbers of Arabs had moved from Arabia to settle in this fertile country, especially in the great garrison towns of Basra and Kufa, and many of them felt that they had been deprived of their rightful shares in the fruits of conquest. They had come in several waves, before and after the *ridda* wars. The early arrivals saw the latecomers as a challenge to their position, while the latter resented the former's privileged status. Vast numbers of men, cut off from their traditional environments, settling in large, newly erected cities and subsisting off government handouts, was not a recipe for a peaceful and contented society.

In Umayyad times, the non-Arabs of Iraq began to convert to Islam in large numbers. These non-Arabs, usually known as *mawali,* found themselves denied the privileges of their Arab co-religionists. Muslims paid lower rates of tax than unbelievers but the government could not afford to grant all these fiscal advantages to new converts. Though many non-Arabs became Muslim, the ruling élite remained almost entirely Arab and very few others were fortunate enough to be enrolled in the *diwan* and hence to receive salaries.

Both these groups were united in Iraq by a feeling of resentment against Syrian rule. Under Mu'awiya, this had not been so oppressive but, with the centralisation of power under 'Abd al-Malik, it became more irksome. Wasit was founded as a base for Syrian troops to keep order in Iraq, the cities were governed by outsiders appointed from Damascus and the local people were no longer masters in their own country.

Iraq was not the only province of the Muslim empire where discontent was widespread. In an effort to reduce over-crowding and political disaffection, large numbers of Iraqi Arabs had been sent to help the conquest of distant Khurasan, and many of them settled. This meant that Khurasan, unlike western Iran or Egypt, had a large Arab population and this accounts in considerable measure for its political importance. The conquest of Khurasan, too, was different from that of western Iran. In the west, the Sassanian state had been a centralised monarchy and with its collapse and the defeat of its armies there was no one to continue resistance. Cities like Isfahan or Hamadhan seem to have had large but mostly passive populations. In the east this was not so. The authority of Sassanian monarchs had been much less effective here. Marw was the eastern outpost of their rule and beyond that there were a whole variety of small principalities. Many of these had rulers of Iranian stock but they did not accept Sassanian rule. It was these princes whom the Arabs met when they had defeated all the

Sassanian armies. Rather than conquer each of these highly independent and often very inaccessible areas, the Arabs made treaties with the existing rulers, which guaranteed them independence and control of their own affairs in exchange for the payment of tribute. This tax was to be collected by the rulers and no effort was to be made to convert their subjects to Islam or to undermine their authority. The Arabs settled in the cities of the plains, especially Marw and Balkh, but also in little towns like Abiward and Nasa, spread out along the edge of the Turkmen steppes. As long as the Arabs remained as garrison troops, living off the taxes of the area, all was well. The problems began when they tried to leave their settlements and become farmers or traders outside. For then they came under the authority of the non-Arab, non-Muslim local rulers and it was to them that they had to pay their taxes.[1]

There were other reasons, too, for the Arabs to feel discontented. They came from Iraq but most of the governors appointed by the Umayyads in far-off Damascus were Syrians and it was easy to feel, with some justice, that the Umayyad governors and the local rulers were acting in concert to deprive the local Arabs of their rights. Then there was the issue of taxation; should the taxes raised in the province be spent there or sent to the central treasury in Damascus? Needless to say, the local Arabs, faced with the difficult problems of frontier life, felt that the money should be spent in the province.

Nor were the Arabs the only discontented groups in the area. As in Iraq, many local people had become Muslims. How far these were genuine conversions and how far people seeking the advantages of joining the ruling group is, of course, impossible to say but, like the *mawali* of Iraq, they found that conversion did not mean that they were relieved of the tax burden they had borne before. In addition, they were still subject to the authority of the local rulers. So, in both Iraq and in Khurasan, there was a large disaffected population, both Arab and non-Arab. Paradoxically, in areas like Egypt and western Iran, where Arab settlement was much smaller and conversion rates seem to have been lower, there was much less trouble.

It was natural that these discontented elements should look for an alternative leadership to replace the Umayyads, who had so signally failed to translate Islamic ideals into reality. The Prophet himself had left no son who might be considered as heir, nor had he left any generally accepted testimony as to who should succeed him as leader of the community. Two questions faced the Muslims in Madina when he died. How should the leader be chosen, and what powers should he have? During the next century, two separate sets of answers emerged to these questions.

The first point of view looked to Arab tribal customs for a precedent and held that the leader should be elected from among the members of the Prophet's tribes, the Quraysh. He would be chosen for his piety but also for his ability to handle the secular affairs of the community. Since he was chosen by men, his authority, like that of the tribal chief, would be limited. Such a ruler could not claim to interpret or modify the Qur'an or the Sunna or to provide religious leadership. This point of view tended to be held by those who were satisfied with the *status quo* and saw no need for radical reform.

The second idea was that authority should be vested in the Prophet's family, *al-Muhammad* or *ahl al-bayt*. Perhaps borrowing ideas from the pre-Islamic kingship of South Arabia, supporters of this argument held that God had chosen this family and man should not interfere in the Divine will. This meant that the ruler's authority would be absolute. Since he was appointed by God, to disobey him would be a form of blasphemy. Correspondingly, this authority was not merely secular and administrative; the leader of the community was to be an *imam* who, because of the powers God had invested in his family, could interpret or supplement Qur'an and Sunna. Naturally, this argument appealed to those who were dissatisfied with the existing order and felt that divine guidance was necessary to establish a truly Islamic society.

The ideal of rule by a member of the family of the Prophet raised a number of other questions. Those which especially concerned early thinkers were: who exactly constituted the family of the Prophet, was it simply direct descendants or a more general and extended family; how should the leader be chosen from among the possible candidates? It was these questions which led to the appearance of different groups among those who supported the claims of the *ahl al-bayt*.[2]

When it came to choosing the *imam*, three distinct theories emerged. The most obvious was that leadership should be hereditary in one particular branch of the family, a point of view which gained currency in the early Abbasid period and provided the ideological basis for the claims of the *imam*s of the family of Husayn b.'Ali, who are generally recognised by the 'twelver' Shi'is today. Secondly, and linked to it, is the idea that that leadership can be transmitted by *nass* – that is, by the designation of the previous leader. If *nass* is given priority, then it would be possible for the imamate to be transmitted to someone other than the son of the previous *imam*, an important point in the Abbasid claim to power. The third view was that leadership should belong to whichever member of the family proved willing and capable of undertaking it. In the circumstances of the Umayyad caliphate, this meant that any member of the family who was prepared to risk leading a revolt against the authorities was thereby worthy to be considered as leader. This last attitude was taken by Zaid b.'Ali, in his unsuccessful revolt of 122 (740), and was thereafter associated with the Zaydiya group. These various ideas had important consequences. If leadership was hereditary, then it was granted by God and could not be challenged by man, whereas the Zaydi version meant the selection of the most efficient and dynamic member of the family, thus placing more emphasis on competence in secular affairs.

These differences in point of view might have remained purely academic if they had not corresponded to divisions within the nascent Muslim community. In Madina, at the time of the death of the Prophet, there were two groups which might reasonably claim a share in the leadership. First, there were the *Muhajirun*, the Makkan emigrants who had come to Madina with the Prophet. Then there were the *ansar*, or native Madinan helpers of the Prophet. The former were determined to keep power in their own ranks, while the latter, because they were not Quraysh, did not feel that they could aspire to the leadership themselves. Instead, they turned to the Prophet's son-in-law and cousin, 'Ali b.Abi Talib. In effect, 'Umar b.al-Khattab and Abu Bakr carried the day by prompt action, but both 'Ali and the *ansar* were left feeling that they had been deprived of their rightful position.[3] In these circumstances, the two rival views about the leadership of the community were developed.

The sanctity of the Prophet's family became more apparent with the arrival of the Umayyads. The Umayyads were disliked for many reasons but the opposition crystallised around the idea that they were unfit to rule because they were not of the family. This view was reinforced by the massacre of Husayn b.'Ali at Karbala in 61 (680), when the favourite grandson of the Prophet was brutally done to death by those who claimed to rule the Muslim community. From the death of Husayn, if not before, many of those who were discontented with the Umayyad regime looked to the family of the Prophet to bring justice and true religion to the community.

Various attempts were made to bring members of the family to power during Umayyad times. In 64 (684), Mukhtar b.Abi 'Ubayd led a rising in Iraq in the name of Muhammad b.al-Hanafiya,[4] which was to have a lasting effect on the development of these opposition movements. Ibn al-Hanafiya was the son of 'Ali, but not by Fatima, the Prophet's daughter. Hence, he was a member of the family but not a direct descendant. It is not clear that Muhammad himself believed in his claim to the leadership but it did represent a widening of the numbers of those who could consider themselves as being of the *al Muhammad*. Ibn al-Hanafiya was described not only as *imam* but also as *mahdi* or messiah. Neither 'Ali nor his sons had been so designated and the term implied something much more activist than the word *imam*; the *mahdi* was going to transform society and bring in the millenium. It was an idea with powerful appeal to the less well-off and established elements in Kufa. In particular, this applied to the *mawali,* the non-Arab converts who were still very much second-class citizens, and the rebellion of Muhktar was the first occasion in Islamic history that such people had become involved with the politics of the *umma* on a significant scale. Among Mukhtar and his followers a variety of beliefs were elaborated, beliefs which came to be looked on with some scepticism by outsiders.

These beliefs included the idea that the *imam* was semi-divine and acquired his powers, not just by heredity or *nass,* but by metempsychosis; that there was a 'soul of prophecy' which had originated with Adam and had passed to Muhammad and then to 'Ali and the *imam*s who succeeded him. This semi-divine *imam* had the task of interpreting the provisions of Qur'an and Sunna and could reveal to his followers the real, hidden meaning *(batin)* of the scriptures, which lay behind the superficial and obvious *zahir,* with which most Muslims were content. These beliefs attracted considerable support in Iraq. To the orthodox they were known as *ghulat* (extremists) or by a variety of sectarian names (Kaysaniya, Saba'iya etc.) and they were regarded with great suspicion. The political collapse of Mukhtar's rebellion did not spell the end of this tradition, however, and the ideas continued to be current in Iraq and, later, in Khurasan.

The next attempt to install a member of the family as ruler had a rather different ideology. In 122 (740), Zayd b.'Ali, a great-grandson of 'Ali and Fatima, rebelled against the Umayyads in Kufa. He claimed the right to lead, not on strictly hereditary grounds, nor yet by *nass,* but simply because he was the boldest and most active member of the family. He was prepared to take the risk and rebel so all those who believed in the rights of the Prophet's family should follow him.[5] Finally, in 127 (744), 'Abd Allah b.Mu'awiya led a rebellion in Iraq and eastern Iran which played an important part in weakening the Umayyads. He was not even a descendant of 'Ali but of his brother Ja'far, but he still attracted a widespread following, especially among the *ghulat.* In later Shi'ite writing, it was made clear who the true *imam*s were at each stage but, in practice, the end of the Umayyad period showed considerable divergence of opinion about which members of the family could claim the right to lead. Set against the idea that there was a line of *imam*s descended from Husayn b.'Ali were the ideas of Zayd, that activism was the best claim to authority, and the ideas of Mukhtar and 'Abd Allah b.Mu'awiya, that direct descent from the Prophet was not essential. Both these ideas were to prove useful to the Abbasids.

The Abbasid claims to rule the Muslim world were based on several different ideas and changed as the movement evolved. The early members of the family do not seem to have been greatly concerned to press their political ambitions. 'Abd Allah b.al-'Abbas had been content to support the rights of 'Ali. After his death, in 68 (687/8), the family retired from Madina to an estate they had at Humayma, now in southern Jordan. Although remote from both Damascus and Iraq, it was conveniently close to the pilgrim routes for maintaining contact with potential supporters and it was here that the Abbasids began to mature their political designs. Muhammad b.al-Hanafiya had died in 81 (700/1) and bequeathed his claims to his son Abu Hashim. Abu Hashim seems to have made little attempt to establish himself as leader but he had inherited a considerable following among the *ghulat*. He died childless in 98 (717/8) and a number of aspirants, including 'Abd Allah b.Mu'awiya, tried to claim his inheritance. Among these claimants was Muhammad b.'Ali, the Abbasid. It was said that Abu Hashim died at Humayma and had designated Muhammad as his heir. Thus Muhammad could claim to be leader of the family by *nass*. Not only did the Abbasids thus inherit a claim, they also inherited a radical ideology whose beliefs included a semi-divine *imam* and a commitment to the equality of all believers, Arab and *mawali* alike. It is not clear how far the *ghulat* who had followed Abu Hashim accepted the leadership of the Abbasids at this stage, but, at least, Muhammad b.'Ali was put in touch with useful contacts in Kufa and Khurasan.[6]

Later, the Abbasids modified their position somewhat. When they were a small underground organisation, adherence to these extreme beliefs might have served to unite them but, as the movement expanded and sought to broaden its base, this narrow affiliation began to be increasingly embarrassing. The propaganda which recruited supporters for the revolutionary army was very broadly based, appealing simply for a *rida* (chosen one) from the family of the Prophet. There was no need to spell out a detailed programme of reform; if the family of Muhammad ruled, and the Qur'an was obeyed, all the other problems which beset the community and gave rise to so much discontent would naturally solve themselves. After the attainment of power, the caliphs, especially the pragmatic Mansur, felt that they had to break completely with the radical past if they were to be accepted as legitimate by the majority of the Muslims, and this led to the working out of a complementary claim. The old emphasis on the testament to Abu Hashim was replaced by an emphasis on the unity of the family. The Abbasids argued three points: that they had had the right in pre-Islamic days to give the pilgrims the waters of Zamzam, that 'Abbas was the nearest male relative of the Prophet and had looked after him as an orphan (a powerful argument in the context of Arab tribal custom) and, finally, an argument borrowed from the Zaydis; according to this, they alone of all the members of the family of the Prophet had succeeded in overthrowing the Umayyads and revenging the martyred Husayn; this activism gave them alone the right to lead. To this end, they made great use of the idea of the Hashimite family. It seems that the Abbasid movement had sometimes been called the Hashimiya, because of the connection with Abu Hashim, mentioned above, and the early Abbasid administrative centres had been called Hashimiya as a result. Later, however, the word was used to describe all the descendants of Hashim b.'Abd Manaf, grandfather of the Prophet. This included both Alids and Abbasids, but not Umayyads. So the idea of the family was extended so that the Abbasids could draw strength from it, as well.[7] Naturally, this process aroused some opposition; groups like the Rawandiya, who belonged to the extremist wing of the movement, felt betrayed by this 'sell-out' to more moderate ideas but it was necessary, if the Abbasids were ever to be generally accepted as leaders of the whole community, not just a small group.

Later historians, like Tabari, suggested that the Abbasid connection with Khurasan dated back to the death of Abu Hashim, but more recent research suggests that it was not until about 126 (743/4) that the leaders of the movement in Khurasan pledged their allegiance to the Abbasid family.[8] The *da'wa* (propaganda) in Khurasan seems to have begun in about 100 (718), when a small group in and around Marw began to put forward the claims of the family of the Prophet. This group was led by twelve *naqib*s and many of the names which appear at this time were to become famous in later Abbasid history.[9] The movement suffered numerous vicissitudes and at least one change of leadership during the next forty years. With the collapse of Zayd b.'Ali's rebellion and the execution of his brother Yahya, in Khurasan, the movement seems to have turned to the Abbasids as possible leaders of the family of the Prophet. In 125 (742/3), a leading supporter of the *al Muhammad* from Kufa, Bukayr b.Mahan, went to the province and won over the leaders of the *da'wa,* notably Sulayman b.Kathir al-Khuza'i and Qahtaba b.Shabib al-Ta'i, to the Abbasid cause. In 127 (745), Sulayman and Qahtaba came west to meet Ibrahim, who had succeeded his father as *imam* in 125 (743) on the *hajj,* bringing with them money collected from Khurasan and returning with a freedman of Ibrahim's, Abu Muslim, who was to act as co-ordinator of the movement.[10] Abu Muslim seems to have been chosen because he had no affiliation with the Arab groups in Khurasan and because his appointment would encourage the non-Arab Muslims of the province to take up the Abbasid cause.[11]

In this way, the leaders of the *da'wa* in Khurasan came to pledge their allegiance to the Abbasid *imam.* Contact was kept up by Bukayr b.Mahan and, after his death, by his successor, Abu Salama, both working in Kufa, and by Qahtaba, who came west a second time to receive instructions. But the propaganda remained unaffected. The *da'wa* called for a *rida min al Muhammad* (a chosen one from the family of Muhammad) and no mention was made of the branch of the family from which he would be chosen.

On his arrival in the east, Abu Muslim began to prepare for active revolution. Having been appointed by Ibrahim, he was dependent on him, rather than on Abu Salama or the Khurasanis, for his authority and he played a vital role, not only in ensuring that the revolution was successful, but also that it remained in the control of the Abbasid family. Khurasan proved to be a very suitable area for such activity. As explained above, it had a large and, in many ways, discontented Arab population along with a fair number of *mawali,* who might also be expected to provide recruits for the cause. Furthermore, a reasonable proportion of the Arabs had military experience. The province was far from the centres of Umayyad power, which meant that government surveillance was necessarily weaker than in other provinces. It had the additional advantage that no other revolutionary group had made it their base. In Iraq, and especially in Kufa, there was a large, discontented population but their first loyalty seems to have been to the Alid family and it was difficult to imagine that the Abbasids would find much support there. So despite the vast distances which separated the centres of Abbasid activity in Khurasan, Kufa and Humayma, it was on the northeastern fringes of the Islamic world that the revolution was born.

The civil wars and rebellions of the reign of Marwan b.Muhammad, the last Umayyad caliph, led to a breakdown of government authority in Khurasan. Various groups tried to take advantage of the inability of the governor, Nasr b.Sayyar, to keep order. At first it seemed as if newly arrived Arabs under Juday' al-Kirmani would take control but, while he was fighting Nasr for the possession of Marw, in Ramadhan 129 (May–June 747) Abu Muslim raised the black banners of the Abbasid *da'wa* in one of the villages surrounding the capital and the Revolution had begun. It may have been the broad-based nature of the Abbasid message, appealing as it did to Arab and non-Arab alike, that enabled Abu Muslim to defeat his rivals in the province. Kirmani was killed and most of his troops incorporated into the Abbasid army, while Nasr was forced to flee to the West. The Abbasids attracted support, above all, from the Arabs settled in Marw and the surrounding villages. It was they who provided the leadership of the army but they were probably joined by considerable numbers of *mawali* from the surrounding areas. The principalities on the fringes of Khurasan, on the other hand, provided few recruits and, on the whole, the *dehqan*s opposed a movement which sought to limit their authority; Khalid b.Barmak from Balkh and Muhammad b.Sul, son of the ruler of Jurjan, are the only members of the native nobility who seem to have joined.

In Jumada II, 130 (February 748), Abu Muslim established himself in Marw and Qahtaba b.Shabib, newly returned from seeing Ibrahim in the West, took command of the army. The Abbasid forces advanced westward and won a series of decisive victories over the Umayyad force in Iran. In Rajab 131 (March 749) a large army under 'Amir b.Dubara was defeated by Qahtaba at Jablaq, near Isfahan, and at the beginning of 132 (August 749) the victorious armies reached the Euphrates near Kufa.[12]

During all this turmoil in the east, Marwan had arrested Ibrahim, who died shortly afterwards in custody. Later sources assert that he passed on his rights to his brother Abu'l-'Abbas, still living with the rest of the family at Humayma. The approach of the armies from the east sparked off revolts against the Umayyads in Iraq. Sufyan b.Mu'awiya, the Muhallabi, made an unsuccessful attempt to take Basra for the Abbasids[13] while, in Kufa, there was a pro-Abbasid coup, led by Muhammad b.Khalid al-Qasri.[14]

In Muharram 132 (August 749), the Abbasid armies crossed the Euphrates after fierce fighting with the troops of the Umayyad governor, Ibn Hubayra, and went on to enter Kufa, where they were welcomed. During the battle, however, Qahtaba was killed. This put the future of the movement in doubt, for Qahtaba was the main link between the armies and the Abbasid family. With Ibrahim and Qahtaba dead, the situation was very uncertain. It was here that the head of the Kufa branch of the *da'wa* saw his opportunity to be a king-maker.

Abu'l-'Abbas and his fellow Abbasids arrived in Kufa but were advised by Abu Salama to stay concealed until things had settled down. There is no doubt that he wanted to be the one to appoint the new caliph and he began negotiations with the Alids. There had been no propaganda commitment to the Abbasids as such and there was no reason to believe that an Alid would be less acceptable to the bulk of the revolutionaries than an Abbasid, but he had reckoned without Abu Muslim. Abu Muslim had remained behind in Khurasan, but he had loyal agents in the army. He was personally connected with the Abbasids and had no wish to see Abu Salama reaping the fruits of victory. It was his agents who discovered the Abbasid family and brought them from hiding to the Great Mosque at Kufa, where Abu'l-'Abbas was proclaimed as first Abbasid caliph.[15]

Notes

1. For the details, see H.A.R. Gibb, *The Arab Conquests in Central Asia* (London, 1923); M.A. Shaban, *The Abbasid Revolution* (Cambridge, 1970); M. Sharon, 'The Abbasid Da'wa Re-examined' in *Arabic and Islamic Studies* (Bar-Ilan University), vol. 1 (1973), pp. 10-14.

2. For the best discussion of these developments, see S.H.M. Jafri, *The Early Development of Shi'a Islam* (London, 1979). See also C. van Arendonk, *Les Debuts de l'Imamat Zaidite au Yemen* (Leiden, 1960), pp. 1-44; M.G.S. Hodgson, 'How did the Early Shi'a become Sectarian?' in *Journal of the American Oriental Society*, vol. 75 (1955); W.M. Watt, 'Shi'ism under the Umayyads' in *Journal of the Royal Asiatic Society* (1960).

3. Jafri, *Shi'a Islam*, pp. 27-53.

4.For Mukhtar and his legacy, see Hodgson, *Early Shi'a*, pp. 4-8; Jafri, *Shi'a Islam*, pp. 235-42; W. Madelung, 'Kaysaniyyah' in EI (2); Watt, *Shi'ism*, pp. 162-5; J. Wellhausen, 'The Religio-Political Factions' in *Early Islam*, ed. R.C. Ostle (Oxford, 1975), pp. 125-40.

5. Van Arendonk, *Imamat Zaidite*, pp. 28-33; Jafri, *Shi'a Islam*, pp. 265-7; Watt, *Shi'ism*, pp. 169-70.

6. For Abu Hashim and his relationship with the Abbasids, see S. Moscati, 'Il Testamento di Abu Hasim' in *RSO*, vol. 27 (1952); T. Nagel, *Untersuchungen zur Entstehung des Abbasidischen Kalifates* (Bonn, 1972), pp. 63-9.

7. Jafri, *Shi'a Islam*, pp. 278-9; Nagel, *Untersuchungen*, pp. 71-87; Sharon, *Abbasid Da'wa*, pp. 6-10.

8. Sharon, 'Kahtaba b.Shabib' in EI (2).

9. *Akhbar al-'Abbas*, ed. A.A. Duri and A.J. Muttalibi (Beirut, 1971), pp. 213-20.

10. Tabari, *Ta'rikh*, vol. 2, p. 1916.

11. Shaban, *Abbasid Revolution*, pp. 153-5.

12. Ibid., pp. 159-63.

13. Baladhuri, *Ansab*, fos. 612-14.

14. Tabari, *Ta'rikh*, vol. 3, p. 18.

15. Ibid., vol. 3, pp. 27-8.

3 SAFFAH: THE LAYING OF THE FOUNDATIONS

The first of the Abbasid caliphs, Abu'l-'Abbas 'Abd Allah b. Muhammad al-Saffah, was proclaimed in the Great Mosque in Kufa, on about 14 Rabi' I, 132 (31 October 749). It was a Friday and the people, both the native Kufans and the newly arrived Khurasani soldiers, were assembled for prayers. The new caliph climbed to the top of the pulpit, accompanied by the most senior of his uncles, Dawud b. 'Ali, who stood on the step below him. He made a short speech, giving thanks to God and those who had helped the cause, before being obliged, either through illness or nervousness, to sit down. His uncle, who was famed for his eloquence, then spoke at some length, expounding the claims of the Abbasids, praising both Kufans and Khurasanis for their support and steadfast opposition to the Umayyads and promising a new era of justice and rule according to the principles of Islam. Then they retired to the palace of the governors next to the mosque, leaving the caliph's brother, Abu Ja'far, to sit and receive the oaths of allegiance from the assembled congregation. It was not until nightfall that the last of these had pledged their loyalty to the new regime.[1]

Despite the triumphant speeches, the new dynasty was far from being securely in control of the empire. The most pressing problem was the need to defeat Marwan himself. His armies had been driven from the Iranian plateau and his governor in Iraq, Yazid b. Hubayra, had shut himself up in Wasit, but the last of the Umayyads was still in control of his power base in northern Syria and the frontier areas, and could count on the allegiance of numerous experienced soldiers. When Qahtaba was leading the victorious Khurasanis down from the Iranian plateau towards Kufa, he had sent 10,000 of them to Shahrazur to discourage any attempt Marwan might make to march into Iraq and join up with Ibn Hubayra. It was a prudent move. Marwan, with a large force, left his base in Harran and came east to the Tigris to face them, while the Abbasid troops, not strong enough to risk battle, stayed some way off on the south bank of the Upper Zab. Marwan crossed the Tigris at Mosul, where he left much of his treasure, and advanced towards them. Meanwhile, both Abu Salama and Saffah had sent reinforcements for the Abbasid troops, and the new caliph also decided that the command of so important an army should be in the hands of a member of his own family; accordingly, he appointed his uncle, 'Abd Allah b.'Ali, to take over. For the first time a member of the Abbasid family had an army at his disposal and it was an important step in making the power of the new dynasty effective. 'Abd Allah does not seem to have had any previous military experience but, aided by his Khurasani advisers, he proved a determined and successful general.[2]

Even allowing for an element of exaggeration in the sources, the Abbasid troops were still heavily outnumbered; estimates vary from 10,000 to 30,000 men while the Umayyads are said to have had between 100,000 and 150,000.

On arriving at the river Zab, Marwan made a move which proved to be a major mistake; he built a bridge and transferred his army to the south bank of the river. The Abbasid commanders were worried about the morale and discipline of their own men and 'Abd Allah was advised to force a battle as soon as possible. Marwan, on the other hand, wanted to play a waiting game but one of his own commanders, anxious to distinguish himself, broke ranks and began the fighting. The battle of the Zab was fought on 11 Jumada II (26 February 750).[3] It was a very close-run thing. 'Abd Allah, worried that his men might break ranks and flee, ordered them to kneel in close formation, with their spears to protect them. These unusual tactics were effective; 'The Syrians attacked us like mountains of iron', one of the Khurasanis recalled later, 'but when we knelt down and prepared our spears, they turned from us like a cloud'.[4] The Syrians fled, and, in his anxiety to make his escape, Marwan destroyed the bridge, leaving many of his men on the other side. More Syrians died by drowning than were killed in battle.

The victory was decisive. Marwan lost his nerve; one of the sources speaks of a head wound he had received during the battle,[5] and his credibility as a military leader was destroyed. He was unpopular in the traditional centres of Umayyad power, like Damascus and Hims, and, when it became clear that he could not defeat the Khurasanis, no one was prepared to fight for him. This was immediately apparent when he reached Mosul. Here, the governor he himself had appointed ordered the city gates to be shut. Marwan and his escort were refused admission on the grounds that they were imposters, 'because', the Mosulis explained, with heavy sarcasm, 'the Commander of the Faithful would not be running away'. In the end, Marwan was forced to abandon his treasure and use the bridge at Balad, some miles to the south. The governor and his family were later rewarded by the Abbasids for their timely initiative with a number of important government posts.[6]

Marwan is said to have considered taking refuge with the Byzantines but was persuaded to try to organise resistance further west.[7] He fled through Harran (his own base), Qinnisrin and the Hims, and was everywhere greeted with indifference or hostility, while many of the Syrians, far from helping him, took the opportunity to pillage his remaining possessions. He fled with the Abbasid forces close on his heels, never able to spend more than a few days in one place before he was forced to move on. Even when he reached Damascus, the old Umayyad capital, he did not stop but left his son-in-law, Walid b.Mu'awiya, to defend the city.

Meanwhile, the Abbasid armies approaching the city had received important reinforcements. Once again, the caliph chose members of his own family, his two uncles, Salih b.'Ali and 'Abd al-Samad b.'Ali, to lead the contingent of 10,000 men who were sent on the direct desert road from Iraq. But Damascus only offered slight resistance and here, as in so much of Syria, it was the conflicts which had plagued the Umayyad regime since the death of Hisham, nine years before, that ensured the success of the Abbasids. The Yamanites, opposed to Marwan, inside the walls enabled the Abbasid forces under 'Abd Allah b.'Ali to enter the city, on 10 Ramadhan 132 (23 April 750), just three months after the defeat on the Zab.

Marwan's position was now hopeless. He was pursued through Palestine, too involved in its own feuds to offer him any assistance, to Egypt. 'Abd Allah b.'Ali remained in Syria to pacify the country and sent his brother, Salih, in pursuit. At the end of Dhu'l-Hijja 132 (early August 750) the last of the Umayyad caliphs was surprised by a small body of enemy troops at the village of Busir in the Delta. Some say he was killed in his sleep but the more general view is that he died in the short, sharp fight which followed.[8]

In Syria, 'Abd Allah conducted a ruthless campaign of extermination against members of the Umayyad family. Despite safe-conducts, many of them were massacred at a banquet given by 'Abd Allah, who calmly continued his meal surrounded by corpses. Even more macabre was the desecration of the Umayyad tombs. Hisham they found still intact and after they had given the corpse a thorough whipping, they burned it. Others were less rewarding; of Maslama, in Quinnisrin, they found the skull, which they duly burned, but of the great Mu'awiya himself only one bone was discovered and tradition does not relate what fate was reserved for it.[9]

This savage treatment of members of the previous ruling family is uncharacteristic of early Islamic history. 'Abd Allah claimed that the massacre of the Umayyads was in revenge for the death of Husayn at Karbala, a move likely to win approval, especially in Iraq. It was a sign, too, that the revolution was going to be more than just a change of caliph, but would mean the complete elimination of the Umayyads and all they stood for. It was also an attempt, at least partially successful, to prevent pro-Umayyad risings in Syria against the new regime. Finally, there were more personal reasons: the Umayyad family possessed vast estates in Syria and Palestine; on their deaths these passed not to the state treasury but to members of the Abbasid family, chief among them the conqueror of Syria, 'Abd Allah, and his brother, Salih.[10]

Pockets of resistance still remained. In Wasit, Ibn Hubayra still held out. He had played an ambiguous role in the drama. He had failed to offer Marwan any effective support, and had rejected advice to leave Iraq and join him, or to attack Kufa; some sources speak of an estrangement between him and the caliph which made him anxious about his position. He was blockaded in the city by the Khurasani army, led by Qahtaba's son, Hasan. Later, as part of his policy of giving important commands to members of his family, Saffah sent his brother, Abu Ja'far, to take control. Ibn Hubayra's purpose in continuing resistance seems to have been to obtain the best terms for himself and his men. When he heard the news of Marwan's death, he made an agreement with Abu Ja'far, who was keen to use the services of this powerful and experienced commander. However, the agreement aroused the resentment of Abu Muslim in distant Khurasan, who feared that the recruitment of large numbers of Syrians into the Abbasid army would reduce his influence in the west. Under pressure, the caliph was forced to disregard the agreement, and the unfortunate Ibn Hubayra and his family were executed.[11]

The other important centre of resistance was in the areas on the Byzantine frontier, where Marwan had first made his reputation and built up his power. The leader was Ishaq b.Muslim al-'Uqayli, who had been one of Marwan's closest advisers, and was, at the time of his defeat, governor of Armenia.[12] He came west, gathered members of the defeated Umayyad armies to him and, with about 60,000 men, established himself at the frontier town of Sumaysat. The local Abbasid governor had only 3,000 men with him, but 'Abd Allah b.'Ali came north from Syria and the caliph sent his brother, Abu Ja'far, now freed from the siege of Wasit. As at Wasit, the object of the resistance was to obtain terms as favourable as possible. The confrontation lasted for seven months, though there seems to have been no actual fighting. At the end of this time, an agreement was reached between Abu Ja'far and Ishaq and his followers;[13] exactly what the terms were we do not know, but many of the rebel leaders appear soon after in the service of 'Abd Allah b.'Ali or Abu Ja'far and Ishaq himself became one of Abu Ja'far's closest advisers.[14] A large and powerful body of Umayyad supporters had now been won over, at least temporarily, to the new regime.

There was sporadic resistance in other parts of the empire; in Syria itself, 'Abd Allah b.'Ali had to crush the rebellion of the pro-Umayyad Abu'l-Ward around Qinnisrin.[15] The Arabian peninsula, with the exception of the independent Kharijite areas of 'Uman, was taken without difficulty and in 134 (751/2), distant Sind was occupied by an Abbasid expedition from Basra.[16] Thus, by the end of 134 (July 752), pro-Abbasid forces were in control of the whole of the Umayyad empire, with the exception of Ifriqiya, which remained in the hands of local Berber rebels until 144 (761/2), and Andalus (Spain), which remained independent under a branch of the Umayyad dynasty.

The success of Abbasid arms had been spectacular: the Umayyads had been eliminated and their supporters either crushed or won over, to the extent that they no longer posed a threat to the new regime. But the political problems they faced were much more intractable. The real issue to be decided was whether the caliph was to be the effective ruler of the state. Would he be a strong monarch on the model of the great Umayyads, Mu'awiya, 'Abd Malik and Hisham, with the added advantage of being a member of the house of the Prophet, or would he simply be a pawn in the hands of those who had brought the dynasty to power, only of use to his powerful protectors as a way of legitimising their authority?

Saffah, and even more his brother, Abu Ja'far, were determined to assert the authority of the dynasty. There were two ways in which this could be done: the first was to keep in check the pretensions and ambitions of their would-be masters; the second was to build up support and a power base of their own, to allow them to act independently.

In the first of these objectives, they were greatly helped by the disunity of those who hoped to manipulate them. Abu Salama and Abu Muslim were bound to be rivals. Abu Muslim, in far-off Khurasan, saw Abu Salama, with his Kufan connections, as a threat to his influence in the west. Abu Salama had played into his hands, he had resisted the proclamation of Saffah and his connections with the Alids must have been suspected, if not widely known. Both Saffah and Abu Muslim had good reason for wanting him out of the way, but it was assassins sent by Abu Muslim who finally killed him, in Rajab 132 (February/ March 750), as he was walking home alone at night after an interview with the caliph. To avoid the opprobrium with which the deed would be regarded by popular opinion, it was publicly ascribed to the Kharijites.[17]

Abu Muslim was in a much stronger position than his rival. He had never compromised his position by negotiating with other dynasties, and it was his agent in Kufa who was directly responsible for the proclamation of Saffah as caliph. Furthermore, Abu Muslim had the powerful military backing which Abu Salama had lacked, he was not defenceless in Kufa and was well-protected in Khurasan. It was essential, at least for the time being, to establish a *modus vivendi* with him.

A virtual division of the empire into two separate sectors was arranged. While the caliph exercised authority in the west, most of the Iranian plateau, except Azerbayjan, in the northwest, was ruled by Abu Muslim from Marw. His area extended far beyond the borders of Khurasan proper, and Sistan, Rayy, Kirman and Fars were all under his control. It was he who appointed and dismissed the governors and, naturally, he chose them from among his own associates. Coins were minted in his name[18] and it is unlikely that any of the taxation from Khurasan ever reached the west. Certainly, he acknowledged the theoretical authority of the dynasty but, in practice, his autonomy was almost complete. When the caliph's brother, Abu Ja'far, visited him in Marw, shortly after the revolution, it was like visiting a friendly but quite independent potentate; the guest had a good opportunity to observe at first hand his host's power and ruthlessness, since it was during his stay that Abu Muslim executed the senior member of the Abbasid movement in the province, Sulayman b.Kathir.[19] Only in Fars was there any dispute about this arrangement. Saffah sent one of his uncles, 'Isa b.'Ali, to take over this province but he was forced to withdraw when Abu Muslim's nominee threatened him with violence, an open rebuff to the caliph's authority.[20] Abu Muslim was, however, unable to assert his authority over Sind; the province was very remote and the land route, either through the wild, hostile mountains of Afghanistan, or the burning deserts of Makran and Baluchistan, almost impossible. Both politically and economically, the province was always connected with Basra by sea and, as we have seen, it was an expedition from Basra which took it for the Abbasids. It fell, therefore, within the caliph's sphere of influence.

Abu Muslim's power extended beyond the area he ruled directly. He interfered actively in the affairs of the caliph's court and we have seen already the role he played in the deaths of Abu Salama and Ibn Hubayra. Abu Ja'far was scarcely exaggerating when he told his brother, 'You will not be caliph and your orders will count for nothing if you leave Abu Muslim and do not kill him.'[21] But Saffah was too cautious to take his brother's advice at this stage.

In Iraq and the west the situation was entirely different. Right from the beginning, Saffah had made sure that control was in the hands of members of the Abbasid family. This was done in three ways; by putting them in command of armies and so allowing them to build up followings among the military, by giving them provincial governorates and by letting them acquire property and settle in the provinces.

The campaign against Marwan had been led by one of his uncles, 'Abd Allah, later joined by two others, Salih and 'Abd al-Samad b.'Ali, while his own brother, Abu Ja'far, commanded the army which besieged Ibn Hubayra, in Wasit, and Ishaq b.Muslim, in Sumaysat. All of them, especially Abu Ja'far, seem to have won the confidence and allegiance of the Khurasani troops they led, and this meant that, for the first time, real military power was in the hands of members of the family.

This pattern of family control was repeated when it came to allotting governorates. Naturally, 'Abd Allah was given charge of Syria, while his brother, Salih, took over Egypt and Palestine.[22] Abu Ja'far was entrusted with the provinces of Jazira and Armenia, difficult frontier areas which provided him with the opportunity to acquire experience and military support. Kufa was at first governed by the caliph's senior uncle, Dawud b.'Ali, and then by his nephew, 'Isa b.Musa, while Basra soon passed into the hands of yet another uncle, Sulayman b.'Ali.[23]

The most striking example of this preference for members of the family, however, comes from the Arabian peninsula. The Holy Cities of Makka and Madina had been entrusted to Dawud b.'Ali, after he had left Kufa, but, on his death the next year, 133 (750/1), the caliph appointed his own maternal uncle, Ziyad b.'Ubayd Allah al-Harithi. What makes this appointment so remarkable is that Ziyad had been second-in-command to Ibn Hubayra in Iraq, and had actually been with him when he was besieged in Wasit, barely a year before. Not only was he given a position full of power and prestige, but he was paid a huge salary, 2,500 *dinar*s a month, we are told; this was equivalent to about 37,500 *dirham*s, at a time when rank-and-file soldiers were paid around 80.[24] The use of the family in this way conflicted strongly with the ideas of the revolution that precedence in the movement should determine seniority. The Abbasid family were different; they were after all the family of the Prophet and they, too, had suffered Umayyad persecution, but the Harithis had actually been part of the Umayyad ruling establishment. Not surprisingly, this was the one appointment which aroused real resentment; on a specious excuse, Khazim b. Khuzayma, a veteran Khurasani leader with many years' service in the movement, attacked and massacred some of Ziyad's Harithi relatives in their camp. In consequence, he was sent to 'Uman to fight the Kharijites as a penance, but otherwise remained unpunished.[25] However, Ziyad was not dismissed and Saffah retained a free hand to make his own appointments, unrestrained by the wishes of the Khurasani army.

Abbasid rule in these early days was very much a co-operative family effort. Saffah was very fortunate in having an extensive immediate family to whom important tasks could be entrusted. At the time of the revolution, he had seven surviving paternal uncles who played a role in politics, either governing provinces or, more discreetly, advising at court, like 'Isa b.'Ali. They ranged vastly in age, from Dawud, who died in 133 (750/1), to 'Abd al-Samad b.'Ali, who survived until 185 (801/2). Then there was his brother, Abu Ja'far, while he could also count on his able and ambitious nephew, 'Isa b.Musa, the governor of Kufa, and on his mother's Harithi relatives, Ziyad (mentioned above) and his cousin, Muhammad b.Yazid, governor of Yaman. This extensive family was a vital element in the establishment of Abbasid control in the west.

After the upheavals of the revolution, the rest of the reign of Saffah was comparatively peaceful, although there were sporadic disturbances in Khurasan, by those who felt that the revolution had been betrayed by the policies of Abu Muslim and his subordinates. There was, also, a rebellion nearer home, led by a disaffected Khurasani soldier, Bassam b.Ibrahim, who, for reasons which are not entirely clear, rebelled in Mada'in in 134 (751/2)[26] but was easily crushed by Khazim b.Khuzayma.

By the time of the caliph's death in 136 (754), the picture of achievement was impressive. Iran, under the control of Abu Muslim and the Khurasanis, was peaceful and, at least nominally, loyal to the government; in the west, the Abbasid family exercised real power, filling almost every post of importance. How much of this can be ascribed to the caliph himself is difficult to assess. Compared with his brother, Abu Ja'far, or his uncle, 'Abd Allah, he emerges as rather a nondescript character. His failure to rise to the occasion and make a great speech in the mosque at Kufa when he was proclaimed caliph suggests that he was a diffident individual. He was also cautious; he refused to let his brother provoke a premature confrontation with Abu Muslim. At the same time, he seems to have been quietly determined to make the authority of the caliph a reality and, by his policies of appointing his family to important positions, he laid the foundations on which his brother was to build.

The last months of his reign were dominated by a growing crisis. Relations with Abu Muslim had been strained from the first. This was particularly true of the caliph's brother, Abu Ja'far. He must have greatly resented Abu Muslim's prevention of his deal with Ibn Hubayra, and his subsequent journey to Khurasan had made him very aware of Abu Muslim's power in the area. What precipitated the confrontation, however, was Abu Muslim's request to come west to make the pilgrimage to Makka, at the end of 136 (June 754).[27] His reasons for doing so remain obscure. He may have wanted to see for himself how matters stood at the caliph's court and he may, too, have wanted to renew contact with those Khurasani military leaders who had remained in the west since the revolution. For Saffah and his brother, this development was both a threat and an opportunity; a threat because, if things went wrong, it might allow the visitor to assert his authority in the west as effectively as he already had done in the east. It was an opportunity, in that Abu Muslim would be away from his power base in Khurasan and the protection of his own troops. Abu Ja'far was determined to make the most of this.

Abu Muslim decided to bring a large escort with him, and set out from Khurasan with about 8,000 men. The Abbasids viewed the prospect of the arrival of so large a body of men with apprehension. The would-be pilgrim was forbidden to bring more than 500 with him: the road to Makka, the caliph explained, could not sustain so many men. Somewhat surprisingly, Abu Muslim agreed, left the bulk of his men in central Iran, on the road between Nishapur and Rayy, and came to Iraq almost defenceless.[28] The question then arose of who was to lead the pilgrims. This had been, and was to remain, the prerogative of members of the ruling house but, if Abu Muslim asked for the honour, it would be, in view of his prestige and the services he had rendered the dynasty, very difficult to refuse. In the present state of relations between him and the Abbasids, they were most reluctant to allow him this privilege and Abu Ja'far decided that the only way to forestall this was to ask to lead the pilgrimage himself. Accordingly, he left his post as governor of Jazira in the hands of a deputy, and came to the caliph's court.

While the ill-assorted travelling companions were away, Saffah fell sick. His brother had been designated as his heir, but there was at least a possibility that Abu Muslim would either murder him or prevent his return from the pilgrimage and so leave himself free to decide the succession. This would, of course, destroy all the achievements of the last four years and, to prevent it, Saffah made a move which, though prudent at the time, was to cause great difficulties later on. He nominated his nephew, 'Isa b.Musa, next in line for the succession; he was powerful, able and, most important, near at hand. If anything happened to Abu Ja'far, he could easily take control. On 13 Dhu'l-Hijja, 136 (8 June 754), the first of the Abbasid caliphs died. He was still in his thirties.[29]

The news reached the pilgrims on the road to Makka. Abu Muslim took the oath of allegiance to the new caliph without demur and they both hurried back to Iraq to take control. Saffah had died at Anbar but Abu Ja'far paused first at Kufa, to preach to the people and receive their oaths, before going on to meet 'Isa b.Musa, who had kept the *diwan*s and the treasury. Then, in Anbar, early in the new year (137), the oath was taken, first to Abu Ja'far, then to 'Isa b.Musa, as his successor.[30]

Notes

1. Tabari, *Ta'rikh*, vol. 3, pp. 23-37; Ya'qubi, *Ta'rikh*, vol. 2, pp. 418-20.

2. For the battle of the Zab, see Tabari, *Ta'rikh*, vol. 3, pp. 38-45; Dinawari, *Akhbar al-Tiwal,* ed. V. Guirgass and I.I. Krachkovskii (Leiden, 1912) p. 363, Azdi, *Ta'rikh,* pp. 125-33.

3. Tabari, *Ta'rikh*, vol. 3, p. 42; Azdi, *Ta'rikh,* p. 127.

4. Tabari, *Ta'rikh*, vol. 3, p. 42.

5. Azdi, *Ta'rikh,* p. 129.

6. Tabari, *Ta'rikh,* vol. 3, p. 47; Azdi, *Ta'rikh,* p. 133.

7. Dinawari, *Akhbar,* pp. 364-5.

8. For his flight and death, see Tabari, *Ta'rikh,* vol. 3, pp. 45, 47-51; Azdi, *Ta'rikh,* pp. 133-7; Ya'qubi, *Ta'rikh,* vol. 2, p. 346; Dinawari, *Akhbar,* pp. 263-5.

9. Tabari, *Ta'rikh,* vol. 3, p. 51, is laconic. The gruesome details are given in Ya'qubi, *Ta'rikh,* vol. 2, pp. 355-7 and Azdi, *Ta'rikh,* pp. 138-9.

10. Baladhuri, *Futuh,* p. 178, and below, pp. 74-5.

11. Tabari, *Ta'rikh,* vol. 3, pp. 20-1, 61-70; Ya'qubi, *Ta'rikh,* vol. 2, p. 353; Ibn Khayyat, *Ta'rikh,* ed. A. Al-Umari (Najaf, 1967), vol. 2, pp. 424-6; Baladhuri, *Ansab,* fos. 597-600.

12. Ya'qubi, *Ta'rikh,* vol. 2, p. 410.

13. Tabari, *Ta'rikh,* vol. 3, pp. 56-8; Ya'qubi, *Ta'rikh,* vol. 2, p. 425; Baladhuri, *Ansab,* fo. 604; Agapius, *'Unwan,* p. 530.

14. Tabari, *Ta'rikh,* vol. 3, p. 281.

15. Ibid., vol. 3, pp. 52-5; Ya'qubi, *Ta'rikh,* vol. 2, p. 425; Azdi, *Ta'rikh,* p. 140.

16. Tabari, *Ta'rikh,* vol. 3, p. 80.

17. Ibid., vol. 3, pp. 59-60; S. Moscati, 'Studi su Abu Muslim' in *RANL* Series 8, vol. 4 (1949), pp. 325-31; D. Sourdel, *Le Vizirat Abbaside* (Damascus, 1949), vol. 1, pp. 65-77; Omar, *Abbasid Caliphate,* pp. 139-53; Shaban, *Abbasid Revolution,* pp. 163-7.

18. G.C. Miles, 'Numismatics' in *Cambridge History of Iran*, vol. 4, p. 369.

19. Tabari, *Ta'rikh*, vol. 3, pp. 58-61.

20. Ibid., vol. 3, pp. 71-2; Dinawari, *Akhbar*, pp. 373-4; Moscati, *Abu Muslim* (1949), pp. 331-2.

21. Tabari, *Ta'rikh*, vol. 3, p. 61.

22. Ibid., vol. 3, p. 72; Kindi, *Wulat*, pp. 97-105.

23. Tabari, *Ta'rikh*, vol. 3, pp. 72-3.

24. Ibid., vol. 3, p. 73; Azdi, *Ta'rikh*, p. 143. The exchange rate used is the fifteen *dirham*s to the *dinar* used by Qudama b. Ja'far in his *Kitab al-Kharaj*, and the comparison is only approximate.

25. Tabari, *Ta'rikh*, vol. 3, pp. 76-8.

26. Ibid., vol. 3, pp. 75; Baladhuri, *Ansab*, fo. 610.

27. Tabari, *Ta'rikh*, vol. 3, pp. 84-7; Moscati, 'Studi su Abu Muslim' in *RANL* Series 8, vol. 5, (1950), pp. 89-91.

28. Tabari, *Ta'rikh*, vol. 3, pp. 86-7.

29. Ibid., vol. 3, pp. 87-8; Baladhuri, *Ansab*, fo. 655.

30. Tabari, *Ta'rikh*, vol. 3, pp. 88-9.

4 MANSUR: THE YEARS OF STRUGGLE

The new caliph, Abu Ja'far Abd Allah b.Muhammad al-Mansur, was in his early forties. In appearance he was tall, spare and swarthy. He was born, probably between the years 90 and 94 (709-13), at Humayma, where the Abbasid family were then in exile.[1] We know nothing of his upbringing but, as a young man, he seems to have travelled fairly extensively in the service of the Abbasid movement. He had been to Mosul and spent some time in Basra but it seems that he had never been to Khurasan, nor had close contacts with the leaders of the Abbasid movement there. His first active political role was during the years 127 to 129 (744-6), when he joined the revolt of 'Abd Allah b.Mu'awiya, a member of the Alid family who had rebelled against the Umayyads in western Iran.[2] He was captured and was lucky to escape with his life. In Shi'ite circles a story was later circulated to the effect that he had sworn allegiance to the Alid leader Muhammad b.'Abd Allah,[3] later to be one of his most dangerous opponents. It seems that, after the collapse of the rebellion, he retired to Humayma and is not heard of again until he came to Kufa, with the rest of his family, at the time of the Abbasid Revolution.

During his brother's reign, he established himself as one of the leading figures in the new regime. As soon as the Abbasids had been proclaimed, he was put in command of the army besieging the last Umayyad governor of Iraq, Ibn Hubayra, in Wasit. This command put him, for the first time, in touch with the leaders of the Khurasani army. Here he met prominent officers, like Khazim b.Khuzayma, al-Tamimi, 'Uthman b.Nahik al-'Akki and the youthful Hasan b.Qahtaba, who were to serve him loyally.[4] After the fall of Wasit, he was given an important command in Jazira and he and his army were sent to mop up the remaining opposition to Abbasid rule in that area. Here, again, he took the opportunity to win military support. He negotiated the surrender of the leader of the Umayyad partisans, Ishaq b.Muslim al-'Uqayli, who became one of his closest advisers.[5] His control also extended to Armenia and he established links with another important local figure, Yazid b.Usayd al-Sulami. Yazid's father had been a companion-in-arms of Marwan b.Muhammad in the Caucasus area, before he became caliph, and, during these campaigns, he had married the daughter of the ruler of the principality of Sisajan, so Yazid inherited a prominent position in the Qaysi army of the last Umayyad caliph and among the semi-autonomous princes of Armenia.[6] Mansur was not a man to allow Yazid's previous loyalty to the Umayyads to deter him and Yazid joined the ranks of his counsellors, offering advice and, we must presume, military support during the confrontations with Abu Muslim and the Alids. By establishing these contacts, Mansur made sure that he commanded the loyalty of a powerful military force, essential if he were to realise his political ambitions.

He also had a coherent political programme which he was determined to push through. His political education had been in the Umayyad world and it was on the great Umayyad rulers, Mu'awiya, 'Abd al-Malik and Hisham, that he modelled himself. He wanted to establish a family-dominated government, similar to the old regime, and based on the secure foundation of a strong and well-paid army. 'He who lacks money', he is reported to have said, 'lacks men and he who lacks men sees his enemies grow powerful'.[7] These ideas were bound to bring him into conflict with many who had hitherto supported the Abbasids but felt that Mansur's policies were a betrayal of the revolution. They found that, instead of a new society, based on the Qur'an, justice and the equality of all Muslims, led by a divinely elected *imam*, they had simply replaced one ruling élite with another and that a substantial section of the old élite had actually been incorporated in the new. These disillusioned elements naturally began to look elsewhere for leadership, especially to members of the family of 'Ali b.Abi Talib. Furthermore, there was no place, in the centralised system Mansur had in mind, for the huge, almost autonomous state which Abu Muslim had established in Khurasan and eastern Iran; Khurasan had to be treated in the same way as any other province. The new caliph was undeterred by the opposition his policies aroused and he moved with skill and determination against those who disagreed with him. Until the defeat of the Alid revolts of the year 145 (762/3), Mansur had to deal with three main threats to his regime: from Syrians unwilling to accept their subordinate role, from Abu Muslim, trying to maintain his position in the east, and from the Alids and those discontented groups who saw them as a potential replacement for the Abbasids.

The Syrians posed the most immediate threat and they found an unexpected ally in the caliph's uncle, 'Abd Allah b.'Ali, who had led the army which had defeated those same Syrians at the battle of the Zab, four years earlier. 'Abd Allah claimed that, when he had volunteered to lead the Abbasid forces from Kufa to meet Marwan, Saffah had promised him the succession to the throne.[8] Whether there is any truth in the story it is impossible to tell, but it is clear that Abu Ja'far, rather than 'Abd Allah, was Saffah's right-hand man for most of his reign. Like his nephew, 'Abd Allah had spent the years since the revolution recruiting supporters. Throughout this period he had been governor of Syria and this brought him into contact with many leading military figures. As luck would have it, the news of the caliph's death reached him when he had just assembled a large army of Syrians and Khurasanis at Duluk, north of Aleppo, with the intention of leading them on a raid against the Byzantines. When he announced his claim to the throne, there seems to have been no opposition in the army and many prominent Syrians and some Khurasanis, including the second of Qahtaba's sons, Humayd, swore allegiance to him.[9] He was, however, supported by only one of his numerous brothers, 'Abd al-Samad, the youngest, while the others, like Salih in Egypt and Sulayman in Basra, remained discreetly neutral – perhaps encouraged by the large subsidies Mansur paid them.[10] Having secured the loyalty of his army, 'Abd Allah set out, at the beginning of 137 (summer 754), to enforce his claims in Iraq.

When Mansur had left his governorate in Jazira to join the pilgrimage, he had left a small garrison at Harran (his headquarters) and these troops showed their loyalty by defying 'Abd Allah's army. 'Abd Allah ignored the advice of his experienced Syrian officers by stopping for forty valuable days, while he forced the city to surrender.[11] The delay was fatal to his chances of success. Mansur used the respite to persuade Abu Muslim to lead a Khurasani army against his uncle.[12] After the fall of Harran, 'Abd Allah moved east, while Abu Muslim moved up the Tigris to Mosul. Divisions began to appear in 'Abd Allah's army. For his Khurasani supporters, it was probably little more than a family dispute, whose outcome would not significantly affect the nature of the regime, and they may well have believed that 'Abd Allah, with his successful military record, would make a better caliph than his nephew. For the more ambitious of the Syrians, however, the issues were much more serious; old associates of Marwan, like Zufar b.'Asim al-Hilali[13] and Ja'far b.Hanzala al-Bahrani,[14] hoped to use 'Abd Allah to defeat the Khurasanis and restore Syrian control over the Islamic state. 'Abd Allah came increasingly under Syrian influence and he began to doubt the loyalty of the Khurasanis in his army. To forestall any possibility of treachery, he had many of them killed and their property handed over to the Syrians; Humayd b.Qahtaba discovered a clumsy attempt on his life and fled to Iraq.[15] By the time of the final battle, 'Abd Allah's troops were almost entirely Syrians, while Abu Muslim's were, of course, Khurasanis. A Christian commentator saw the conflict in racial terms, between the Arabs and the *'ajam* (Iranians).[16]

The two armies confronted each other at Nisibin and, for five months during the late summer and autumn of 754, there was little more than skirmishing. Abu Muslim attempted to cause further divisions in the ranks of the opposition by claiming that he had come not to attack 'Abd Allah but simply because he had been appointed governor of Syria and had to obey orders. The Syrians nearly panicked. How could they remain at Nisibin while Abu Muslim by-passed their army and occupied their homeland?

Then, around the beginning of Jumada II, 137 (late November 754), a real battle developed. Abu Muslim outmanœuvred the Syrians by pretending to concentrate all his troops on one wing while preparing an attack on the other. At this point the lack of mutual confidence between 'Abd Allah and his army became apparent; he fled precipitately and the Syrians were completely routed. 'Abd Allah fled to Basra, where he took refuge with his brother Sulayman, who protected him from the caliph's wrath.[17] He was still considered dangerous in 145 (762/3), when Mansur refused his help against the Alid rebels. With the death of Sulayman in 142 (759/60), however, he became more vulnerable and he was killed in 147 (764) when the house he was staying in 'collapsed'.[18] He was able and ambitious but rash, and lacked his nephew's understanding of the political situation. His opportunism was his undoing. By relying on the Syrians, he had united the Khurasanis behind Mansur, but it was less than five years since he had defeated those same Syrians and it seems that, while both he and they were prepared to work together, they did not really have confidence in each other. 'Abd al-Samad fled to his great-nephew, 'Isa b.Musa, the governor of Kufa, who gave him presents and released him. He outlived all the other participants by many years but was never allowed to play a major political role or to be trusted with an important independent command.[19] With the Syrians, Mansur reached an agreement. They were useful to him to balance the influence of the Khurasani military and he did not wish to alienate them. They were to be stationed as garrisons on the Byzantine frontier.[20] They retained their strength and organisation; their leaders remained entirely unpunished and continued to enjoy real political power, Ja'far b.Hanzala becoming a close adviser of the caliph, while Zufar b.'Asim became governor of Madina and later of Jazira.[21] They had not destroyed Khurasani dominance, and feelings between the two groups still ran high, but they had secured for themselves a useful, if secondary, place in the new power structure. It was a measure of the success of this agreement that not until the confusion which followed the death of Harun, in 193 (809), was there any serious threat to Abbasid rule in the area.

'Abd Allah and the Syrians had ceased to be a threat to Mansur's authority and he was now free to tackle the formidable problem of Abu Muslim. Relations between the two men had never been good. Since Abu Muslim had largely confined his activities to Khurasan, it was unlikely that he and Mansur had met before the revolution, but they came into conflict almost as soon as the Abbasid forces occupied Kufa.[22] It had not been easy for the caliph to persuade Abu Muslim to lead the army against the rebels. Some of Abu Muslim's advisers had urged him to let uncle and nephew fight it out and then, from the security of Khurasan, to pledge allegiance to the victor.[23] It is not clear why he rejected this advice, but it was probably because he felt that he would lose his influence in the west, especially if 'Abd Allah and the Syrians were to prove victorious. During the campaign Mansur had him closely watched; two of the Khurasani generals most closely connected with the caliph, Hasan b.Qahtaba and Khazim b.Khuzayma, were despatched to join Abu Muslim's army.[24] After the defeat of the rebels, Abu Muslim's intention was to return to Khurasan as soon as possible. It was vital for Mansur to prevent this if he were to have any chance of eliminating his rival.

The caliph began by being deliberately provocative; the booty captured from the Syrians was distributed not by Abu Muslim but by an agent sent by the caliph for the purpose. Abu Muslim was naturally furious. Mansur then offered him the governorate of either Syria or Egypt. This was a shrewd move; if he accepted, he would be isolated from his supporters in Khurasan and under the watchful eye of the caliph, but he could hardly refuse without putting himself in the wrong.[25] The caliph cannot have been surprised when the offer was rejected and Abu Muslim set out for Khurasan. When he reached Hulwan, at the start of the road through the Zagros mountains, he hesitated, not wishing to break completely with the caliph. Mansur moved to Mada'in and from here he directed to Abu Muslim a stream of letters from members of the Abbasid family and erstwhile colleagues urging him to obey the caliph and come to court. His own advisers said otherwise. 'Go to your own province', said Malik b.al-Haytham, one of his most prominent Arab supporters, 'and do not return for if you go to him he will kill you'. 'Go to Rayy', said Nayzak, a leading eastern Iranian noble, 'and wait there, for the area between Rayy and Khurasan is in your hands and there are your troops, not one of whom will betray you'.[26] As the argument went on, the caliph produced his trump card. He had not spent the five months while Abu Muslim was occupied in defeating 'Abd Allah's rebellion in doing nothing and had prepared his next move with his usual thoroughness. He had been in correspondence with Abu Muslim's second-in-command in Khurasan, Abu Dawud Khalid b.Ibrahim, who now wrote saying that he would not allow Abu Muslim to return to the province until he had made his peace with the caliph.[27] The unfortunate man was left with no choice. Reluctantly, he left his baggage with Malik at Hulwan and returned, almost unaccompanied, to meet the caliph. When he arrived, on 23 Sha'ban 137 (10 February 755), he was informed that the caliph was 'busy' and he was kept waiting. After he was finally admitted to the caliph's presence, Mansur began to accuse him of a number of trivial and possibly fictitious slights against Saffah and himself before giving the signal for the Khurasani captain of the guard, 'Uthman b.Nahik, and his men to come in and execute him.[28]

So died the man who perhaps more than any other single individual had been responsible for the success of the Abbasid Revolution. His rise to power had been meteoric and, at the height of his influence in the years after the revolution, he was probably more powerful than the caliph himself. But his position was more fragile than it appeared. He had made a large number of enemies in Khurasan. It seems that he attempted some sort of *rapprochement* with the local aristocracy and had alienated many who had served the revolution well. The period of his rule in the east was one of constant rebellion and bloodshed and, almost without exception, his opponents were disillusioned members of the Abbasid movement. He had also lost control of the Khurasani army in Iraq and the west. Mansur had been amazingly successful in winning the loyalty of the leading figures in this army. By the time Abu Muslim came west such senior commanders as Hasan b.Qahtaba were firmly attached to the caliph's cause. Abu Muslim had been chosen for his role because he was a man without connections, whom everyone could accept as a leader for the movement; herein, perhaps, lie the causes of his downfall. He belonged to no group or tribe. There were those who supported him when it suited their interests but ultimately he was a loner and the weakness of his position became disastrously apparent at Hulwan.

He has remained a controversial figure. Within a few months of his death he had been adopted as a symbol of anti-Arab feeling in Iran, but there is no evidence that he was himself hostile to the Arabs or wanted to expel them from the country. Right to the end, some of his closest supporters were Arabs, but his relations with the Iranian *dehqan*s and his apparently conciliatory attitude to the *herbadh*s and *mobadh*s (priests) of the Zoroastrian hierarchy may have given rise to this belief.[29] Nor is there any evidence that he was a 'heretic', except in so far as anyone who opposed the caliph was *ipso facto* heretical. Of his religious beliefs we know nothing, but the fact that the most serious revolt against his rule in Khurasan was raised in the name of the Alids suggests that he had no leanings in that direction.

It is easy to accuse the caliph of gross ingratitude but this does not really do justice to the difficulties of his position or the clarity of his political vision. Abu Muslim's conduct as ruler of the east had made it clear that Iran could never be incorporated into the caliphate as long as he retained control. Equally, his refusal to accept appointment to Syria or Egypt showed that he was not prepared to compromise and accept the role of an ordinary provincial governor. These attitudes left the caliph with very little choice politically, and, even in moral terms, it is hard to find great fault with Mansur. Abu Muslim had been responsible for many thousands of deaths in Khurasan and gloried in his role as a slaughterer. Dante would surely have consigned him to the lowest circle of the *Inferno* for his treatment of his own benefactors, Abu Salama and Sulayman b.Kathir. Mansur was, in contrast, very sparing in his use of assassination and murder as political weapons, only employing them when there seemed no alternative.

The execution of Abu Muslim was a risk but, like all Mansur's risks, it was a carefully calculated one. There were no disturbances among the Khurasani army in the west, showing once again how loyal this army was to the caliph, while even in the east the response was much more muted than might have been expected. In Khurasan itself, the new governor, Abu Dawud, remained firmly in control and even the leaders most closely associated with Abu Muslim were soon to be found serving the caliph. Muhammad b.al-Ash'ath, who had driven Saffah's governor from Fars, was fighting for the government against rebels in Iran the next year,[30] while, by 141 (758/9), even the most devoted of his Khurasani officers, Malik b.al-Haytham, was reconciled with the caliph.[31]

Only in central Iran was there any serious attempt to avenge the dead man. The rebellion was led by an Iranian by the name of Sunbadh.[32] It seems that he originally came from Nishapur, or one of the villages nearby, and Nizam al-Mulk calls him a *ra'isi* (chief), which suggests that he came from the *dehqan* class. According to some sources, he had been with Abu Muslim in Hulwan and had escaped to the east following his master's death. When he reached Nishapur he raised the standard of revolt and moved along the road through Qumis to Rayy, gathering recruits among the troops Abu Muslim had been forced to leave there on his fatal journey to the west. As with many other rebellions of the time, it is not easy to understand what Sunbadh's objectives were, but two things are clear: he was closely connected with Abu Muslim, whose death was the immediate cause of the outbreak, and he sought to revive the old Persian religion and drive the Arabs out of the country, an aim summed up in his declared intention of sacking the Ka'aba. This openly anti-Muslim stand attracted considerable support in Rayy and Jibal, and the local ruler, or *isbahbadh*, of Tabaristan, an area as yet almost unaffected by Muslim penetration, gave assistance.

To begin with, the movement was very successful: Rayy was taken and the *Majusiya*, or Zoroastrian religion, restored; the governor of Qumis was defeated and Sunbadh could write to the ruler of Daylam that he had destroyed the *mulk* (rule) of the Arabs. He was, however, over-optimistic. Mansur sent against him, not the Khurasaniya, who might have felt some sympathy for his cause, but the people who had most to lose from his success, the Arabs of western Iran, led by Jahwar b.Marrar al-'Ijli. The 'Ijlis were the most powerful Arab tribe in the area of Jibal[33] and they followed Jahwar, along with the troops of Fars, Khuzistan and the lightly armed troops of Isfahan and Qum, numbering some 10,000 altogether. In the speech he is said to have made before the battle, Jahwar made the issues quite plain to his men, urging them to fight those who wished 'to exterminate your religion and expel you from your worldly possessions'. Sunbadh's army seems to have been many times the size of the Muslim one but it was, nonetheless, defeated with huge slaughter, between Rayy and Hamadhan, and Sunbadh himself was killed, probably when he tried to take refuge with the ruler of Tabaristan.

Perhaps the most curious feature of this rebellion, from our point of view, is the connection with Abu Muslim. There is no evidence that Abu Muslim had any intention of ending Arab rule or restoring Zoroastrianism. It is possible that this was no more than a device to attract support but there is probably more to it than that. It does seem that Abu Muslim had tried to maintain something of a half-way position between Arabs and Iranians; of his closest advisers, one, Malik b.al-Haytham al-Khuza'i, was an Arab while the other, Nayzak, was an Iranian. He had also sided with the Zoroastrian *mobadh*s against the reformer Bihafarid. Furthermore, he had hoped to rule Iran from Marw, not from some essentially Arab capital on the plains of Iraq. Many non-Arabs who had hoped for great things from the revolution regarded him as their spokesman and were outraged when he was killed. Sunbadh took advantage of these emotions. After his death the real Abu Muslim became obscured and he became adopted in Iran as an anti-Arab, anti-Muslim hero. According to Nizam al-Mulk, a late source but one which gives considerable new information and probably reflects popular belief, Sunbadh claimed that Abu Muslim would appear again, along with the mahdi of the Rafidis and the Mazdak, to lead his people to victory.[34] We are a long way here from the calculating but ultimately unsuccessful politician of the first years of Abbasid rule.

The third major problem the caliph faced was more insidious: the question of his relationship with those who wanted a more religious leadership and more radical political reform than Mansur was prepared to grant. As has been pointed out, his policies had little to offer those who looked to the revolution to provide charismatic leadership. He aspired to no religious authority and claimed no divine guidance for his actions and this was bound to disappoint many who had originally favoured the Abbasid cause. The first of these to take action was the small and mysterious group known as the Rawandiya. Their name derives ultimately from the small eastern Iranian town of Rawand and the group was founded by one 'Abd Allah al-Rawandi, who is listed among the earliest supporters of the Abbasids. It is clear that they belonged to the extreme Messianic fringe of the Abbasid movement, believing in transmigration of souls, and they ascribed semi-divine powers to the caliph.[35] Their heterodox views had led Abu Muslim to take action against them in Khurasan in 135 (752/3) and they are heard of no more in the province. However, they reappeared a few years later in the west where, in 141 (758/9), a group of them in the army staged a riot in the then capital of Hashimiya. The immediate cause of the trouble seems to have been the imprisonment of some of their leaders but their longer-term discontent was probably due to the failure of Mansur's low-key pragmatic approach to come up to their expectations. Despite the smallness of their numbers, their proximity to the palace and the inadequate security in the capital meant that, for a while, they posed a serious threat to the caliph, who was only just able to escape with his life. After this, the sect was ruthlessly exterminated by loyal troops and disappeared as a group, but their history serves to highlight an important source of discontent with the new regime among its former adherents.

The Rawandiya were a small, compact group who seem to have attracted no widespread support outside their own ranks and so were easily contained. The claims of the Alid family were a much more serious matter. The propaganda of the Abbasid Revolution had simply demanded a ruler 'from the House of Muhammad' and the Alids had, of course, as good a claim to this title as the Abbasids. Mansur had himself come into contact with the Alids during the rebellion of Ibn Mu'awiya, before the revolution, and he was fully aware that at least some members of the family were prepared to take militant action to secure the leadership of the Muslim community. The chief threat of the Alids lay in their unpredictability. There was no one generally accepted leader; the family was large and diffuse and any member of it could claim descent from the Prophet and hence the right to lead, which meant that it was very difficult for the government to watch them all. Furthermore, there was at this time no group of people who could be confidently identified as Shi'ites and therefore likely to support an Alid claimant. The situation was very fluid and the history of the period is full of men who supported the Alids at one time and the Abbasids at another. Each Alid rebellion of the period seems to have drawn on different sorts of support from different areas. The problem that faced the caliph and his advisers was, then, that, while they could be sure that there would be pro-Alid disturbances, it was very difficult to predict when and where these would occur. But this strength of the Alids was at the same time a source of weakness. Communication between different groups of rebels was often bad and they frequently had nothing in common beyond a desire to change the Abbasid regime. In addition, they could not call on any body of experienced and disciplined troops to face the well-organised Abbasid armies.

The Alids had already shown that they were a potential threat to the regime when Abu Salama had made his ill-fated approach to them at the time of the revolution and the first two caliphs were faced with the problem of safeguarding themselves against this menace. There were two possible approaches to the problem, both tried at different times. The first was to take a soft line; by inviting the Alids to court, honouring them and paying them allowances they could be persuaded to accept Abbasid rule, the incentive to revolt would be reduced and the government could keep them under surveillance. The second approach was to take a hard line; to track down and imprison the Alids and their supporters and so prevent revolts, even if it meant making more martyrs for the cause.

Saffah, in keeping with his more cautious policy, had tried the first alternative: leading members of the Alid family were encouraged to come to court and give their advice.[36] Nor did the accession of Mansur immediately change this, but he became increasingly anxious about the activities of two members of the family, Muhammad b.'Abd Allah, known as Nafs al-Zakiya (The Pure Soul), and his brother, Ibrahim. Even before the revolution, Muhammad's father had been putting him forward as the leader of the family and people swore allegiance to him as 'mahdi'. Pro-Alid sources even allege that Mansur himself had sworn allegiance to him in Umayyad times.[37] Muhammad remained immune to the blandishments offered by the caliphs and by 138 (755/6) he and Ibrahim had vanished. The caliph's cousin, Fadl b. Salih, was sent to Madina to track them down but was informed that they were away hunting.[38] In fact, the two brothers wandered extensively in Iraq and as far away as Sind and Aden, both to avoid Mansur's agents and to look for potential support.[39] For the caliph their disappearance was a major headache. At first, he concentrated on finding the brothers but, when this proved impossible, he changed his strategy. He began to put pressure on Muhammad's relatives to induce the brothers to give themselves up or to come out in premature rebellion. Towards the end of Ramadhan 144 (December 761), acting on the advice of his Syrian counsellors, he sent Riyah b.'Uthman al-Murri as governor of Madina.[40] Riyah was from Syria, a Qaysi and a hard man, with none of the scruples about maltreating members of the Prophet's family which had worried his predecessors. His appointment was itself a provocation and he followed it up by arresting many of Muhammad's family, including his aged father, and sending them to Iraq, whence reports of the ill-treatment they were receiving were circulated.[41]

The combination of increasing government pressure in Madina, where he had returned after his wanderings, and the sufferings of his family had the desired effect. About the beginning of Rajab 145 (25 September 762), Muhammad declared himself. That night, he and his companions took over the prison and the treasury and Riyah was arrested. He then made public his take-over by preaching in the Mosque of the Prophet and appointing a governor for the city, a *qadi*, a *sahib al-shurta* and, more ambitiously, governors for Makka, Yaman and even Syria.[42] Then, to the disgust of some of his more experienced supporters, he sat back to await the inevitable attack.

The news reached the caliph when he was occupied in building his new city of Baghdad. He was delighted and with good reason. 'I have lured the fox from his hole', he is reported to have said.[43] By declaring himself in Madina, Muhammad destroyed any real chance he might have had of overthrowing the regime. The area was isolated from the centres of power, too small in population to raise a significant army and heavily dependent on grain imports from Egypt. Furthermore, there was very little support elsewhere. His brother, Ibrahim, delayed fatally in Basra while an attempted coup in Egypt was easily put down.

During this crisis, the caliph had turned increasingly to Syrians for help and advice. Many of them had had great military experience and, unlike the Khurasanis, their hostility to the Alids could be guaranteed. Veteran Qaysis and ex-Umayyad supporters, like Salm b.Qutayba b.Muslim al-Bahili, son of the great governor of Khurasan, and Ja'far b.Hanzala al-Bahrani, are found helping the caliph, while even the opinions of the ex-rebel, 'Abd Allah b.'Ali, were sought though he was still considered too dangerous to be allowed a military command.[44] Mansur now took action in two ways. He sent a military force of some 4,000 men (a small army by Abbasid standards) under the command of his nephew, 'Isa b.Musa, to attack the rebels, but he also sent men to Wadi'l-Qurra, in the northern Hijaz, to interrupt the grain supplies from Egypt.[45] By the time 'Isa b.Musa and Muhammad met in battle, in mid-Ramadhan 145 (November 762), Muhammad's support in the city was much reduced and he had only about 300 men with him when he faced the Abbasid armies. The outcome was a foregone conclusion: the rebel leader died fighting bravely and so added another name to the long list of Alid martyrs.[46]

Muhammad's brother, Ibrahim, had not been inactive. Looking for a base from which to launch a revolt, he had decided on Basra. The choice seems strange. The city had no tradition of involvement with the Alid cause, but Kufa, the most obvious centre for Alid activity, was so heavily policed by Mansur's troops that it proved impossible to organise a mass movement there. The support which Ibrahim received in Basra probably owed more to local grievances against the government than to any long-term commitment to the Alid cause and it melted away as suddenly as it had appeared. At the time, however, the revolt posed a much more dangerous threat to the government than had Muhammad's. At the beginning of Ramadhan 145 (23 November 762), only about two weeks before his brother's death, Ibrahim led a mass revolt in the city. The timing is important; there can be no doubt that the two brothers had intended that their rebellions should coincide but pressure from the government had forced Muhammad's hand before his brother was ready. A co-ordinated attack from Basra and the Hijaz might have made life very difficult for Mansur. Even so, it was a bad moment for the caliph. The Abbasids seem to have been wholly unprepared for trouble from that quarter and the area was much more populous and closer to the centre of government than the Hijaz. The governor of the city was unable or unwilling to oppose them and Ahwaz, Fars and Wasit fell without serious resistance.[47]

Mansur was caught off his guard. The military forces at his disposal were very small. He had only 1,000 men with him and the remainder of the Abbasid army was widely scattered; 30,000 were with the caliph's son, Mahdi, in Rayy, 40,000 with Muhammad b. al-Ash'ath, in Ifriqiya, and the rest with 'Isa b.Musa, in the Hijaz.[48] The caliph made his head-quarters in Kufa and immediately set about gathering troops from all quarters. 'Isa was ordered to leave everything and return. Reinforcements were hurried from Rayy, including Khazim b.Khuzayma, one of Mansur's closest collaborators among the Khurasani leaders, and Salm b.Qutayba al-Bahili,[49] who had extensive property and family connections in Basra. The 2,000 men of the garrison at Mosul were rushed south and troops were also despatched from Syria.[50] But the most determined opponents of the Alid take-over of Basra were those members of the Abbasid family who had interests in the city. The caliph's uncle, Sulayman b.'Ali, had established his power in the city and after his death in 142 (759/60) his position had been inherited by his sons, Muhammad and Ja'far. They were in the city at the time of the Alid coup but were forced to withdraw to the country. From there they wrote to the caliph, who sent them reinforcements, and they continued to resist the attempts of the rebels to establish their authority.[51]

Despite the lack of preparation, the Abbasids emerged victorious. This was due, partly to the division within the ranks of the rebels, between the Basrans and those who arrived from Kufa, but also to the speed with which the caliph acted. In this emergency, the support he had built up over the previous thirteen years among different groups in the army really showed its value and both Khurasani veterans of the revolution and their ex-opponents from Syria hurried to support the regime. Ibrahim was persuaded to leave Basra and march on Kufa. At the height of the rebellion his pay-roll was said to have been as high as 100,000 men but dissatisfaction among the Basrans had drastically reduced this by the time his army met the Abbasids, on 25 Dhu'l-Qa'ada 145 (14 February 763). Ibrahim is said to have had some 10,000 men under his command, while the Abbasid forces, once again commanded by 'Isa b.Musa, numbered 15,000. Despite their numerical weakness and their lack of military experience, the Alids gave a good account of themselves in the battle which developed at Bakhamra, on the road

between Kufa and Basra. They defeated the Abbasid advance guard
and forced its leader, Humayd b.Qahtaba, to flee ignominiously from
the field, but, in the end, the government forces prevailed and, when
Ibrahim was fatally wounded by a stray arrow, his army broke and
fled. There was no further resistance.[52]

There were many reasons for the failure of this major Alid attempt.
Perhaps the most crucial was their inability to co-ordinate the two
rebellions, but in both cases divisions within the ranks led to bad
decision-making and the lack of training and military experience must
have played its part as well. The role of the caliph must not be under-
estimated, however. It was he who kept so firm a hand on the situation
in Kufa that no rebellion could be mounted in that most Alid of cities,
and it was he who forced Muhammad into the open before he was
ready. Although he did not lead the Abbasid armies in person, it was
he who assembled them and decided their strategy.

By the end of 145 (March 763), Mansur had overcome the three
major threats which had faced him at the outset of his reign. He had
done this by a mixture of military force and political shrewdness but
it was careful planning rather than the chance of battle which
decided the outcome. But he had achieved more than this. He had
ensured that the Abbasid caliph was to be the real and effective ruler
of the empire and he established Abbasid rule on foundations which
were to remain secure until after his grandson's death. It is to the
positive and constructive side of Mansur's rule that we shall turn in
the next chapter.

Notes

1. Tabari, *Ta'rikh*, vol. 3, pp. 390-1.
2. Baladhuri, *Ansab*, fo. 617; Shaban, *Islamic History*, vol. 1, pp. 161-3.
3. Isfahani, *Maqatil*, p. 209.
4. Tabari, *Ta'rikh*, vol. 3, pp. 62, 64-5.
5. Ibid., vol. 3, pp. 56-8; Ya'qubi, *Ta'rikh*, vol. 2, p. 425; Baladhuri, *Ansab*,
fo. 604.
6. Tabari, *Ta'rikh*, vol. 3, p. 162; Baladhuri, *Futuh*, pp. 242, 244.
7. Ya'qubi, *Ta'rikh*, vol. 2, p. 466.
8. Tabari, *Ta'rikh*, vol. 3, pp. 92-3.
9. Ibid., vol. 3, pp. 92-3; Baladhuri, *Ansab*, fo. 577; Azdi, *Ta'rikh*, p. 163.
10. Baladhuri, *Ansab*, fo. 578.
11. Tabari, *Ta'rikh*, vol. 3, pp. 93-4; Baladhuri, *Ansab*, fos. 578, 620.
12. Tabari, *Ta'rikh*, vol. 3, pp. 93-4, 100-1; Ya'qubi, *Ta'rikh*, vol. 2, p. 438.
13. Tabari, *Ta'rikh*, vol. 3, p. 94; Baladhuri, *Ansab*, fos. 577-8. His father had
governed Armenia under Marwan: see Ya'qubi, *Ta'rikh*, vol. 2, p. 404.
14. Tabari, *Ta'rikh*, vol. 3, p. 224; Baladhuri, *Ansab*, fo. 620.

15. Tabari, *Ta'rikh*, vol. 3, pp. 94-5, 101; Baladhuri, *Ansab*, fos. 578, 580.

16. Agapius, *'Unwan*, p. 534.

17. Tabari, *Ta'rikh*, vol. 3, pp. 97-9; Baladhuri, *Ansab*, fo. 579.

18. Tabari, *Ta'rikh*, vol. 3, p. 330.

19. Ibid., vol. 3, p. 98.

20. Baladhuri, *Ansab*, fos. 579-80.

21. Tabari, *Ta'rikh*, vol. 3, pp. 125, 224, 291, 482, 500; Azdi, *Ta'rikh*, pp.243-4.

22. See above, p. 54.

23. Tabari, *Ta'rikh*, vol. 3, pp. 93-4, 100-1; Ya'qubi, *Ta'rikh*, vol. 2, p. 438.

24. Tabari, *Ta'rikh*, vol. 3, pp. 95, 96.

25. Ibid., vol. 3, pp. 98, 103; Ya'qubi, *Ta'rikh*, vol. 2, p. 339.

26. For these negotiations, see Tabari, *Ta'rikh*, vol. 3, pp, 100-8; Ya'qubi, *Ta'rikh*, vol. 2, pp. 438-42; Azdi, *Ta'rikh*, pp. 165-6; Baladhuri, *Ansab*, fo. 629. See also the discussion in Moscati, *Studi su Abu Muslim* (1950), pp. 95-105, and Omar, *Abbasid Caliphate*, pp. 163-81. Both modern authors treat the dispute as a conflict of personalities while ignoring the much more fundamental issue of the status of Khurasan within the empire.

27. Tabari, *Ta'rikh*, vol. 3, p. 107.

28. Ibid., vol. 3, p. 115; Ya'qubi, *Ta'rikh*, vol. 2, p. 441; Baladhuri, *Ansab*, fos. 628-30.

29. At the time of the Bihafarid movement. See Biruni, *Athar*, vol. 2, pp. 210-11; Sadighi, *Mouvements*, pp. 111-31; Amoretti in *Cambridge History of Iran*, vol. 4, pp. 489-90.

30. Tabari, *Ta'rikh*, vol. 3, p. 122.

31. Ibid., vol. 3, pp. 117-18.

32. For Sunbadh's revolt, see Tabari, *Ta'rikh*, vol. 3, pp. 119-20; Baladhuri, *Ansab*, fo. 651; Nizam al-Mulk, *Siyasatnameh*, ed. H. Darke (Tehran, 1962), pp. 260-1; Ibn Isfaniyar, *History of Tabaristan*, trans. E.G. Browne (London, 1905), pp. 117-18; Agapius, *'Unwan*, p. 537; Sadighi, *Mouvements*, pp. 132-49.

33. Ibn al-Faqih, *Buldan*, p. 261, gives some details of their arrival in the area. Further indication of their importance can be seen in the career of Abu Dulaf, pp. 139-40, below.

34. Nizam al-Mulk, *Siyasatnameh*, p. 261. See also I. Melikoff, *Abu Muslim* (Paris, 1962).

35. Tabari, *Ta'rikh*, vol. 3, pp. 129-33.

36. Baladhuri, *Ansab*, fo. 608; Ya'qubi, *Ta'rikh*, vol. 2, pp. 431-2.

37. Isfahani, *Maqatil*, pp. 207, 209.

38. Tabari, *Ta'rikh*, vol. 3, p. 147.

39. Ibid., vol. 3, p. 149.

40. Ibid., vol. 3, pp. 162-3.

41. Ibid., vol. 3, pp. 173-5; Isfahani, *Maqatil*, pp. 205-29.

42. Tabari, *Ta'rikh*, vol. 3, pp. 190-202; Isfahani, *Maqatil*, p. 260; Ya'qubi, *Ta'rikh*, vol. 2, p. 452.

43. Tabari, *Ta'rikh*, vol. 3, p. 206.

44. Ibid., vol. 3, pp. 206-7, 224.

45. Ibid., vol. 3, pp. 223-5.

46. Ibid., vol. 3, pp. 236-41; Isfahani, *Maqatil*, pp. 268-9.

47. Tabari, *Ta'rikh*, vol. 3, pp. 298-304; Isfahani, *Maqatil*, pp. 324, 331-2; Ya'qubi, *Ta'rikh*, vol. 2, p. 454.

48. Tabari, *Ta'rikh*, vol. 3, p. 305.

49. Ibid., vol. 3, p. 305; Isfahani, *Maqatil*, pp. 325-8.

50. Tabari, *Ta'rikh*, vol. 3, p. 296.

51. Ibid., vol. 3, pp. 300, 306.

52. Ibid., vol. 3, pp. 315-16; Ya'qubi, *Ta'rikh*, vol. 2, pp. 454-5. There are a number of anecdotes about the battle in Isfahani, *Maqatil*, pp. 345-9, but they do not add up to a connected account.

5

MANSUR: THE CONSOLIDATION OF POWER

The Abbasid caliphs attemped to rule a vast area stretching from the Indus valley to the plains of Tunisia, from Aden to the mountains of Armenia.Within this area, there was a huge diversity of races, languages and religions among the subject peoples. Communications, although efficient by the standards of the day, were still very slow. All these factors meant that a caliph who wished to govern effectively had to attract the support and co-operation of many different groups and individuals, who could be trusted to represent him and uphold his authority in distant provinces. In return, these people expected financial rewards and that government policy should be responsive to their needs. When the government became too dependent on one particular group, as the late Umayyads did on the Qaysis of northern Syria, or the later Abbasids did on the Turks, then other elements became disaffected and the system broke down. In a real way, early Abbasid government was a coalition of different interests, brought together by Mansur in the service of the dynasty; the entry of new groups into the coalition and the removal of others, the growth and decline of power and influence within it were the causes of most of the political tensions of the period.

The Abbasid family were among the most prominent supporters of the caliph. The family was extensive and included a number of men of great ability. Mansur's closest surviving relatives were his brothers, 'Abbas and Yahya. 'Abbas acquired enormously valuable properties in Baghdad and Wasit but never became a political figure of great importance; neither his brother nor later caliphs seem to have had great faith in his ability and he was rarely allowed an independent command. He is reported to have survived until 186 (802) and was certainly active in the reign of Hadi, which probably means he was still a young man at the time of the revolution.[1] The career of the other brother, Yahya, was even less distinguished; in the year after the revolution, he was appointed as governor of Mosul and was responsible for the appalling massacre of the local citizens by the Abbasid garrison.[2] After this, he was dismissed and never given another post.

Much more influential were the caliph's uncles, the sons of 'Ali b.'Abd Allah b.al-'Abbas. Of these six ('Abd Allah, Salih, Sulayman, 'Isa, Isma'il and 'Abd al-Samad) played an important role in the life of the caliphate. Then there was the caliph's nephew, 'Isa b.Musa, and a distant cousin, Quthm b.al-'Abbas b.'Ubayd Allah b.al-'Abbas, governor of Yamama for many years before his death in 159 (775/6). The family sometimes acted as a concerted pressure group; the Banu 'Ali used their influence to protect their brother, 'Abd Allah, from the caliph's wrath in the years following his unsuccessful rebellion and, when Isma'il b.'Ali fell out of favour in 155 (772), it was members of the family who saved him from permanent disgrace.[3] Mansur was noted for his generosity to his family and took great pains to ensure their continued loyalty and support.

Mansur built on the foundations his brother had laid during his short reign. Saffah had appointed members of the family as governors of various western provinces and they and their descendants tended to remain in those areas to acquire property and form local sub-dynasties. Often members of the local dynasty were appointed as governors of their provinces but this was not always the case, and the fact that they did not provide governors for a period did not necessarily mean that they had lost their influential positions. For example, after the dismissal of 'Isa b.Musa as governor of Kufa in 147 (764), no member of his family held office in the city for the next twenty years but they were still powerful and influential there during the reign of Harun and after. Sometimes their power was based on their role as military leaders; this was especially true of the family of Salih b.'Ali in Syria, who often commanded the troops on the Byzantine frontier, but even the sons of Sulayman b.'Ali, in the comparatively peaceful area of Basra, could raise 600 men in an emergency to oppose the Alid take-over of the city during the rebellion of 145 (762). They were often great property owners in their areas, as well; in Syria the family of Salih b.'Ali had taken over most of the Umayyad family lands, while the Basran branch seems to have been particularly wealthy. They might also represent the interests of their areas at court; 'Abd al-Malik b.Salih clearly emerges as the spokesman of the Syrian 'interest' in the reign of Harun. As links between the provinces and the Abbasid caliphs, the members of the family were of major importance.

Probably the most important of these sub-dynasties was the family of Salih b.'Ali. After the defeat of his brother 'Abd Allah's rebellion, Salih abandoned his Egyptian interests almost entirely and moved to take over his lands and position in Syria; like his brother, he established close links with the Qaysi leaders of the frontier areas. Not only did

Salih take over Umayyad property, but he also married Marwan's ex-wife. The family built extensively at Salamiya, east of Hims, in and around Aleppo and at Manbij, on the Euphrates, where 'Abd al-Malik b.Salih built a much-admired castle.[4] Besides leading the annual expedition against the Byzantines on many occasions, the family were active in restoring and garrisoning frontier fortresses; Salih himself rebuilt Malatya, Mar'ash, Massissa and Adhana.[5] His daughter married Mahdi to strengthen ties with the main branch of the family[6] and he minted coins in his own name.[7] Before his death in 152 (769), his power and the number of his supporters was causing the caliph some anxiety.[8] His son, Fadl, inherited his position and maintained the power of the family until his own death twenty years later. He was succeeded by his brother 'Abd al-Malik, who became one of the most important figures at the court of Harun. His mother had been Marwan's wife and gossip had it that he was not really Salih's son at all.[9] Able, austere and puritanical, he was a complete contrast, both personally and politically, with the Barmakids and their faction. He raised the power of the family to new heights and this proved to be his undoing, as he aroused the suspicions of the caliph. In 187 (803) he was arrested and spent the next six years in prison,[10] but with the accession of Amin, who badly needed support in Syria, he was sent there to raise an army. There is no more striking illustration of the power and influence of the family than the way in which the Syrians flocked to Raqqa to serve under him.[11] The victory of Ma'mun reduced their influence, but they played a significant role in the politics of the Aleppo region throughout the third (ninth) century.

Though they did not enjoy the same independence, the family of Sulayman b.'Ali were prominent in Basra throughout the early Abbasid period, both Sulayman himself and his son Muhammad being frequently appointed as governors of the city. The family also had extensive lands in the area and Sulayman was given the property of 'Abbasan, which had belonged to the Muhallabi family in Umayyad times. He built a new governor's palace and we know that he had at least one private house in the city. He spent large sums on public works, especially bringing badly needed drinking water to the town and cultivating waste-land.[12] On occasion he took the side of the citizens in a dispute with the caliph. He died in 142 (759/60) and his position was inherited by his son, Muhammad. Though still in his early twenties, Muhammad led the only effective opposition to the Alid take-over[13] and, under him, the power and influence of the family reached its zenith. As with the family of Salih, they were linked to the main branch of the dynasty by marriage, when Muhammad married a daughter of Mahdi. He had many government appointments, being at times governor of Fars, Kufa, Ahwaz and the Basran dependency of Sind. But the real centre of his power and influence was the city itself, now at the height of its prosperity as a great trading centre, and it was there that he died in 173 (789); the sixty million *dirhams* confiscated by the caliph on that occasion are testimony to his fabulous wealth.[14] After his death, the family's fortunes declined. It seems to have been part of Harun's policy to reduce the influence of such branches of the family and he seized this opportunity.

At the end of 132 (summer 750), 'Isa b.Musa was appointed governor of Kufa, a post he held without interruption for the next fifteen years, the second longest tenure of any governor during the early Abbasid period – the longest being the twenty-one years, from 184 to 205 (800 to 820/1), when Dawud b.Yazid al-Muhallabi was governor of Sind. During this period, he was one of the most powerful men in the Abbasid state. Saffah singled him out to take control after his death if anything should happen to Mansur[15] and it was he who was chosen, probably because he was close at hand, to lead the Abbasid armies against the Alids, in 145 (762/3). Despite his disgrace in 147 (764), when Mansur removed him from the succession, his family remained influential in the city, his son Musa being governor no less than four times before his death in 183 (799/800). If, as seems probable, it was 'Isa b.Musa who built the vast desert palace at Ukhaydir during his retirement, it demonstrates to this day the power and wealth of the family.[16]

Other members of the family, Isma'il b.'Ali in Mosul, for example, developed links with different provinces, though they never became as important as the three just discussed. Others, like 'Isa b.'Ali, were active at court advising the caliph and it was the gout-ridden 'Isa who assured the smooth accession of Mansur.[17] In short, the family played a vital role in the formation of the Abbasid regime. Early Abbasid government was, like Umayyad government, very much a family business.

It was the army from Khurasan which had brought the dynasty to power and, along with the ruling family, they remained its principal support. They had a controlling interest in many areas of the caliphate. After the fall of Abu Muslim, the governors of Khurasan were always chosen from their numbers and their leaders also provided governors for provinces, like Armenia and Azerbayjan, where disturbances could be expected. In 144 (761/2) a leading Khurasani commander, Muhammad b.al-Ash'ath al-Khuza'i, took Ifriqiya for the Abbasids. He had with him some 40,000 men, many of whom settled in the province, where they subsequently produced their own dynasty, the Aghlabids.[18] In the capital, members of the leading Khurasani families usually commanded the two élite groups of the *shurta* (police) and *haras* (guard), in attendance on the caliph and under his direct orders.

The army was fundamental to the survival of the state; without it the numerous local disturbances could never have been contained and the vast empire would have dissolved into its constituent parts. Its leaders were among the most important and influential political figures in the state and the payment of the troops must have been one of the largest items in the budget. And yet we know almost nothing about the recruitment and organisation of this force and are dependent on the information we have from scattered, incidental references in chronicles. Much of what follows here must therefore be very speculative but, unless a new type of source suddenly appears, such speculation will remain our only way of attempting to understand this most important of institutions.

We have very little guide to the total numbers. Faced by the Alid rising in Basra in 145 (762), Mansur bemoaned the fact that he was almost defenceless. His armies were widely scattered; 4,000 with 'Isa b.Musa, fighting Muhammad b.'Abd Allah in Madina, 30,000 under his son Mahdi in Rayy, the 40,000 already mentioned in Ifriqiya and the 1,000 he had with him in Kufa.[19] This gives us a total of some 75,000 men, but we know that there were others, whom the caliph did not mention: the 2,000 who formed the standing garrison to protect Mosul from the Khawarij brigands of the surrounding steppe-lands, for example.[20] There must also have been a rather larger number of troops stationed on the Byzantine frontier – probably over 25,000 – although many of these were local Syrians rather than Khurasanis.[21] In addition, difficult provinces like Armenia and Azerbayjan must have had garrisons at important centres. This would give us an overall total of about 100,000 salaried Khurasani soldiers in the reign of Mansur. The pattern changed over the years; new troops may have been recruited for the military settlements in Baghdad and Raqqa and we know that 50,000 additional men were raised in Khurasan during the reign of Harun.[22] Conversely, the troops in North Africa ceased to be an integral part of the army. Some expeditions against the Byzantines are said to have involved very large numbers of men: 95,793 in 165 (781/2) and 135,000 in 190 (806).[23] These numbers seem very high, even though many of the participants would have been *muttawi'ah* (volunteers) rather than regular soldiers. When 'Ali b.'Isa b.Mahan raised between forty and fifty thousand men to fight Ma'mun in 195 (811), people in Baghdad said that it was the biggest army they had ever seen.[24] These troops were concentrated in fairly large garrison towns (Baghdad and Raqqa), and in Khurasan. Some provincial centres, like Mosul, had small garrisons, while others, like Basra, Fars and Ahwaz, seem to have had none at all. When Husayn b.'Ali rebelled in Madina, in 169 (786), there were only two hundred government troops to oppose him.[25] In Egypt the locally recruited *jund* seems to have been the only military force normally available to the governor. The forces consisted of both horsemen and foot-soldiers, usually with twice as many foot as horse.

The members of the regular army whose names were on the *diwan* were paid on a monthly basis. The basic rate was eighty *dirham*s a month for most of the early Abbasid period. In many cases they were also given grants of land known as *qati'a*, in Baghdad or on the frontier. These were neither fiefs, in the western sense, nor *iqta'* of the sort that later developed in Islam. They were plots of land held in absolute ownership and were both heritable and alienable. We have the dimensions of some of these grants in frontier areas and they seem to have been very small, just big enough to build a house on. The importance of this is that it shows that soldiers were dependent for their income on their salaries, fixed by the government, rather than on revenues from land. These salaries were comparatively generous by the standards of the time; labourers helping in the building of Baghdad were paid between one and two *dirham*s a month and, although skilled workers could make much more, the soldiers were still better off than the majority of the population. The Khurasani soldiers were determined to keep this privileged position and were prepared, if necessary, to fight any group which might rival them. The recruitment of other elements into the army would be more than just a political threat; it would also be a threat to their livelihood.[26]

Command and organisation in this army were in the hands of men known in the Arabic sources as *quwwad* (plural of *qa'id*), a term which could be translated as generals or commanders. In the armies of the early Abbasid period most of these *quwwad* were drawn from families of Arab origin settled in Khurasan. Many of those who later became famous had been among the small nucleus of *nuqaba'* who had founded the *da'wa* in the year 100 (718/19).[27] Military command was largely hereditary; senior appointments were made for political reasons and were not promotions based on military ability. When Qahtaba, who had led the Abbasid armies west from Khurasan, was killed during the crossing of the Euphrates, early in 132 (late summer 749), he was succeeded not by another senior *qa'id* but by his son Hasan, still a comparatively young man.[28] In 142 (759/60), the commander of the *shurta* in Baghdad, Musa b.Ka'b, died and the position was given to another prominent Khurasani, Musayyab b.Zuhayr, but Musa's son, then in Sind, was so enraged at being deprived of the office he must have considered rightfully his, that he started a rebellion.[29] This pattern is continued throughout the early Abbasid period and command of the Khurasani troops remained in the hands of about half a dozen prominent military families: the family of Qahtaba himself, of Khazim b.Khuzayma al-Tamimi, of Musayyab b.Zuhayr al-Dabbi, of Malik b.al-Haytham al-Khuza'i, of 'Uthman b.Nahik al-'Akki and of the latecomer and outsider, 'Ali b.'Isa b.Mahan. Since these men played a central role in the political events of the period, it might serve some purpose to examine the histories of two of these families in detail.

The family of Qahtaba b.Shabib al-Ta'i was naturally among the most prominent of the Arab military families. Qahtaba had been one of the original *nuqaba'* and had been a member of the delegation from Khurasan which came west in the years before the revolution to make contact with Ibrahim and the Abbasid family. He rose to pre-eminence in 130 (747/8), when Abu Muslim appointed him as leader of the army he sent to the west.[30] He proved his ability as a general in numerous encounters with the enemy in the course of the long march across Iran and down to the Iraqi plains; then, just as victory seemed in his grasp, he was killed, and it was left to his son, Hasan, to lead the victorious armies to Kufa. Hasan was then sent to command the armies besieging Ibn Hubayra and it was here that he came into contact with the future caliph, Mansur, and attached himself firmly to his cause. When Mansur was appointed as governor of Jazira,[31] Hasan went with him and was used in the difficult pacification of Armenia; then, when Abu Muslim was leading the Khurasanis against 'Abd Allah b.'Ali, Hasan was called south by the caliph to keep an eye on him. Thereafter, he was employed mostly on the Byzantine frontier, leading military expeditions and building up the defences[32] but playing little part in active politics, until his death in 181 (797), at the ripe old age of 84.[33] Like all the leaders of the army, he was rewarded with grants of property in Baghdad, and Ya'qubi records a street, *rabad* (quarter) and houses belonging to him.[34] He was obviously a man of great wealth; when Malatya was being rebuilt in 140 (757/8), he was able to feed all the workmen at his own expense, to the considerable irritation of his fellow commander, the Abbasid 'Abd al-Wahhab b.Ibrahim, who felt that he was getting above himself.[35]

If Hasan's career was smooth and successful, his brother's was much more stormy. As Hasan attached himself to Mansur, so Humayd served 'Abd Allah b.'Ali. He participated in the early stages of 'Abd Allah's revolt but this does not seem to have adversely affected his career for in 142 (759/60) he was briefly governor of Egypt.[36] In 145 (762/3) he served with 'Isa b.Musa against the Alids in Madina and Basra, and his flight from the battlefield of Bakhamra nearly caused a fatal panic among the Abbasid forces.[37] Three years later, he was sent to Armenia and his career culminated in his appointment as governor of Khurasan, a post he held from 151 (768) until his death in 159 (776).[38] Like his brother, he had property in Baghdad.

The third generation continued to be important. One of Hasan's sons was sent to Khurasan by Ja'far, the Barmakid, as his deputy, while one of Humayd's was *sahib al-haras* to the same Ja'far, in Syria.[39] Despite this Barmakid connection, however, members of the family played an important role in the struggle against Ma'mun. 'Abd Allah b.Humayd led an abortive expedition against Tahir when he was approaching Iraq, while his cousin, Sa'id b.al-Hasan, was put in charge of East Baghdad in 201 (816).[40] As with most families in a similar position, the civil war marked the end of their political influence. That they retained some of their wealth, if not their power, is suggested by the fact that Dawud b.'Abd Allah b.Humayd is recorded as being a patron of translators in the third century.[41]

Another good example is the family of Malik b.al-Haytham al-Khuza'i. Like Qahtaba, Malik had been one of the original *nuqaba'* but, after the revolution, he had thrown in his lot with Abu Muslim. Abu Muslim had made him his *sahib al-shurta* and Malik had tried to persuade his master into returning direct to Khurasan after the defeat of 'Abd Allah b.'Ali, rather than agreeing to see the caliph. After Abu Muslim's murder he was arrested but was able to regain the favour of the caliph at the time of the riot of the Rawandiya, in 141 (758/9), when he came to the caliph's aid at a crucial moment.[42] He then did a three-year spell as governor of Mosul,[43] but disappears from the sources after 145 (763) and we must presume that he died about then. Nonetheless, he had established his family's position and was given land on the East Bank at Baghdad.

Three of his sons had distinguished careers in the administration. The eldest, Nasr, was *sahib al-shurta* to Mahdi, until his death in 161 (777/8), and was given land in the new development in East Baghdad. He was succeeded in office by his brother, Hamza, who was in turn replaced by the third brother, 'Abd Allah, before the end of Mahdi's reign.[44] Hamza, who died in 181 (797), rose to be governor of Khurasan during 176/7 (793/4). 'Abd Allah survived his brothers to be one of the most prominent figures of Hadi's reign and was one of the military leaders who urged that caliph to execute Yahya, the Barmakid. Naturally, the accession of Harun and the Barmakid ascendency was a severe blow to him but, after the fall of the Barmakids in 187 (803), he was again in command of the *shurta* and two years later was given a very extensive governorate in western Iran. He was one of the leading military figures with Ma'mun in Marw when Harun died, but was gradually reduced to a subordinate position by Fadl b.Sahl, though he was present when the caliph finally entered Baghdad in 204 (819).[45] His son, Muttalib, played a very tortuous role in the civil war and was one of the leaders of Baghdadi resistance to Ma'mun in the years 201/3 (816/19).[46] Perhaps the most famous member of the family was Ahmad b.Nasr, who assumed the leadership of those in Baghdad who protested about the imposition of the doctrine of the creation of the Qur'an in the reign of Wathiq.[47]

The two families of Qahtaba and Malik are typical of the group. They were almost all founded by men who had joined the Abbasid movement early; they produced generals and governors for the caliphs; they all had land in Baghdad; finally, they all lost their privileged position in the long civil war which followed the death of Harun. Until that period, however, they formed a loyal and effective military élite and one of the main props of the dynasty.

There was no regimental organisation in the army and no career structure of the sort that Nizam al-Mulk describes for Saljuk times. Although the troops were paid by the government, they were led and probably recruited by the *quwwad,* to whom they owed their first loyalty. It may be significant that members of the leading military families often returned to Khurasan during their careers and it is possible that one of the objects of this was to recruit new men. In Baghdad, they were all given areas of land where they could settle their followers.

The most detailed example of the make-up of one of these contingents comes from the career of Khazim b.Khuzayma. He was a Tamimi tribesman, from the town of Marwrudh in Khurasan, and it was these two connections which provided him with his men. When, in 134 (751/2), he was sent to 'Uman, to fight the Kharijite rebels there, his forces consisted of men from his *ahl* (family), his *'ashira* (tribe), his *mawali* (freedmen or clients), the people of Marwrudh and some Tamimis from Basra, who joined him just before he set out.[48] All these men were in some way related to or dependent on him personally. Four years later, he was fighting Kharijite rebels again, this time in Jazira, and he had with him 8,000 of the men of Marwrudh. In 141 (758/9), he was ordered back to Khurasan to fight the governor, 'Abd al-Jabbar al-Azdi, who had rebelled against the caliph; on his approach, the people of Marwrudh rose against the rebel, captured him and handed him over to Khazim, showing that, despite some ten years' absence in the west, he still retained close links with the area.[49] When he died, his power and position passed to his son Khuzayma, who was able to raise 5,000 armed supporters in Baghdad on the night in 170 (786) when the caliph Hadi died.[50] It should be noted that, while Khazim himself was an Arab, he spoke Persian to his troops and had a Persian brother-in-law.[51]

We have, then, the picture of a man who could raise an effective fighting force from his own connections and put it at the service of the government, somewhat like the clan regiments raised by Scottish chiefs and landowners in the late-eighteenth century. An important consequence of this method of raising troops was that the commanders were men of considerable political weight. They were not employees to be ordered about and dismissed at will but were rather leaders of small private armies — hired, as it were, to the government — and it was only natural that the leadership of these armies tended to remain in the families of those who had originally raised them. The caliph retained control over them because he paid them and, to that extent, they depended on him, but, at the same time, he had to treat these leaders with care and pay attention to their wishes.

In addition to the Abbasids and the Khurasanis, already discussed, there were a number of other, Arab, groups who played important roles in the system established by Mansur. In most cases, these had not played an active part in the revolution, but had been attracted to Abbasid service later, either because they had a record of opposition to the Umayyads, or because they commanded the allegiance of important areas or groups.

The Muhallabi family falls into both these categories. Muhallab b.Abi Sufrah al-Azdi had been one of the great leaders of the Islamic conquest of Iran and, although his son, Yazid, had fallen foul of the Umayyads and Hajjaj had destroyed his power, the family continued to be prominent in and around Basra. Their influence was based on their position among the Azd of Basra, who were important as traders in many parts of the Islamic world, and they had contacts in places as far apart as Sind and Ifriqiya. At the time of the Abbasid Revolution, a

member of the family, Sufyan b.Mu'awiya, made an unsuccessful attempt
to drive out the last Umayyad governor of the city, while his cousins,
Yazid and Rawh b.Hatim, joined Mansur at the siege of Wasit. Sufyan
was rewarded for his efforts with a spell as governor of Basra and the
return of at least some of the lands confiscated by the Umayyads. He
disgraced himself by failing to offer effective opposition to the Alid
take-over of the city in 145 (762) and was never given another post,[52]
but other members of the family remained influential. Yazid b.Hatim
was governor in Azerbayjan (where he encouraged Azdis and others to
come from Basra and settle), Egypt and, finally, Ifriqiya, where he died,
in 170 (786/7). Ifriqiya, indeed, came near to becoming a family
possession; Yazid succeeded a Muhallabi, 'Umar b.Hafs, as governor and
was succeeded in turn by his brother Rawh. Yazid was very successful
in pacifying the unruly Berbers and is said to have revived trade, probably
as a result of his contacts with the merchants of Basra.[53] Rawh had
been governor of Basra, Kufa and Sind, before his appointment to
Ifriqiya.[54] His death four years later marks the effective end of the
family's role and, under the rule of Harun, their influence declined.
Only in Sind, a province always closely connected with Basra, did they
remain important as late as 216 (831), when the last Muhallabi governor
of the province was dismissed.[55]

Another influential family with connections in Basra was that of
Qutayba b.Muslim al-Bahili, the conqueror of much of Khurasan for the
Umayyads. His son, Salm, was the last Umayyad governor of Basra and
vigorously opposed the Abbasid advance. After the success of the
revolution, he seems to have retired to his estates in Rayy, but Mansur
was quick to let bygones be bygones when it came to recruiting
influential men and Salm helped him to defeat the Alid rebellion in
Basra, using his contacts in the city. He was made governor for a brief
spell, as a reward, and, when he died four years later in Rayy, no lesser
person than the caliph's son and heir prayed over his body.[56] His son,
Sa'id, was a close confidant of the short-lived Caliph Hadi but was,
nonetheless, appointed by Harun to some of the most difficult governorates in the caliphate, Armenia and Jazira among them, although he
never succeeded to his father's position in Basra.[57] The civil war saw
the power of the family greatly weakened and, though Sa'id's son,
Ahmad, was governor of the Thughur province on the Byzantine frontier
as late as the reign of Wathiq,[58] the family was no longer part of the
ruling élite.

While Basra was the base for three families of major importance
(those of Sulayman b.'Ali, the Abbasid, the Muhallabis and Salm

b.Qutayba), Kufa was less well represented in the ruling groups. This may be a reflection of the declining importance of the town, especially after the foundation of Baghdad, and perhaps, also, of the heavy hand that the government kept on the city, in order to prevent disturbances. Apart from the Abbasid family of 'Isa b.Musa, which had a somewhat chequered record, the only Kufan family which seems to have been of any importance were the descendants of Ash'ath b.Qays al-Kindi, who are mentioned several times, both as deputies for 'Isa b.Musa and as governors in their own right; Ishaq b.al-Sibah, father of the famous philosopher, Ya'qub b.Ishaq al-Kindi, was briefly governor in 159 (785/6), while his nephew, Fadl b.Muhammad, is mentioned as being in the same post in 202 (817).[59] Though, no doubt, influential in their own town, the Kindis were never as important in the rest of the empire as the great Basran families were.

In Syria, we have already seen how Mansur won over many of the leaders of the Qays faction who had been Marwan's closest supporters. Even those who had supported 'Abd Allah b.'Ali in his abortive rebellion were not punished but continued to play a part in expeditions against the Byzantines. Some, like Zufar b.'Asim al-Hilali, were given important government posts, Zufar being governor of Madina and Jazira, while others,[60] like Ja'far b.Hanzala al-Bahrani, made their mark as advisers to the caliph. Syrian troops played a useful if secondary role in the Abbasid army, principally on the frontier but also fighting the Alids in Basra or suppressing rebellions in Khurasan. It seems probable that they, like the Khurasanis, were recruited and led by their traditional leaders and that this accounts for the influence that such leaders enjoyed in government.

Not all the magnates on whom the government relied were based on particular areas. Some of them derived their power from their position as tribal leaders. It is easy to assume that, after the Abbasid Revolution, Arab tribes and tribal feelings ceased to be of real importance for the political life of the Muslim community. There is some truth in this but there still remained tribal leaders, relying on the support of their tribesmen, who were prominent figures. The most important of these was Ma'n b.Za'ida, whose tribe of Shayban roamed the steppe-lands of Jazira. Ma'n had been an important supporter of Marwan's regime and claimed that it was he who had killed Qahtaba when the Abbasid armies were crossing the Euphrates. Not surprisingly, he went into hiding after the victory of the Abbasids but he was too useful a man for Mansur to neglect. He was instrumental in saving the caliph's life at the time of the riot of the Rawandiya, in 141 (758/9), and was thereafter employed as a strong-arm man in such difficult areas as Yaman and Sistan. It was here that he was killed, in 152 (772/3), when Kharijites dug through the roof of his house and surprised him,[61] but his position was inherited by his son, Yazid b.Mazyad, who also inherited the feud with the Kharijites, who pursued him to Baghdad and attacked him on the bridge of boats over the Tigris. Yazid survived to become one of the leading military figures of the age. In the latter part of Mahdi's reign, he became closely attached to the heir apparent, Musa al-Hadi, and, when he became caliph, Yazid was among the military leaders who urged that Harun should be removed from the succession and Yahya, the Barmakid, killed. Naturally, the accession of Harun saw him in deep disgrace and it was not until Harun was faced by a serious Kharijite threat in Jazira, in 179 (795/6), that Yazid, against the advice of the Barmakids, was again given a military command. He led his *'ashira* against the rebel and killed him. Thereafter, he served Harun in Khurasan, on the Byzantine frontier and in Armenia, where he finally ended his spectacular career, in 185 (801).[62] Both Ma'n and Yazid were celebrated in poetry and legend; to the popular imagination they were held up as examples of the old Arab virtues of bravery in battle and generosity. Their role as representatives of 'Arabness' comes out clearly in the career of Yazid's son, Asad, known as *'faris al-'arab'* (the 'knight of the Arabs').[63] Yazid had been a determined opponent of the Barmakids and all they stood for, so it was natural that he and his family supported Amin, while urging him to give preference to Arabs over Khurasani soldiers.

The Early Abbasid system, then, depended on many different people and groups around the empire, of whom only a sample has been discussed. Many different people saw it in their interest that the Abbasid regime should continue, and this gave it a wide and firm power base, which contrasts strikingly with the militarily dominated regime of the next century. At least under Mansur, power was to an extent decentralised. The most important people in the state after the caliph himself were the governors of the great provinces. Of course the caliph had advisers at court, some of whom were very influential, like 'Isa b.'Ali, his uncle, or Ja'far b.Hanzala; he had also secretaries, like Abu Ayyub al-Muryani, financial officials, like Khalid b.Barmak, and personal servants, like Rabi' b.Yunus, but these had none of the controlling influence that their successors had in later reigns. Power lay with the army and the provincial governors, not with the bureaucracy or the palace.

As a result of this widely diffused support, early Abbasid government was very successful. It was a period of comparative peace and growing prosperity. In the whole of Iraq there was only one major rebellion, the Alid rising in Basra, between the accession of Saffah and the death of Rashid. In Syria, perhaps because of the integration of Syrian leaders into the Abbasid hierarchy, there were no major disturbances after the defeat of 'Abd Allah b.'Ali. This is not to say that peace reigned everywhere. Khurasan remained a largely unsolved problem and rural discontent was endemic among the Arabs of Jazira and the Copts of the Egyptian Delta, but, considering the slender resources at the disposal of the dynasty in 132 (750), the achievement is very impressive.

The best-known and most lasting of Mansur's achievements was the foundation of the city of Baghdad.[64] Since the revolution, the Abbasids had founded or attempted to found cities at no less than four different sites in the area of Kufa and Anbar. All these sites were known as Hashimiya, in honour of the dynasty, but each of them proved unsuitable. It was not until the year 145 (762) that Mansur finally decided on the site of Baghdad. There was no large settlement in the area but a number of small villages, one of which gave its name to the future metropolis.

There were several reasons for seeking to found a new capital in open country. The most pressing of these was the need for security, which became especially apparent at the time of the riot of the Rawandiya, in 141 (758/9); this need could only be satisfied by the construction of a fortress-palace which could easily be defended. Secondly, there was the desire felt by so many dynasties, both Islamic and pre-Islamic, in the area to have a new capital to demonstrate their identity and prestige. The Middle East is full of the ruins of these grandiose enterprises and it is a tribute to the foresight of its founder that Baghdad is one of the few to have survived after the dynasty had gone. The Abbasids also needed a base where they could settle their Khurasani followers. Clearly, if they had chosen any existing city, there would inevitably be tensions between the original inhabitants and the newcomers, as Mu'tasim was to find three-quarters of a century later, when he attempted to settle his Turks in Baghdad. Finally, it enabled the caliph to reward his followers at very little cost to himself. He could give them plots of land on which they could settle themselves and their followers and which they could let out to merchants. For the caliph, land was very cheap but once the court and the administration were established in the area, the same land became very valuable. Vast fortunes could be made and, to some extent, the foundation of such a new capital was a gigantic property speculation.

The Abbasids seem to have decided right from the beginning that their new capital should be in Iraq. Khurasan was too far from the centre of the empire to be a practical choice and the location of centre of government in that area would have made them over-dependent on the Khurasanis. Iraq had a long tradition of opposition to the Umayyads and support for the house of the Prophet, if not necessarily for the Abbasid branch. In addition, Iraq provided by far the largest share of the revenues of the caliphate. For political and military reasons the Umayyads had kept the centre of government in Syria but it had been one of the major weaknesses of their state that they were dependent financially on Iraq, a considerable distance from the capital; this was not to happen under the Abbasids.

Since the third millenium BC, the capitals of Iraq had been in the centre, near the point where the Tigris and the Euphrates approach each other most closely; Sargon's capital of Akkad was probably near here and so was the Babylon of Hammurabi and Nebuchadnezzar. Slightly to the west lay the Kassite capital of Aqar-Kuf, while to the southeast was the Seleucid and Sassanian centre of Seleucia/Cteisphon. Mansur was following a very ancient tradition. But it was practical considerations which made up the caliph's mind, and of these practical considerations, communications were the most important. It was vitally important for the caliph to keep in close touch with Khurasan and the new site was ideal for this; it was a comparatively short journey, up the fertile Diyala valley, to Hulwan and the beginning of the long road through the passes in the Zagros to the Iranian plateau.

The city was on the banks of the Tigris, which provided a means of communication to the north, to Mosul and thence to Armenia and Jazira, or south to Basra, the Gulf and distant Sind. In addition, the site was connected to the Euphrates by a number of canals, especially the Sarat, which dated from Sassanian times. This meant that goods, especially grain, could be brought by water from Raqqa and Jazira and provided a route to Syria and the Byzantine frontier.

Communications were also very important for commercial reasons, as the caliph was very well aware. During the next half-century, Baghdad became a great trading centre and the cross-roads of the Islamic world. In addition, water transport was very important for supplying the city. As the population grew, it could no longer be fed from the surrounding countryside; grain had to be imported in large quantities from the Jazira, and Baghdad, on the Tigris and connected to the Euphrates by canal, was in an ideal situation for this. The site is superbly chosen and the sources show that Mansur was keenly aware of the strategic and economic factors which were to make his city so successful.[65]

The heart of the new capital was the Round City which contained the palace, the main mosque and some administrative buildings and quarters for troops. The palace and mosque were together in the middle of the central courtyard and the palace was surmounted by a green dome over the audience chamber. Both Hisham's palace at Rusafa and Hajjaj's at Wasit had had green domes and it seems that Mansur was deliberately symbolising the transfer of sovereignty.[66] Originally, there had been markets within the Round City, but these were removed shortly afterwards for security reasons. While the Round City remained the administrative centre, the caliph soon decided to build palaces outside the walls, where there was more room for expansion and they could take advantage of cool breezes from the river. Mansur himself built a palace called the Khuld (Eternity), between his city and the river. Mahdi began by living in the palace at Rusafa, on the East Bank, but he, too, built a retreat at 'Isabadh, on the same side of the river. During his short reign Hadi continued to use 'Isabadh, but Harun, on the rare occasions when he lived in Baghdad, returned to Khuld and his son, Amin, made it his permanent residence.[67] Other members of the family had palaces by the river; Mansur's uncle 'Isa b.'Ali had one to the south of Khuld, while two of his sons, Sulayman and Salih, had them to the north.

Beyond the walls of the city a large number of suburbs were developed and it was here that most of the population lived. Much of the land was distributed among the leaders of the Khurasani army, who settled their followers there, especially in the area known as the Harbiya, to the northwest of the original city. These Khurasani soldiers and their descendants were the most influential inhabitants of the city and dominated its political life. Some members of the Abbasid family had property, notably the caliph's brother 'Abbas, who owned the island called 'Abbasiya, in his honour, but it is interesting to note that those members of the family who established themselves in the provinces were not given land in Baghdad. Some palace officials were granted areas to develop, especially the caliph's *hajib* and faithful servant, Rabi' b.Yunus, who owned much of the commercial area of Karkh. The new capital soon attracted other inhabitants trying to make their fortunes. There were the substantial merchants of the Karkh area but there was also a large number of people of humbler status who flocked to the city and formed a non-military, urban proletariat. The city grew very fast; population estimates are very difficult, but a figure of half a million inhabitants by the end of the century is quite possible,[68] and Baghdad must have suffered from all the social problems and tensions found in rapidly growing cities today.

In addition to this West Bank city, there appeared a parallel settlement on the east side of the Tigris. Whereas the West Bank had been developed by Mansur to house his supporters, the East Bank was created by his son and heir, Muhammad al-Mahdi. In 151 (769), Muhammad returned from Rayy, where he had ruled as viceroy of Khurasan for ten years, and he brought with him many who had attached themselves to his cause during this period. He now used the new development, originally called 'Askar al-Mahdi (the Military Camp of Mahdi), to house and reward his followers. Some well-established figures, like Khazim b.Khuzayma, had land on both sides but Mahdi also gave plots to people who were attached to him particularly, such as his *wazir*, Abu 'Ubayd Allah Mu'awiya, and, above all, the Barmakids, all of whose extensive properties lay on the East Bank. The population of this area differed somewhat from that of the West Bank and they tended to be later recruits to the Abbasid élite. There was no equivalent to the Round City on this side of the river but Mahdi had a fine palace built for himself, in the area known as Rusafa, and this was flanked by a large mosque to complement the one on the other bank. The East Bank city grew as fast as the West Bank and, after the civil war, it seems to have become more populous and the normal residence of the caliphs.

With the city built on both sides of the river, the bridges were of great importance. There seem to have been three by the reign of Harun, all of them pontoon bridges built on boats because of the fast current and muddy bottom of the river. But the river, despite all the benefits it brought in terms of communications and the provision of drinking water, was also a menace and floods were a constant danger from the Abbasid period until the twentieth century.[69] From the time of the Sumerians, mud-brick was the normal building material of the area, there being no workable stone and baked brick being expensive. It was cheap and flexible but when not maintained quickly degenerated into the shapeless mounds so typical of the Mesopotamian landscape. Sieges, wars and flood damage have combined to destroy all traces of the city of Mansur, which now survives only in literary descriptions.

On the middle Euphrates, some 750 kilometres from Baghdad, Mansur founded the town of Rafiqa, near Raqqa, which was complementary to the capital on whose plan it is said to have been modelled. Unlike Baghdad, the ground plan of the fortifications of Rafiqa can still be recovered and one of the city gates, dating from the time of Harun, still survives.[70] The new city was begun ten years after Baghdad, in 155 (772). Like Baghdad,[71] its purpose was, at least in part, military.

It was a city to house Khurasani troops, to reinforce the Byzantine frontier, if necessary, and to keep an eye on the provinces of Syria and Jazira. Unfortunately, we have none of the detailed information about the inhabitants which we have for Baghdad. It is clear, however, from accounts of the fighting of the year 195 (811/12) that they were largely Khurasanis, in contrast with the Syrian population of the old city of Raqqa, from which it was still separated by open ground.[72] It also had an economic function, as a centre for collecting the grain of Jazira for transport down river to Baghdad, though it never became a great commercial centre like Baghdad. Rafiqa, which gradually took on the name of the old city and was known as Raqqa, enjoyed its heyday under Harun, who also used it as his residence, from 180 (796) onwards.[73]

After the great struggles of the first half of Mansur's reign, the period after the final defeat of the Alids was one of comparative quiet. Internally, it was a period of comparative peace and only in Khurasan and Egypt were there serious disturbances. In 151 (768), Ustadhsis, who seems to have been a local *dehqan* in Badhghis in southern Khurasan, led the people of his remote and mountainous area in rebellion, largely as a protest against increasing Arab penetration.[74] In Egypt, there were sporadic rebellions among the rural Christian population, resentful about high levels of taxation. On the frontiers, too, things were comparatively peaceful. The Byzantine frontier had been severely weakened by the campaigns of Constantine V, in the difficult times during and immediately after the revolution, but, since then, the position had been restored and Muslim outposts re-established. In 147 (764), the Caucasus frontier was disturbed when people who are referred to as Turks, but were probably Khazars, invaded and took Tiflis. The limited Abbasid forces in the area were defeated and their leaders killed but, the next year, when Humayd b.Qahtaba led a punitive expedition, the invaders had retired and did not trouble the Muslims for the rest of the reign.[75] The caliph spent most of his remaining years in Baghdad, developing and improving it. The year before his death, 157 (774/5), he removed the merchants from the Round City to Karkh, which then became the great commercial district, and he built the new palace called the Khuld.[76] In 152 (769), he led the pilgrimage and stopped at Basra for forty days on the way home, to organise the war against the pirates of Kurk, probably Abyssinians who were threatening Jidda.[77] In 154 (771), he visited Jerusalem and the site of his future town at Rafiqa.[78]

All this activity, however, was overshadowed by the last great political problem of the reign, the question of the succession. When Saffah was dying, he was very concerned lest his chosen successor,

Mansur, should not return from the pilgrimage he was making with his arch-enemy, Abu Muslim. If Mansur were to die for any reason, Abu Muslim would then be in the position of king-maker, to choose whichever member of the family he wanted as caliph, and this would undo all the work Saffah had done to strengthen Abbasid power. In order to avoid this, he decided that another Abbasid should be chosen to succeed Mansur so that, if anything did happen, power could pass swiftly and without dispute to another member of the dynasty. The man selected for this role was 'Isa b.Musa. He was still fairly young (probably thirty-four), but had proved his ability as governor of Kufa during the previous four years and he was near at hand to take over without delay. In the event, the need did not arise and Mansur returned safe and well to take control, but 'Isa remained Mansur's heir, serving him loyally as governor of Kufa and as his leading general against the Alid revolts of 145 (762/3). After his position had been made secure, however, Mansur decided to arrange for the succession of his own son, Muhammad, later known as Mahdi.[79] He had probably been contemplating this step for some time and his son had been well-groomed for the succession.[80] In 141 (759/60) he had been appointed viceroy of the east, living at Rayy and supervising Khurasan, and this enabled him to make close contacts with many of the leading figures in the Khurasani army. This connection with the Khurasanis was to prove very important for Mahdi and it was pressure from the army which allowed him to replace 'Isa. There were, doubtless, personal reasons why Mansur wanted his own son rather than his nephew to succeed to the state he had virtually created, but there is no doubt that Mahdi had made himself very popular in the army and among many who had achieved wealth and fame under Mansur and wanted to ensure that the system which he had established continued.

We can be fairly clear as to who supported Mahdi; it is much more difficult to discover who wanted 'Isa b.Musa as caliph and why the Khurasanis were so fiercely hostile to him. Circumstantial evidence suggests that we should look to Khurasan for an explanation. He is never recorded as having visited the area but he does seem to have had contacts there. He is said to have been a friend of Abu Muslim, which may well have meant that they had met before the revolution. When 'Isa b.Musa was removed from his position as heir apparent, there was trouble in the province. His removal is said to have been the immediate cause of the rebellion of Ustadhsis and, in 153 (770), a small group of Khurasanis, among them Harthama b.A'yan, was brought to Baghdad in chains as a punishment for supporting 'Isa's cause.[81] Ustadhsis seems to have been a local *dehqan,* or princeling, in Khurasan and Harthama certainly had links with the *dehqans.* This suggests that his candidacy may have been supported by the *dehqans,* against whom the Abbasid Revolution had, at least in part, been directed. This would account to some extent for the strength of the opposition to him, especially from 'Ali b.'Isa b.Mahan, later to emerge as the scourge of the *dehqans.* This hypothesis receives some support from the fact that the family of 'Isa b.Musa was the only branch of the Abbasid family to support the pro-*dehqan* party of Ma'mun during the civil war.

From the defeat of the Alid rebellions onwards, Mansur tried to persuade 'Isa to give precedence to Mahdi; 'Isa was still to be Mahdi's heir, though, clearly, his chances of outliving his great-nephew and thus inheriting the caliphate were small. 'Isa rejected a straightforward approach and Mansur realised that he would need to use more than simple persuasion to achieve his end. His first move was to look for allies and persuade others to put pressure on 'Isa. He began by entrusting him with the supervision of 'Abd Allah b.'Ali, who had been more or less a prisoner since the collapse of his rebellion ten years before. 'Abd Allah owed his life, at least in part, to the pressure of his formidably powerful brothers, the Banu 'Ali. Mansur decided to use this pressure against 'Isa and secretly ordered him to execute his prisoner. Fortunately, 'Isa, or rather his secretary, saw the trap. When the Banu 'Ali, on the caliph's instigation, asked to see their brother, Mansur sent for 'Isa, confident that he would by now have executed the prisoner, and ordered that he be produced. 'Isa, of course, said that he had been ordered to kill him; the caliph, for his part, denied any such order and was preparing to allow his uncles their legitimate revenge when 'Isa produced the supposed victim and the caliph's plan was exposed.

But Mansur's determination was not undermined. 'Isa was deprived of the governorship of Kufa, which he had held for fifteen years, and never given another government appointment. The caliph then began to intimidate 'Isa, threatening and humiliating him in public in an effort to provoke him to anger or to renounce his rights. 'Isa's response was one of dignified restraint and he refused to give in; it was not for himself, he explained, that he was holding out, but for the sake of his son and all those Muslims who had sworn oaths of allegiance to him. Mansur now turned to the Khurasani military, who, at the same time, extolled the virtues of Mahdi and made it clear to 'Isa that, whatever the formal arrangements were, he would never, in practice, be allowed to exercise power. This show of force succeeded where persuasion and intrigue had failed. According to one version, it was Khalid b.Barmak who tricked 'Isa out of his rights; according to another, Salm b.Qutayba was the middle man. In 147 (764), Mahdi was finally acknowledged as heir apparent and the long-suffering 'Isa finally renounced his rights, in exchange for vast financial compensation and the position of heir to Mahdi.[82]

The whole incident is very revealing and gives a foretaste of things to come. It shows clearly the way confusion over the succession polarised opinion within the governing classes. It also suggests that the *dehqan*s of Khurasan were still a force to be feared; if 'Isa had not had powerful backers, all the intrigue and manœuvre would have been unnecessary. 'Isa retired into private life but he was still on the caliph's mind; on his death-bed, Mansur is reported to have said that the only two men he was anxious about were 'Isa b.Zayd, the Alid, and, despite all the promises and guarantees he had given, 'Isa b.Musa.[83]

In 158 (775), the caliph, now in his mid-sixties, decided to lead the pilgrimage in person for the fifth time. He took with him leading members of his family, including 'Isa b.'Ali, 'Isa b.Musa and Muhammad b.Sulayman, his *hajib*, Rabi' b.Yunus (an increasingly influential figure in the last years of his reign) and a military escort. He became ill on the road and died at Bi'r Maymun, a few miles from the Holy City, towards sunrise on 6 Dhu'l-Hijja, 158 (7 October 775).[84] He had reigned for almost twenty-two Muslim (just over twenty-one solar) years. During this time he had laid the foundations of the Abbasid state. His combination of political vision and pragmatic approach had led to the development of a powerful secular monarchy. But this power, impressive and broadly based though it was, could lead to problems. The division between the ruling élite and the bulk of the Muslims, which had been typical of Umayyad rule, remained. Mansur secured the dynasty; he did not satisfy the aspirations of those who wanted a community led by a divinely guided *imam*. It was left to his successors to try to bridge this gap.

Notes

1. Tabari, *Ta'rikh*, vol. 3, pp. 374-5, 495, 557; Ya'qubi, *Buldan*, pp. 243, 252; Yaqut, *Mu'jam*, vol. 3, p. 601, vol. 4, p. 835.
2. Tabari, *Ta'rikh*, vol. 3, pp. 72, 74; Azdi, *Ta'rikh*, pp. 145-54.
3. Tabari, *Ta'rikh*, vol. 3, pp. 329-30, 374-5.
4. Baladhuri, *Futuh*, pp. 159, 170; Ibn al-'Adim, *Zubdat*, p. 59; Yaqut, *Mu'jam*, vol. 4, p. 655.
5. Tabari, *Ta'rikh*, vol. 3, p. 122; Baladhuri, *Futuh*, pp. 197, 199, 223, 225.
6. Tabari, *Ta'rikh*, vol. 3, p. 466.

7. Ibn al-'Adim, *Zubdat*, p. 60.

8. Ya'qubi, *Ta'rikh*, vol. 2, p. 461.

9. Jahshiyari, *Wuzara'*, pp. 262-3.

10. Tabari, *Ta'rikh*, vol. 3, p. 688.

11. Ibid., vol. 3, p. 842.

12. Baladhuri, *Ansab*, pp. 569-71; *Futuh*, pp. 429, 433, 454, 456.

13. Tabari, *Ta'rikh*, vol. 3, p. 300.

14. Ibid., vol. 3, pp. 607-8.

15. Ibid., vol. 3, pp. 87-9.

16. Creswell, *Early Muslim Architecture* (Oxford, 1932-40), vol. 2, pp. 96-8. I do not find the arguments advanced by W. Caskel, 'Al-Uhaidir' in *Der Islam*, vol. 39, 1964, convincing.

17. Ya'qubi, *Ta'rikh*, vol. 2, p. 437; Baladhuri, *Ansab*, fo. 619. The sources often confuse 'Isa b.'Ali with 'Isa b. Musa.

18. Baladhuri, *Futuh*, p. 271; Ibn Idhari, *Bayan*, vol. 1, p. 72. cf. Tabari, *Ta'rikh*, vol. 3, p. 74, where this event is put ten years too early. For further details, see below, pp. 189-90.

19. Tabari, *Ta'rikh*, vol. 3, pp. 304-5.

20. Azdi, *Ta'rikh*, pp. 194-5.

21. Baladhuri, *Futuh*, pp. 194-203, 219-29.

22. Tabari, *Ta'rikh*, vol. 3, p. 631. See also below, pp. 120, 181.

23. Tabari, *Ta'rikh*, vol. 3, pp. 504, 709.

24. Ibid., vol. 3, p. 818.

25. Ibid., vol. 3, p. 554.

26. Baladhuri, *Futuh*, p. 201; E. Ashtor, *Histoire des Prix et des Salaires* (Paris, 1969), pp. 64-5.

27. For lists of the *nuqaba'*, see Tabari, *Ta'rikh*, vol. 2, p. 1358, *Akhbar al-'Abbas*, pp. 213-20.

28. Tabari, *Ta'rikh*, vol. 3, pp. 12-18.

29. Ibid., vol. 3, pp. 138-9.

30. Tabari, *Ta'rikh*, vol. 2, p. 2000.

31. Tabari, *Ta'rikh*, vol. 3, p. 95.

32. Ibid., vol. 3, pp. 353, 493, 495; Baladhuri, *Futuh*, pp. 223, 261, 296; Yaqut, *Mu'jam*, vol. 4, p. 167.

33. Tabari, *Ta'rikh*, vol. 3, p. 646; Ibn al-Athir, *Ta'rikh*, vol. 6, p. 109.

34. Ya'qubi, *Buldan*, p. 246.

35. Baladhuri, *Futuh*, p. 223.

36. Tabari, *Ta'rikh*, vol. 3, p. 141.

37. Ibid., vol. 3, p. 313.

38. Ibid., vol. 3, pp. 353, 369, 459.

39. Ibid., vol. 3, pp. 639, 644; Hamza Isfahani, *Ta'rikh*, p. 143.

40. Tabari, *Ta'rikh*, vol. 3, pp. 797, 840, 1002.

41. Ibn al-Nadim, *Fihrist*, p. 244.

42. Tabari, *Ta'rikh*, vol. 2, pp. 1358, 1959, vol. 3, pp. 112-18, 130.

43. Azdi, *Ta'rikh*, pp. 177-8.

44. Tabari, *Ta'rikh*, vol. 3, p. 491; Ya'qubi, *Ta'rikh*, vol. 2, p. 474; Yaqut, *Mu'jam*, vol. 3, p. 201.

45. Tabari, *Ta'rikh*, vol. 3, pp. 602, 692, 734, 905; Azdi, *Ta'rikh*, p. 269; Jahshiyari, *Wuzara'*, pp. 278, 309, 314; Ibn Tayfur, *Kitab Baghdad*, p. 18.

46. Tabari, *Ta'rikh*, vol. 3, pp. 1011-12, 1016.

47. Tabari, *Ta'rikh*, vol. 3, pp. 1345 ff.

48. Ibid., vol. 3, p. 78.

49. Ibid., vol. 3, pp. 123, 135.

50. Ibid., vol. 3, p. 602.

51. Isfahani, *Maqatil*, pp. 326-9.
52. Tabari, *Ta'rikh*, vol. 3, pp. 21, 299; Baladhuri, *Ansab*, fos. 612-17.
53. Tabari, *Ta'rikh*, vol. 3, pp. 142, 370, 372, 569; Ya'qubi, *Ta'rikh*, vol. 2, p. 446; Ibn Idhari, *Bayan*, vol. 1, pp. 76-84; Kindi, *Wulat*, pp. 111-15; Azdi, *Ta'rikh*, pp. 217-19.
54. Tabari, *Ta'rikh*, vol. 3, pp. 461, 467, 482, 505, 609; Ibn Idhari, *Bayan*, vol. 1, p. 84.
55. Tabari, *Ta'rikh*, vol. 3, p. 1105.
56. Ibid., vol. 3, pp. 319, 326; Dhahabi, *Ta'rikh*, vol. 6, pp. 31, 71. Ibn Qutayba gives a detailed account of the family, with their Basran and Khurasani connections, in *Ma'arif*, p. 407.
57. Tabari, *Ta'rikh*, vol. 3, pp. 587, 597, 645, 647; Ya'qubi, *Ta'rikh*, vol. 2, p. 518; Ibn Tayfur, *Kitab Baghdad*, p. 13; Azdi, *Ta'rikh*, pp. 269-70.
58. Tabari, *Ta'rikh*, vol. 3, p. 1352.
59. Ibid., vol. 3, pp. 465, 1022; Baladhuri, *Ansab*, fo. 593.
60. Tabari, *Ta'rikh*, vol. 3, pp. 378, 482, 500; Azdi, *Ta'rikh*, pp. 243-4.
61. Tabari, *Ta'rikh*, vol. 3, pp. 16, 63, 129-30, 368, 369, 394-7; Baladhuri, *Futuh*, p. 494; Ya'qubi, *Ta'rikh*, vol. 2, pp. 448, 462; Ibn al-Athir, *Ta'rikh*, vol. 5, p. 464; Isfahani, *Aghani*, vol. 10, pp. 84-6.
62. Tabari, *Ta'rikh*, vol. 3, pp. 519, 602, 638, 650; Baladhuri, *Futuh*, pp. 247, 494; Ya'qubi, *Ta'rikh*, vol. 2, pp. 515-19; Isfahani, *Aghani*, vol. 10, pp. 94-100.
63. Tabari, *Ta'rikh*, vol. 3, p. 735.
64. The most important sources on the foundation of Baghdad are Tabari, *Ta'rikh*, vol. 3, pp. 271-82, 319-26; Ya'qubi, *Buldan*, pp. 238-54; Khatib al-Baghdadi, *Ta'rikh Baghdad* (Beirut, 1967), published in English translation, by J. Lassner, *The Topography of Baghdad in the Early Middle Ages* (Wayne State, 1970), pp. 45-110. For modern accounts see Duri, 'Baghdad' in EI (2); Creswell, *Early Muslim Architecture*, vol. 2, pp. 4-38; Le Strange, *Baghdad under the Abbasid Caliphate* (Oxford, 1900); M. Jawad and A. Sousa, *Kharitah Baghdad* (Baghdad, 1958); S. El-Ali in *The Islamic City*.
65. Tabari, *Ta'rikh*, vol. 3, pp. 273-6.
66. Lassner, *Baghdad*, pp. 134-7.
67. Ibid., p. 134.
68. Ibid., pp. 160, 282-3.
69. See A. Sousa, *Fayadanat Baghdad* (Baghdad, 1963).
70. Creswell, *Early Muslim Architecture*, vol. 2, pp. 39-45.
71. Tabari, *Ta'rikh*, vol. 3, p. 373.
72. Ibid., vol. 3, pp. 843-5.
73. Ibid., vol. 3, p. 645.
74. See below, pp. 183-4.
75. Tabari, *Ta'rikh*, vol. 3, pp. 327, 353; D.M. Dunlop, *The History of the Jewish Khazars* (Princeton, 1954), pp. 179-84; Bosworth, 'Kabk' in EI (2).
76. Tabari, *Ta'rikh*, vol. 3, p. 379.
77. Ibid., vol. 3, pp. 369, 370; Omar, *Abbasid Caliphate*, p. 319.
78. Tabari, *Ta'rikh*, vol. 3, p. 372.
79. Muhammad had been given the title 'mahdi' in 145 (762/3), two years before he was officially acknowledged as heir; see G.C. Miles, *Numismatic History of Rayy* (New York, 1938), p. 26.
80. Tabari, *Ta'rikh*, vol. 3, p. 116. For a discussion of the whole affair, see J. Lassner, 'Did the Caliph Abu Ja'far al-Mansur murder his uncle 'Abd Allah b.'Ali?' in *Studies in Memory of Gaston Wiet*, ed. M. Rosen-Ayalon (Jerusalem, 1977).
81. Tabari, *Ta'rikh*, vol. 3, p. 371; Ya'qubi, *Ta'rikh*, vol. 2, p. 457.
82. Tabari, *Ta'rikh*, vol. 3, pp. 328-52; Baladhuri, *Ansab*, fos. 655-6.
83. Tabari, *Ta'rikh*, vol. 3, p. 448.
84. Ibid., vol. 3, pp. 387-9.

THE REIGNS OF MAHDI AND HADI

The new caliph, Abu 'Abd Allah Muhammad b.'Abd Allah, called Mahdi, was now in his thirties. He was born, probably in 126 or 127 (743/5) in the obscure town of Idhaj, in Khuzistan in the foothills of the Zagros, perhaps because his father was then involved in the ill-fated rebellion of 'Abd Allah b.Mu'awiya against the last Umayyads. His mother, Arwa, was a free-born Arab from a Yamani family of no great distinction.[1] After the collapse of the rebellion, in 129 (746), the young boy went with his father to Humayma, whence he came with the rest of the Abbasid family to Kufa after the revolution. In 141 (758/9), when he was no more than fifteen or sixteen years old, he was sent in charge of operations in Khurasan against the rebel governor, 'Abd al-Jabbar al-Azdi. For the next ten years he was based at Rayy, supervising the affairs of eastern Iran and building a new government quarter in the city, known as Muhammadiya in his honour. In 144 (762), he returned briefly to the west to marry Rita, the daughter of Suffah. By the time of the Alid revolts of late 145 (762), he was back in Rayy and he did not return to Baghdad until Shawwal 151 (October/November 768), when he began the building of Rusafa on the east bank of the Tigris at Baghdad, as a settlement for his followers. He had been given a place in the succession after 'Isa b.Musa as early as 141 (758/9), but it was not until 147 (764) that 'Isa was forced to give up his position and Mahdi became next in line to the throne. In Rayy he had had his own administration and *wazir,* Abu 'Ubayd Allah Mu'awiya, and, on his return to Baghdad, he was given a ceremonial welcome by Mansur and members of the Abbasid family and a *sahaba,* or group of advisers.[2] The rest of his father's life he spent in the west, assisting the caliph.

By the time of his accession he had had considerable poli⁺ical experience and contacts with many of the most powerful men in the state. The death of a caliph was usually a time of crisis but Mahdi's take-over could hardly have been smoother. He was already in charge in Baghdad, serving as his father's deputy, while his only possible rival, 'Isa b.Musa, was far away in the Hijaz, under the watchful eye of the *hajib,* Rabi' b.Yunus. Rabi' had been the only figure of importance with the old caliph, at the time of his death, and he took care to extract oaths of allegiance to Mahdi, then to 'Isa b.Musa, as his heir, from all the most important people in the camp. Only when he had done this did he make the news public. Once again, 'Isa b.Musa's unpopularity among the troops became apparent and it was only after 'Ali b.Isa b.Mahan had been threatened with force that he agreed to acknowledge his rights. Then Hasan al-Sharawi was despatched with the caliphal insignia, the staff and mantle of the Prophet, to Baghdad.[3]

The new reign began auspiciously; the treasury was full and the Muslim world was at peace. The caliph was a more popular figure than his father and, even before his accession, he had cultivated a reputation for generosity and open-handedness, in contrast to Mansur, who was notoriously mean.[4] He also celebrated his accession by releasing numbers of political prisoners, and stressed his role as the champion of Islam, again in contrast to his father, whose outlook was more secular. One of the first acts of his reign was the completion of the mosque at Rusafa and, in 161 (777/8), he ordered that the mosque of Basra be enlarged. In 163 (779/80), after a tour of Jazira and the frontier provinces, he visited Jerusalem and gave orders for the remodelling of the Aqsa Mosque; he also ordered the rebuilding and extension of the mosque at Makka. He ordered the removal of *maqsuras* (enclosures within the mosque to separate rulers or other dignitaries from the rest of the worshippers), which had always caused great offence to the pious, from all mosques, and that *minbars* (pulpits) should be no higher than the one in the Prophet's mosque in Madina.[5] He was much concerned, too, for the problems of the pilgrims; for most of his reign the *hajj* occurred in high summer and the problems of thirst were acute. After his first pilgrimage, in 160 (777), he ordered repairs to the road from Iraq to the Hijaz and the provision of new water supplies; but these, however, were clearly not effective for, when he went again in 164 (July/August 781), the people were once more much troubled by thirst and further measures were necessary.[6] In contrast to his father, the new caliph participated personally in campaigns against the Byzantines.

But this concern for Islam had a negative side as well. Religious dissenters were suppressed with a determination hitherto unknown in Islam. This particularly affected those known as Zindiqs. This term seems to have been originally applied to those who held Manichaean beliefs but was used in this period to cover any form of rejection of Islam. Those accused of this offence do not seem to have come from any particular group and included members of the Abbasid family and sons of leading men in the state as well as poets and men of letters.

They seem to have been harmless and to have had no real organisation and certainly did not pose a threat to the regime in the way radical pro-Alid groups did. Nonetheless, the caliph invoked the full severity of the law against apostasy and numbers of them were executed.[7] He also showed his concern when he came into contact with the Christian tribe of Taghlib, during his visit to Aleppo in 163 (779/80). It was repugnant to the caliph that an Arab tribe should have refused to accept Islam and, very unusually for the time, he gave them the alternative of conversion or death. Apart from this isolated incident, the caliph, following the precepts of the Qur'an, seems to have treated the Christian population well.[8]

When the caliph took office, his most pressing problem was to settle the question of the succession. Once again, 'Isa b.Musa was the next in line to the throne; once again, the Khurasani military found this an intolerable situation and they were determined to change it as soon as possible. The caliph summoned 'Isa to court but he refused to attend. He was now in his mid-fifties and something of a recluse, living in his vast desert palace and only coming to Kufa, the nearest large town, twice a year for the two great religious festivals, at the end of Ramadhan and the *hajj*. It was on one of those occasions in 159 – probably Dhu'l-Hijja (September/October 776) – that he was apprehended by a party of soldiers from Baghdad and taken to the capital. Here the troops made no secret of their dislike for him, and by riots and demonstrations forced him to give up his position.[9] In Muharram 160 (November 776), he was compelled to attend the public swearing of allegiance to Musa, the caliph's son (later to reign as Hadi), in the great mosque of Rusafa. Here he made a public renunciation of his rights and signed a written declaration to this effect. He was promised a vast sum of money (ten million *dirhams*) and estates at Kaskar and on the upper Zab, to sweeten the pill, but he no longer had any place in the succession.[10] He was a broken man and retired completely from public life until his death, some eight years later, in Dhu'l-Hijja 167 (summer 784).[11] Once again, the caliph's natural desire to be succeeded by his son and pressure from the army had combined to deprive him of his rights, but his family were to continue to play a considerable role in Abbasid politics. It is perhaps important to emphasise the humane way in which this was achieved. There was no use of the silken bow-string the Ottomans would have employed to solve this problem; the Abbasid family was still a unit and its members were still to be treated with respect.

The new caliph's most important political initiative concerned relations with the Alid family. Despite the defeat of the rebellions of 145 (762/3) and, despite the pacific and largely non-political outlook of many of the leading members of the family, like Ja'far al-Sadiq, the Alid family still remained a powerful threat and the only viable alternative to Abbasid rule. Their descent from the Prophet meant that they represented an alternative legitimacy, while the continuous crop of martyrs they produced in each generation strengthened their popular appeal against the authorities. The caliph knew, as well, that a few Alids were still actively working to overthrow the government, chief among them being 'Isa b.Zayd and the small militant group who gathered around him in Kufa, known as the Zaydiya. As always, there was a choice of policies. We have already seen that Mansur pursued a hard line to dispose of the threat of Muhammad and Ibrahim but there is some evidence to suggest that, later in his life, perhaps on his son's advice, he became more conciliatory. For five years, 150-5 (767-72), an Alid, Hasan b.Zayd, was governor of Madina, a city where the Alids had always been popular.[12]

Mahdi decided to pursue this policy much more intensively and actively. His own title was the very one claimed by Muhammad, 'The Pure Soul', and its choice was probably a conscious attempt to provide some of the charismatic religious leadership which the Alids offered but which Mansur had largely eschewed. He decided to seek out members of the Alid family and win them over with pensions and estates. In this way, he could hope to neutralise the threat they presented and even turn them into supporters of the regime. When he went on the *hajj* in 160 (777), Hasan b.Ibrahim, who had been in prison since the failure of his father's rebellion in Basra, fifteen years before, but had recently escaped, gave himself up. Mahdi was 'extremely generous' to him and gave him wealth from the *sawafi* (state lands) in the Hijaz.[13] The estate at Fadak, which had belonged to the Alid family before the Umayyads confiscated it, was returned to them.[14] Nor did his generosity end with members of the family. He made a real effort to win over the Alids' traditional supporters among the people of Madina; massive largess was distributed and five hundred of the men of the city, dignified with the ancient title of *ansar,* or helpers of the Prophet, were recruited as a special guard for the caliph and given salaries and property in Baghdad.[15] This buying over of the people of Madina seems to have been largely successful and, when Husayn b.'Ali rebelled in 169 (785/6), he attracted none of the popular support in the city which his predecessor had done in 145 (762). The attempt to win over the Alids failed, however, to move 'Isa b.Zayd and, despite the blandishments of the caliph and the efforts of his police, he remained at liberty and a constant source of anxiety.

The middleman in negotiations with the Alids was Ya'qub b.Dawud.[16] Ya'qub's father had been secretary to the last Umayyad governor of Khurasan, Nasr b.Sayyar, so his unfortunate children, Ya'qub and his elder brother 'Ali, despite their excellent education, were unable to find a government appointment. In these circumstances they were attracted to the Alids and, especially, to the Zaydiya group. They joined the rebellion of Ibrahim b.'Abd Allah in 145 (762/3); after the defeat of the rebels, Ya'qub was imprisoned in the notorious *matbaq,* the dungeon in Baghdad. Ironically, however, this proved to be the making of him since among his fellow prisoners were several notable Alids, including Hasan b.Ibrahim and the Zaydi thinker, Ishaq b.al-Fadl b.'Abd al-Rahman.[17] In the amnesty which followed Mahdi's accession, Ya'qub was released while his Alid fellow prisoners were not. However, Ya'qub seems to have kept in contact with the Alids for, when Hasan escaped from custody the next year, Ya'qub approached the caliph with an offer to find him. The meeting was effected on the pilgrimage of 160 (777) and Ya'qub thereby gained the confidence of the caliph, whose chief adviser he became. He became immensely powerful, controlling correspondence between the caliph and the provinces and appointing his own agents as a sort of parallel admini-stration. For six years, 160-66 (777-82/3), he remained the caliph's most influential adviser and, in 163 (779/80), replaced Abu 'Ubayd Allah as *wazir.* Eventually he fell victim to the ambiguity of his position, which depended on keeping on good terms with the Alids while retaining the confidence of the caliph, and the policy failed to win over the most dangerous Alid of them all, Isa b.Zayd. Ya'qub's power and authority had annoyed many people at court who felt that he had usurped their authority. Chief among these were the newly powerful *mawali,* who were instrumental in bringing him down. Different versions are given of the immediate cause of his downfall. One is that he was ordered to kill a recalcitrant Alid, as a test of his ultimate loyalty, but that, instead, he secretly released him, whereupon the man was recaptured and his duplicity exposed. Others say that he planned to hand over the caliphate to the Zaydiya and that the break came when he proposed his mentor, Ishaq b.al-Fadl, as governor of Egypt.[18] Much of this was, no doubt, malicious slander but it had its effect; Ya'qub was brutally punished and barely survived the ordeal of prison. Released by Harun, five years after his accession, he refused any further government appointments and retired to the Hijaz, where he lived in retirement until his death in 187 (803). His career is important for two reasons. It marks the most sustained attempt before the time of Ma'mun to close the gap between the Abbasids and the Alids and to restore the unity of the family of the Prophet. It also marks an important advance in the powers of the *wazir*. Mansur and Mahdi had both had secretaries who were, in their own spheres, influential and competent men, but Ya'qub was the first member of the bureaucracy to decide policy and the first to make appointments to provincial offices, a position which gave him great powers of patronage. His career was short; it ended in failure and he left no pupils to continue his work, but it foreshadowed in many ways the powers enjoyed by later Abbasid *wazir*s.

The reign of Mahdi saw also important changes in the composition of the ruling élite. New groups appeared to challenge the influence of the Abbasid family, of the Khurasaniya and of other military groups who had been so powerful under Mansur; this, inevitably, led to rivalries and stresses — stresses which were eventually to destroy the regime.

It was in this reign that the bureaucracy of government secretaries, known as the *kuttab,* became, for the first time, an important political pressure group. Increasingly, as well, the Syrian element which had been so important under the Umayyads and early Abbasids was replaced by men of Iranian extraction. These developed a considerable *esprit de corps,* which they expressed by harking back to the glories of the pre-Islamic past and, whether consciously or not, they tried to recreate the powerful élite bureaucracy of the late Sassanian period. The building up of this party was largely the achievement of the Barmakid family; its members play a colourful role in the stories of court life which come down to us in the *Kitab al-Aghani* and the *Arabian Nights.* For later generations, they symbolised the opulence and culture of the Golden Age of Baghdad but, in fact, their origins lay far to the east. 'Barmak' was the hereditary title enjoyed by the keepers of the Buddhist shrine at Balkh, a position of great prestige; the geographer, Ibn al-Faqih, stressing their noble origins, compares them with Quraysh (guardians of the shrine at Makka in pre-Islamic times).[19] In late Umayyad times, they had become Muslims, with the result that they lost their status among their fellow *dehqan*s in the Oxus valley and were obliged, for a time, to go into exile. This may be why they, almost alone of their class, decided to join the Abbasid Revolution. Khalid b.Barmak played an important part in the westward march of the Abbasid forces, being in charge of the distribution of the booty. After the new dynasty was established in Kufa, he became chief of the *diwan al-kharaj* (taxation department).[20] He was not always in the capital, being governor, at various times, of Tabaristan, Fars and Mosul.[21] Under Mansur, he enjoyed a fairly modest position but he seems to have been on good terms with Mahdi from early on and the family were rewarded with a large grant of land in the new settlement of Rusafa.[22] It was not always easy going. He had many enemies at court, like Mahdi's chief secretary Abu 'Ubayd Allah Mu'awiya, himself a Palestinian, who resented his increasing influence; then he owed much to the talents of his son, Yahya. Yahya had begun his career as his father's assistant when the latter was governor of Tabaristan and in this way he came into contact with Mahdi, who was then at Rayy. It was while he was there that the infant Harun and his own son Fadl became milk-brothers: that is to say that Harun was suckled by Fadl's mother and vice versa. This curious custom had started in the previous generation when Khalid's daughter had been nursed by Saffah's wife. It is difficult to say why it began or what importance to attach to it but the Barmakids were the only family thus honoured and the practice continued through three generations.[23] Yahya became firmly attached to the young Harun and, in 161 (777/8), he was made both *wazir* and *katib* to the prince. As such, he became a very influential figure and, when Harun was sent on a raid deep into Byzantine territory in 163 (780), it was Yahya and his father who organised the army.[24] Khalid died on this expedition but his son's position remained unaffected. His power was based on his close relations with Harun (by this time proclaimed as heir to the caliphate, after his brother Musa), on his experience and friends in the bureaucracy and on his contacts with the *dehqan* party, in Khurasan, and the merchant community in Baghdad and elsewhere.

Another group who became powerful during this reign was the *mawali*.[25] This word has a variety of meanings in the early Islamic sources. The basic root is connected with ideas of dependence and clientage. In pre-Islamic times, *mawali* were men who attached themselves to a tribe to seek its protection while not becoming full members of it. After the Islamic conquests, many non-Arab Muslims became *mawali* to Arab tribes as a way of integrating themselves into the new ruling élite and the word is often used for all non-Arab Muslims, whether they had formal ties with an Arab tribe or not. After the Abbasid Revolution the distinction between Arab and non-Arab was much eroded and the old meaning of the term fell into disuse. From Mansur onwards, however, the Abbasid caliphs began to employ freed slaves for certain administrative purposes, often in charge of the *barid* (postal service) or financial administration but occasionally as provincial governors. They were useful because, unlike members of the ruling dynasty or leading Khurasanis, they had no family connections or political allegiance which could interfere with their obedience to the caliph. Like the freed men of early imperial Rome or the *ministeriales* of twelfth-century Germany, they were dependent on the ruler alone and could be expected to identify exclusively with the interest of their master.

It is during the reign of Mahdi that the use of such men increased and we find them, for the first time, holding posts as provincial governors and, like the *kuttab* in the same period, they became a powerful pressure group. They, too, provoked resentment; 'You have given them [the *mawali*] charge of all your affairs and favoured them by night and day', Mahdi was told by his uncle, 'Abd al-Samad b.'Ali, who went on to warn him that the loyalty of the army was being eroded by this favour.[26]

As the Barmakid family emerged as leaders of the *kuttab* so the family of Rabi' b.Yunus were leaders of the *mawali*. Rabi''s origins were very obscure and his parentage the subject of gossip and rumour, but it seems clear that he started life as a slave in the Hijaz, where he was bought by the governor, Ziyad b.'Ubayd Allah al-Harithi, and presented to Saffah.[27] Thereafter, he was attached to Mansur's first *hajib*, Abu'l-Khasib and, when he died, some time after 142 (760), Rabi' stepped into his shoes. The *hajib* was always a man of consequence; being close to the caliph he was always in a position to give messages and ask favours and, most of all, he controlled access to his master. Until 153 (770), Mansur's secretary was Abu Ayyub al-Muryani but Rabi' used his position to allow the secretary's enemies access to the caliph and it was at least partly due to him that Abu Ayyub was disgraced. Thereafter he was himself appointed as *wazir,* though his powers were limited, while his son Fadl took on the post of *hajib*. When the caliph died, Rabi' was the only man with him; it was he who organised the swearing of allegiance to Mahdi and it was he who later handed the keys of the treasury to the new caliph.[28]

The reign of Mahdi marked the high point of the power of the *mawali* and consequently of their leader, Rabi'. His vast and valuable property in Baghdad, where he owned most of the market quarter of Karkh, his position in charge of the caliph's household, the *dar al-khilafa* and of the *dar al-raqiq,* where the palace slaves lived, made him a formidable political power.[29] Relations between him and the *kuttab* were often strained. He played an important part in the dismissal of

Mahdi's first *wazir*, Abu 'Ubayd Allah, in 163 (779/80), and the *mawali* were instrumental in the fall of Ya'qub b.Dawud, three years later.[30] His relations with the Barmakids, on the other hand, were generally friendly.

While the *mawali* and the *kuttab* were becoming a power in the state, changes were taking place within the army. The chief of these was the emergence of the *abna'*. This term is short for *abna'al-dawla* or 'sons of the state' and it seems to be used by the new generation of Khurasanis, whose fathers had settled in Baghdad after the revolution and who now regarded the city as their home. Many of them were property owners and had, no doubt, become involved in commerce and trade but their military salaries were still very important to them. They had two over-riding political concerns. The first was to make certain that they, and they alone, were the main military prop of the dynasty and that their salaries were paid, while the second was to ensure that their city, Baghdad, remained the capital of the empire. If they felt that either of these interests were being seriously threatened, they were prepared to take up arms to defend them. The emergence of the *abna'* is connected with the emergence of two new military leaders, whose families were to play a crucial role in future political events, 'Ali b.'Isa b.Mahan and Abu Khalid al-Marwazi.

The reputation of 'Ali b.'Isa has suffered from the fact that almost all contemporary sources are hostile to him, but it is possible to read between the lines and reach some understanding of why he was such a powerful figure. To do this we must first consider the career of his father. 'Isa b.Mahan was an Iranian who joined the Abbasid movement very early. He had been one of the original *naqib*s in Marw[31] and was one of the few non-Arabs to hold an important position in the movement. After the revolution he remained in Khurasan but became increasingly dissatisfied with the way things were going in the province. In 135 (752/3), Abu Muslim discovered some letters to a member of his own staff, in which 'Isa complained of the conduct of his own immediate superior, Abu Dawud Khalid b.Ibrahim, the governor of Balkh.[32] Abu Dawud was accused of three faults; plotting to revolt, putting the Arabs and his own *qawm* (tribe) above the people of the Abbasid movement (*da'wa*) and having thirty-six tents in his camp for *musta'mina* (see below). Of these charges, the first is commonplace but the other two are very interesting. In the second, he was protesting against Abu Dawud's practice of following the old Arab tradition and promoting his relatives and fellow Arabs to important commands, and it is interesting to see so clear a statement of racial differences. 'Isa, and those who thought like him, wanted command to be given to those who had precedence (*sabiqa*) in the Abbasid movement; that is to say that, just as in the early Muslim community, the earliest converts should enjoy the highest status. Participation in the movement, not family connections, should be the criterion for choosing leaders. Then there were the *musta'mina* (literally, those who have asked for an *aman*, or safe-conduct). Their presence in the camp suggests that Abu Dawud was seeking to incorporate them in his army. In the years since the revolution, Abu Dawud had led a number of expeditions into the small mountain principalities north of the Oxus, where he had captured many prisoners, and it seems likely that he was encouraging such prisoners to join his army.[33] 'Isa could not but see this as a threat to the people of the *da'wa,* the Abbasid movement, and feel that Abu Dawud was trying to replace him and his fellows. The discovery of the letters sealed 'Isa's fate and he was savagely beaten to death, but his cause did not die with him. He spoke for the forgotten men of the revolution, for the rank and file of the Iranian soldiers who were not really represented by the Arab leaders of the Khurasaniya and bitterly resented the continuing influence of the *dehqan*s in their province.

'Ali inherited his father's position. He first appears at the time of Mansur's death, when he and Abu Khalid al-Marwazi led the opposition among the military to the swearing of allegiance to 'Isa b.Musa. Thereafter, he rose to prominence in the entourage of the young heir apparent, Musa al-Hadi, and, in 163 (779/80), he was appointed as his *sahib al-haras* (commander of the guard) and remained one of his closest military advisers throughout Mahdi's reign.[34]

The second of the new leaders, Abu Khalid al-Marwazi (or Marwrudhi), was an older man than 'Ali and had fought in the battle of the Abbasid Revolution; he and the Marwrudhiya were given land to the west of the Round City when Mansur founded Baghdad. He soon became a spokesman for the interests of the troops and, in 152 (769), he led an army mutiny in Ifriqiya. He joined 'Ali b.'Isa's protest at the time of the death of Mansur and is last heard of defeating a Kharijite rebel at the beginning of the reign of Harun.[35] It must be presumed that he died soon after this but, as with 'Isa b.Mahan, his role passed to his son Muhammad b.Abi Khalid. While both these families stood for the interests of the *abna'*, the family of Abu Khalid seems to have had most following among the troops of the Harbiya quarter on the West Bank in Baghdad, while 'Ali b.'Isa's family had more support in the newer quarters on the other side of the river.

These developments led to a gradual polarisation of interests within the ruling class. There is evidence of conflict between the military and the 'civil' administration from the time of Mansur. In 150 (767), for example, when the military leader, Khazim b.Khuzayma, appointed to lead the expedition against the rebel Ustadhsis in Khurasan, refused to do so unless he had complete control, Mahdi's civil administrator, Abu 'Ubayd Allah Mu'awiya, was forbidden to interfere.[36] This rivalry became more intense as the two groups became organised in the time of Mahdi. The issues between them were basically the control of power. Should the effective rulers of the state be the *kuttab* and *mawali* of the central administration, or the military leaders and provincial governors? Naturally, the *kuttab* wished to centralise power, since their influence was at the centre, while the military, since many of them served as provincial governors and commanders, were anxious for more local control. The conflict is very similar to the tension between civil and military aristocracies which was so disastrous in the Byzantine empire of the eleventh century. This antagonism was reinforced by the Khurasani factor. The bureaucracy was increasingly under the control of the Barmakids, a *dehqan* family, while the fathers of the *abna'* had joined the revolution to destroy the influence of such men. As always, the politics of Baghdad and Khurasan were inseparable.

Despite these ominous developments at the centre, the reign of Mahdi was, with some exceptions, especially in Khurasan, one of peace and prosperity. On the frontiers, Islamic armies were on the offensive. Mahdi sent his son Harun to lead expeditions against the Byzantines, in 163 (780) and 165-6 (782), which proved the largest and most far-reaching since Umayyad times.[37] In addition, a force set out from Basra in 159 (776), to attack the unbelievers in Sind. Mahdi appointed a commander to organise the expedition and 2,000 troops from Basra and they were joined by some 7,000 volunteers, some from as far away as Syria. The campaign was not an unqualified success; the city of Barbad was sacked, with very few casualties on the Muslim side, but, on the return journey, many of the ships were wrecked on the south coast of Iran and some of the passengers drowned.[38] On the eastern frontiers of Khurasan, as well, Islamic troops were active; one Ahmad b.Asad attacked Farghana, and Ya'qubi gives a long list of eastern princes who, he claims, gave allegiance to the caliph and which includes, rather ambitiously, the kings of Tibet, China and India.[39]

As always, the succession was a crucial question and reflected the political divisions which had emerged in the state. Two of Mahdi's sons had emerged as candidates for the throne. As early as 160 (776) his son, Musa, had been made heir apparent to replace the unacceptable

'Isa b.Musa, while Harun had been introduced as successor to his brother in 166 (182/3).[40] Both brothers were the sons of Mahdi's favourite wife, the dominating Khayzuran. They were both born in, or near, Rayy and were close in age; Hadi was probably born in 147 (764) and his brother in 149 (766).[41] From an early age, Hadi had been trained for his role. In 160 (777), he had been left in charge in Baghdad while his father was away on the *hajj,* while the next year he himself led the pilgrims. In 163 (780), he was again left in Baghdad while his father accompanied Harun to Syria. In 167 (783/4), he was sent in command of an army to settle the affairs of Jurjan and was still in the province when his father died.[42] As the most likely successor to the throne, he had collected supporters from an early stage; the most important and influential of these came from the military. 'Ali b.'Isa b.Mahan was, as we have seen, one of the earliest and most steadfast of these; he was, after all, instrumental in removing 'Isa b.Musa from the succession, but he also cultivated links with older-established military families.

Harun's advancement did not begin until rather later. In 163 (780), when still only about fifteen, he was appointed to lead a great expedition against the Byzantines. Naturally, he had advisers, chief of whom were Yahya b.Khalid and Rabi' b.Yunus.[43] After this expedition, he was given formal overlordship of all the western provinces. After his second expedition against the Byzantines, he was given the title of Rashid and his place in the succession. The two brothers, then, had quite different groups of supporters, each anxious that their man should enjoy power after the death of the caliph. They seem to have been quite different in character as well; while Hadi was forthright and sure of himself, Harun was diffident and easily persuaded. He was also his mother's favourite, a fact of some political as well as personal importance.

At first sight it is difficult to see why Mahdi should have nominated two sons in this way and it seems like a sure recipe for trouble; yet it may have been more reasonable than might at first appear, and there are, perhaps, three motives which ought to be considered. The first is the security of the dynasty. No matter how young or healthy he was, the caliph's chosen successor might suddenly die by accident or disease. Since there was no law of primogeniture or established rule of succession, there would be no generally accepted candidate to replace him; the result could well be civil war, or the choice of caliph falling to the army, as happened in the next century when Wathiq failed to name an heir. For administrative reasons, too, it might have seemed a good idea; Mahdi had served for many years as his father's heir and viceroy in the east and the arrangement had worked well. Perhaps some of the problems of administering the vast area could be solved if Harun were to perform the same function for his brother in the west. The third reason was probably pressure from Khayzuran, who is said to have wielded considerable influence over her husband, and from Yahya b.Khalid and Fadl b.al-Rabi', who could expect little favour from Hadi. To complicate matters still further, there were rumours to the effect that Mahdi was considering replacing Hadi by Harun at the time of his death.

His death seems to have caught everyone by surprise. According to the most probable version, he had left Baghdad to escape the summer heat and had gone hunting at Masabadhan, in the foothills of the Zagros; one day, his hounds were pursuing a gazelle through some ruins and, while the caliph was following them, he struck his forehead on the lintel of a door. He died on 22 Muharram (4 August) and was buried, as modestly as all the early Abbasids, at the foot of a nut-tree he used to sit under.[44]

With Mahdi, in his country retreat, were his son Harun, with his mentor Yahya b.Khalid, the Barmakid, as well as a number of palace servants and *mawali*. All these people could be expected to be friendly to Harun, while Hadi and his supporters were many hundreds of miles away in Jurjan. Nonetheless, there was no attempt at a coup d'état, and the insignia of office were despatched to Hadi while the rest of the party returned to Baghdad. The news had preceded them and troops in the city had begun to riot, both to demand bounty to which they felt entitled on an occasion such as this and to express their dislike of Rabi' b.Yunus, who had been left in charge in the city and whose house they burned. Rabi', in consultation with the new caliph's mother, Khayzuran, agreed to meet their demands and calm was restored before Harun reached the city. When he received news of his father's death, Hadi returned as quickly as possible to Baghdad, taking only twenty days on the journey.[45]

The new caliph was only about twenty-two years old, tall and of fair complexion with a marked hare-lip.[46] His character is difficult to assess, since the sources tend to compare him unfavourably with his brother, but he was certainly determined, forceful and, on occasion, hasty and ill-tempered. In particular, his relations with his mother were, from the outset, extremely bad. It is not clear why this was so, but he may have suspected her of prejudicing his father against him in favour of her other son, Harun. From the very beginning, he made it clear that he would tolerate no interference from that quarter. When he heard, on his way from Jurjan, that Rabi' had acted in consultation with her, he threatened him with death and was only dissuaded when the old *hajib's* son, Fadl, was sent to meet him with massive gifts.

In many ways Hadi's reign was a reaction against many of the developments of his father's time. The military leaders, especially 'Ali b.'Isa b.Mahan and Sa'id, son of Salm b.Qutayba al-Bahili, were naturally his closest advisers, while the *mawali* and the *kuttab* were reduced to secondary roles. The eclipse of the *mawali* was aided by the death of their leader Rabi'.[47] The new caliph saw the advantages of winning over so powerful and experienced a figure and had made him *wazir* on his arrival in Baghdad, over the heads of the secretaries who had been with him in Jurjan. Rabi''s appointment had been an attempt to win over Hadi's enemies in Baghdad but the caliph seems to have quarrelled with him and so deprived himself of a man who could have proved a useful mediator. Rabi' had served Mansur and Mahdi personally for over thirty years, supervising their households and giving them advice. Of all the figures at court he was perhaps the most consistently influential and never out of favour. He was a skilled intriguer and completely ruthless in disposing of rivals like Abu Ayyub al-Muryani, secretary to Mansur, or Mahdi's *wazir,* Abu 'Ubayd Allah Mu'awiya. Nonetheless, to the caliphs he was a loyal and devoted servant, having no family or regional ties and concerned only with the status and position of his fellow *mawali.*

Hadi also broke with his father's policy towards the Alids. The pensions and favours which Mahdi had lavished on the family were withdrawn and it seems to have been this cessation of financial support, as much as the oppressions of the local governor, which led to the rebellion of Husayn b.'Ali. The rebellion, which broke out in Madina, in Dhu'l-Qa'ada 169 (May 786), was neither as well-planned nor as well-supported as the rebellion of Muhammad b.'Abd Allah, twenty years before. Husayn declared himself in the mosque but lack of enthusiasm in the city and the opposition of local members of the Abbasid family forced him, after eleven days, to leave for Makka. Here he tried to rally the slaves of the city by promising them their freedom and the *badu* of the surrounding area, but the response was disappointing. Meanwhile, the pilgrimage caravan was approaching with several senior members of the Abbasid family, including Muhammad b.Sulayman, the fabulously wealthy governor of Basra. Hadi wrote to him instructing him to take command of the war. The troops in the caravan and local Abbasid supporters were sufficient to defeat the pathetically small army of Husayn at the Battle of Fakhkh — 8 Dhu'l-Hijja (11 June) — where the rebel leader was killed. The behaviour of the victorious Abbasids was very moderate and few prisoners were executed.[48] The incident did, however, have an important repercussion: two members of the Alid family who had taken part in the revolt fled to outlying parts of the Muslim world. They were both brothers of the unfortunate Muhammad b.'Abd Allah, who had led the previous revolt in the Hijaz — Idris and Yahya. Idris b.'Abd Allah made his way to Morocco, where he established himself among the local Berber tribes, thus founding the dynasty of the Idrisids, the first independent Muslim rulers in the area. Yahya fled to Daylam, the mountainous area at the southwest corner of the Caspian Sea. Here he preached the Alid cause to the local, mostly non-Muslim inhabitants and so established the Alid cause in the area.

Apart from this disturbance, the reign was largely peaceful. On the Byzantine frontier, the enemy had taken the city of Hadath, driving out both governor and merchants, but the summer expedition of 169 (786) seems to have restored the position.[49] The caliph continued, and even intensified, his father's persecution of the Zindiqs. He spent most of his time in the palace of 'Isabadh and it was here that he died, probably on 16 Rabi' I, 170 (15 September 786), aged only twenty-three.

The circumstances of his death were confusing and dramatic, and were closely connected with the succession dispute which dominated the thirteen months of his reign. His only known expedition outside the capital had been cut short by illness[50] and it is quite possible that the dispute was intensified by the knowledge that the caliph did not have much longer to live. The chronicler Tabari furnishes us with a detailed picture, though the chronology is vague.[51] He sees it very much as a personal drama. On the one hand, there is the caliph, under pressure from his leading military supporters to take strong action to ensure the succession of his own son Ja'far, and, on the other, Harun, eager himself to retire into private life but urged to resist by his mentor, Yahya b.Khalid, and his mother, Khayzuran. There is, no doubt, much truth in this picture but, like all such disputes, it had wider political ramifications. The move to depose Harun had strong support from the military leaders, who had no wish to see a Barmakid-dominated government; Tabari explains, 'He [Hadi] was supported in this decision by the *quwwad*, among them Yazid b.Mazyad, 'Abd Allah b.Malik, 'Ali b.'Isa b.Mahan and others like them.'[52] The choice of names is significant. Yazid b.Mazyad al-Shaybani was one of the leading non-Khurasani army commanders; 'Abd Allah b.Malik, the son of Abu Muslim's adviser, Malik b.al-Haytham, came from one of the leading families of the Arab-Khurasan élite; 'Ali, of course, represented the *abna'*. Not only was 'Ali commander of the caliph's guard, he had also been put in charge of the *diwan al-jund* (ministry of the army).[53] This, then, is a representative cross-section of the Abbasid military leadership: the chronicler is saying that the bulk of the military of all groups was behind Hadi. It is even said that these *quwwad* had gone so far as to swear allegiance to the young Ja'far in private but fate intervened before there could be any public change in the succession.

Hadi hoped to act with his brother's consent rather than having to resort to force and he had good reason to hope that this consent would be forthcoming. Despite his long apprenticeship as leader of expeditions against the Byzantines and as governor of the west, Harun at this stage seems to have had no real taste for power. 'Would not my pleasures and comforts be left to me?' he argued to Yahya b.Khalid, and suggested that he could retire and live peacefully with his cousin, with whom he was very much in love. But Yahya was firm: it might not matter to Harun if he did not enjoy the power to which he was entitled, but it mattered to Yahya very much. Even if he was not to succeed for many years, he was still governor of the west and heir apparent. Yahya had gambled heavily on Harun and knew that his future depended on him. Hadi's attitude to Yahya varied. He recognised his ability and power and tried to win him over. When this proved unsuccessful, he began to threaten him and, according to some accounts, he was actually imprisoned. Hadi accused him of alienating his brother, a charge not without foundation, and Yahya had good reason to fear for his life. He remained firm, however, and this firmness was rewarded, largely because of the actions of the third leader of the opposition, Khayzuran.

Khayzuran was a slave from the Yaman who had been purchased by Mansur and given to his son, Mahdi, probably when he was in the west in 144 (761). She went with Mahdi to Rayy, where both Musa and Harun were born to her soon after, and she married the caliph in 159 (775/6), after his accession.[54] She had very considerable influence over Mahdi and ensured the promotion of both her sons and her family. Her brother, Ghitrif b.'Ata, enjoyed one of the most spectacular 'rags to riches' careers of the period, beginning as an ill-clad farm labourer and ending as governor of Khurasan for a brief period, after his sister's death.[55] Hadi refused to allow her to interfere in affairs of state and this contributed further to the coolness between the two. Matters are said to have come to a head when he discovered that she had promised political favours to 'Abd Allah b.Malik before she had even asked the caliph. Hadi harangued his troops on the iniquities of maternal inter-ference and excluded her completely from power.[56] Her attachment to

Harun was, however, based as much on affection as political calculation and she is said to have preferred that he renounce his rights rather than risk death in a political struggle.[57] It is difficult to assess her real influence over the course of political events. Her power was considerable but circumscribed and, given the limitations imposed by social custom, it had to be exercised indirectly. This power derived, at least in part, from her great wealth, but even more from the fact that she could have access to the caliph in a way in which even the most favoured politicians and generals did not. Khayzuran used this position to build up a network of patronage; by offering to speak to the caliph on someone's behalf, she could make herself useful to the great men of the state and become, albeit vicariously, a great power in the land. But her position was very vulnerable; if the caliph decided, as Hadi had done, that none should be allowed to visit her, or, as happened in the reign of Harun, the *wazir* was on such good terms with the caliph as to be able to dispense with such an intermediary, then her power was destroyed.

By Rabi' I, 170 (September 786) Hadi, his resolve strengthened by the persuasion of senior army officers, was preparing the decisive move: the removal of Harun from the succession and the appointment of his own son Ja'far as heir apparent. Then one night — 16 Rabi' I (14-15 September) — the caliph suddenly died, in his palace of 'Isabadh. Some said he died from a stomach ulcer; others, less charitably, suggested that his own mother, Khayzuran, had arranged for him to be murdered by a slave girl.[58] Whether she was responsible for her son's death can never be known. She certainly had the motive and the opportunity, and the speed and efficiency with which Hadi's enemies exploited his death suggests that it was not entirely unexpected. On the other hand, he had been ill shortly before and this may have been a more severe recurrence of the same complaint.

The order of events that night is confused.[59] Harun was with the caliph at 'Isabadh and it seems that Yahya was imprisoned there too. According to one version, it was Harthama b. A'yan, the Khurasani *dehqan* who had supported 'Isa b. Musa, who fetched Harun and appointed him caliph. Another source says that Khayzuran herself immediately released Yahya and it was he who woke the startled and frightened Harun and told him he was now caliph. He then advised him to go to Baghdad with all possible speed and wrote to all the provincial governors telling them of Harun's accession. There remained Hadi's young son Ja'far, to whom many had already taken the oath as heir apparent. He was hauled from his bed by Khuzayma b. Khazim, accompanied by a large number of armed *mawali*, and forced to renounce his rights publicly. Khuzayma was one of the *quwwad* who had been also one of Hadi's firmest supporters but he had probably been alienated when his brother was dismissed from the position of *sahib al-shurta* by the caliph. The coup was swift and effective and the dead caliph's supporters were presented with a *fait accompli*. What was decided at court was accepted without demur in the provinces.

Notes

1. Tabari, *Ta'rikh*, vol. 3, pp. 442, 526-7; Yaqut, *Mu'jam*, vol. 1, pp. 416-17.
2. Tabari, *Ta'rikh*, vol. 3, pp. 133-4, 143, 304-5, 355, 364.
3. Ibid., vol. 3, pp. 451-6.
4. S. Moscati, 'Nuovi Studi sul Califatto di al-Mahdi' in *Orientalia*, vol. 15 (1946), pp. 174-7.
5. Tabari, *Ta'rikh*, vol. 3, pp. 486, 502, 520.
6. Ibid., vol. 3, pp. 486, 502.
7. On the persecution of the Zindiqs, see Vajda, *Les Zindiqs RSO*, vol. 17 (1938), and Omar, *al-Mahdi*, p. 145.
8. Moscati, *Nuovi Studi*, p. 168; Omar, *al-Mahdi*, p. 145.
9. Tabari, *Ta'rikh*, vol. 3, pp. 455-6.
10. Ibid., vol. 3, pp. 467-71.
11. Ibid., vol. 3, p. 519.
12. Ibid., vol. 3, pp. 359, 377.
13. Ibid., vol. 3, p. 482.
14. 'Fadak' in EI (2).
15. Tabari, *Ta'rikh*, vol. 3, p. 483; Khatib, *Ta'rikh Baghdad*, vol. 1, pp. 88-9.
16. For Ya'qub b.Dawud, see Tabari, *Ta'rikh*, vol. 3, pp. 461-4, 482, 506-17; Jahshiyari, *Wuzara'*, pp. 155-63; Ya'qubi, *Ta'rikh*, vol. 2, p. 473; Sourdel, *Vizirat Abbaside*, vol. 1, pp. 103-11; Moscati, *Nuovi Studi*, pp. 164-7; Omar, *al-Mahdi*, pp. 148-9.
17. On Ishaq, see Nagel, *Untersuchungen*, pp. 167-9.
18. Tabari, *Ta'rikh*, vol. 3, pp. 509, 511-13; Jahshiyari, *Wuzara'*, pp. 160-2.
19. Ibn al-Faqih, *Buldan*, pp. 323-4; Sourdel, *Vizirat Abbaside*, vol. 1, pp. 129-33.
20. Tabari, *Ta'rikh*, vol. 3, p. 72; Jahshiyari, *Wuzara'*, pp. 87, 89.
21. Tabari, *Ta'rikh*, vol. 3, p. 371; Jahshiyari, *Wuzara'*, pp. 99, 136; Ibn al-Faqih, *Buldan*, p. 311; Azdi, *Ta'rikh*, pp. 207-9, 224, 226.
22. Khatib, *Ta'rikh*, vol. 1, p. 93.
23. Jahshiyari, *Wuzara'*, pp. 89, 136; Ibn 'Abd Rabbihi, *'Iqd al-Farid*, ed. A. Amin *et al.* (Cairo, 1940), vol. 5, p. 65; Sourdel, *Vizirat Abbaside*, vol. 2, p. 722; Talbi, *L'Emirat Aghlabide* (Paris, 1966), pp. 83-4.
24. Tabari, *Ta'rikh*, vol. 3, pp. 492, 497-8; Jahshiyari, *Wuzara'*, p. 150.
25. For the *mawali*, see P. Crone, 'The Mawali during the Umayyad Period' (unpublished PhD thesis, School of Oriental and African Studies, London, 1973); D. Ayalon, 'The Military Reforms of al-Mu'tasim' (unpublished paper in the Library of the School of Oriental and African Studies, London); F. Omar, 'The Composition of Abbasid Support' in *Bulletin of the College of Arts, Baghdad*, vol. 2 (1968).
26. Tabari, *Ta'rikh*, vol. 3, p. 531.
27. Jahshiyari, *Wuzara'*, p. 125; Ibn Rusteh, *Kitab al-A'laq al-Nafisa*, ed.

M.J. de Goeje (Leiden, 1892), pp. 207-9; Sourdel, *Vizirat Abbaside*, vol. 1, p. 88.
28. Tabari, *Ta'rikh*, vol. 3, pp. 112, 388-9; Ya'qubi, *Ta'rikh*, vol. 2, pp. 469, 475; Jahshiyari, *Wuzara'*, p. 116; Baladhuri, *Ansab*, fo. 650; Sourdel, *Vizirat Abbaside*, vol. 1, pp. 87-90.
29. Ya'qubi, *Buldan*, pp. 248, 252.
30. Tabari, *Ta'rikh*, vol. 3, pp. 487-80, 495, 508.
31. *Akhbar al-'Abbas*, p. 220.
32. Tabari, *Ta'rikh*, vol. 3, pp. 82-3; Baladhuri, *Ansab*, fos. 609-10.
33. Tabari, *Ta'rikh*, vol. 3, pp. 74, 79, 82.
34. Ibid., vol. 3, pp. 389, 455, 494, 519.
35. Tabari, *Ta'rikh*, vol. 2, p. 2004, vol. 3, pp. 21, 369, 455, 606; Ya'qubi, *Buldan*, p. 247.
36. Tabari, *Ta'rikh*, vol. 3, p. 355.
37. Ibid., vol. 3, pp. 494-8, 503-5.
38. Ibid., vol. 3, pp. 460-1, 476-7.
39. Ya'qubi, *Ta'rikh*, vol. 2, p. 479.
40. Tabari, *Ta'rikh*, vol. 3, pp. 472-3, 506.
41. For the conflicting evidence, see N. Abbott, *Two Queens of Baghdad* (Chicago, 1946), pp. 23-5.
42. Tabari, *Ta'rikh*, vol. 3, pp. 482, 492, 518-19.
43. Ibid., vol. 3, p. 494.
44. Ibid., vol. 3, pp. 523-6, 544-7; Ya'qubi, *Ta'rikh*, vol. 2, pp. 484-5.
45. Tabari, *Ta'rikh*, vol. 3, pp. 544-8; S. Moscati, 'Le Califat d'al-Hadi' in *Studia Orientalia*, vol. 13 (1946), pp. 5-7.
46. Tabari, *Ta'rikh*, vol. 3, p. 580.
47. Ibid., vol. 3, pp. 548, 598-9.
48. Ibid., vol. 3, pp. 551-60; Ya'qubi, *Ta'rikh*, vol. 2, p. 488; Isfahani, *Maqatil*, pp. 440-9; Van Arendonk, *Imamat Zaidite*, pp. 62-5; Omar, *Abbasid Caliphate*, pp. 252-7. See also below, pp. 205-6.
49. Tabari, *Ta'rikh*, vol. 3, p. 568.
50. Ibid., vol. 3, p. 578.
51. Ibid., vol. 3, pp. 569-80. See also Moscati, *Al-Hadi*, pp. 18-23.
52. Tabari, *Ta'rikh*, vol. 3, pp. 571-2.
53. Ibid., vol. 3, p. 548.
54. Abbott, *Two Queens*, pp. 22-5.
55. Tabari, *Ta'rikh*, vol. 3, pp. 612, 626; Ya'qubi, *Ta'rikh*, vol. 2, pp. 481, 488.
56. Tabari, *Ta'rikh*, vol. 3, pp. 569-71.
57. Ibid., vol. 3, p. 575.
58. Ibid., vol. 3, p. 569.
59. Ibid., vol. 3, pp. 599-603.

7 HARUN AL-RASHID

So it was by a mixture of good fortune and planned *coup d'état* that Abu Ja'far Harun b. Muhammad, known as Rashid, became the fourth Abbasid caliph on 16 Rabi' I (15 September 786). Because of his role in the stories circulating in such collections as the *Kitab al-Aghani* and the *Arabian Nights* none other of the Abbasid caliphs has left such an impression in the popular mind, and the 'good Haroon al-Rasheed' is the only member of his dynasty to be widely remembered outside the Muslim world. The reasons for this are not hard to find. His reign was, on the whole, a period of peace — particularly in contrast with the long years of suffering and civil war which followed his death — and his court was wealthy and cultured. The sources comment on his good looks, and he was extravagantly generous to poets and singers, who earned their rewards by immortalising his name.

Despite, or perhaps because of, all this publicity, his personality and policies are difficult to assess. In speculating on his character and abilities, it is important to recognise that these changed and developed as his reign progressed. His rule can be divided into three phases. In the first, up until about 180 (796), he allowed himself to be dominated by the Barmakids, who had done so much to bring him to power, and he himself showed little interest in affairs of state. In the second phase, he moved away from the Barmakids and, while they were still important, he began to rely more on Fadl b.al-Rabi' and the military leaders who had supported his brother. In the third phase, after the fall of the Barmakids, there was no single powerful minister and the caliph himself played a larger part in political life. Throughout his reign, however, he tended to distance himself from day-to-day affairs, which meant that vast power was left in the hands of ministers like the Barmakids or Ibn al-Rabi'.

There were two exceptions to this general lack of interest. The first was in the war against the Byzantines, in which he had been closely involved since his father's reign, when he had himself made two large-scale expeditions against the enemy. After his accession, he continued to take a lively interest, not only in arranging campaigns, but in the administration of the frontier areas as well and he was the first of the

Abbasid caliphs to devote any attention to naval warfare. His other main interest was in financial administration. He was an extravagant spender, on poets, on women and on building, but still contrived to leave an enormous surplus in the treasury when he died.[1] This was done by the ruthless taxation of the provinces, the confiscation of the wealth of private individuals and the buying up of estates in different provinces. The court may have been cultured and luxurious but, in the scattered townships of Jazira and the huddled villages of the Egyptian Delta, they were made to pay the price, and expressed their resentment in many small-scale insurrections.

Was Harun a great caliph? Certainly there were areas in which he showed his ability (in frontier warfare, for example) and he was the only reigning caliph who sought to solve the problems of Khurasan by visiting the province in person. On the other hand, he seems to have suffered from a certain laziness; there are no stories of his working all night as his grandfather had done, and he left too much to subordinates. As long as they produced the revenues and caused no trouble, then he was content to leave them be. The result of this was that he lost touch with the administration and, in provinces like Ifriqiya or Khurasan, this had disastrous results. So the verdict must be mixed; he was neither a fool nor a nonentity but, at the same time, he failed to use his talents and energies to the best advantage and cannot be considered a truly great ruler as Mansur had been.

Once victory was assured, Harun and his advisers were surprisingly lenient with their opponents. There seem to have been only two executions, neither of the victims being very prominent men, and a couple of Hadi's advisers were arrested, among them Ibrahim al-Harrani, his *wazir,* and chief rival to the Barmakids among the *kuttab.*[2] Most of the military leaders who had advocated the removal of Harun from the succession were in temporary disgrace; Abd Allah b.Malik, his chief of police, thought it advisable to go on foot to Makka to demonstrate his humility,[3] while Yazid b.Mazyad and 'Ali b. 'Isa b.Mahan were not given any important appointments for the next decade.

Political life in the new regime was dominated by the Barmakids and their protégés. Harun referred to Yahya as his father and was entirely dependent on his advice; for the next ten years Yahya b.Khalid ruled the empire almost as if it were his own.

The power of the Barmakids was based on their control of the administration, of the *diwan*s and the following they built up among the *kuttab* who worked there. Members of the bureaucracy were given charge of all the government departments except for the caliph's seal (*khatam*), which, however, passed into the hands of the Barmakid family on the death of the existing holder the next year (171).[4] Never before had one family acquired such a complete grip on the administration. Yahya remained the head of the family but he was ably assisted by his two sons, Fadl and Ja'far, who took over the seal. In addition, there was Yahya's brother, Muhammad, famous (unlike the rest of the family) for his meanness, who took over the office of *hajib* (chamberlain) in 173 (789/90), thus completing the family monopoly of important posts. In addition to members of the family, the Barmakids filled the administration with their followers, who were to carry on Barmakid policies and traditions long after the fall of the family itself. Two examples will show how the system worked. Fadl b.Sahl was the son of a small landowner from the Sawad near Kufa. He came to the notice of the Barmakids when Yahya decided a case about the family land in his favour. He began as *qahraman* (household steward) to Yahya's grandson, Fadl b.Ja'far, but was employed by Yahya because of his ability to translate from Persian to Arabic. He was then sent to Ja'far, who brought him into contact with the young prince, Ma'mun, a contact which enabled him to survive the disgrace of his patrons. It is interesting to note that he did not even become a Muslim until after the fall of the Barmakids.[5] Ahmad b.Abi Khalid, on the other hand, owed his successful career to the fact that his father had helped Yahya during a period of poverty early in his career, with the result that Ahmad and his sons were given training and positions in the bureaucracy.[6] We know of these two examples as both later became famous, but there must have been many more, humbler men, who, nonetheless, owed their positions and their loyalty to the family. This pattern changed the character of the Abbasid administration considerably, and it meant that the bureaucrats acquired a unity and an *esprit de corps* which made them a powerful influence in the counsels of the caliph, which the individual secretaries of previous reigns had lacked.

The Barmakids were also powerful because of their close connections with the Abbasid family. Yahya's relations with Harun were almost paternal, while his son Ja'far became the caliph's closest companion. In addition, both Yahya's sons were given charge of the two young princes, who were being groomed for the succession, Fadl taking Amin and Ja'far, Ma'mun.[7] The custom of milk-brotherhood, alluded to above, was continued into the third generation, Fadl's and Ja'far's sons being linked in this way to the sons of the two young princes.

Barmakid control was control at the centre; members of the family seldom held provincial governorates and, with the exception of Fadl's period in Khurasan,[8] they paid little attention to them when they did. Ja'far, for example, was appointed at various times to Egypt and Syria. Egypt he never visited at all and Syria he went to only once, in 180 (796/7), to crush a rebellion.[9] He made no effort to turn the province into a power base. The consequence of this was that Harun's reign saw a noticeable decline in the importance of provincial governorates and an increasing centralisation of power, a process which had begun under Mahdi and which reached its logical conclusion only after the civil war. There are various signs of this. Chroniclers pay less attention to appointments in the provinces and we are very badly informed about changes of governor in Harun's reign, compared with that of his grand-father. Governors were also appointed for shorter periods, which prevented their building up local influence; in Basra, there were fifteen appointments during the twenty-three years of Harun's reign and only ten during the twenty years of his grandfather's, furthermore the latter figure is distorted by three very quick changes at the time of the Alid rebellion of 145 (762/3). In Kufa, the contrast is more striking, with eleven changes under Harun as compared with three under Mansur and, in Egypt, the pattern is repeated, with twenty-two compared with eight. The power of the provincial 'dynasties' of the early years of the Abbasid state was also undermined. In 173 (189/90), Muhammad b.Sulayman, whose branch of the Abbasid family had been prominent in Basra since the revolution, died; his vast wealth was confiscated and the family position in the city effectively destroyed.[10] The power of the other major Abbasid sub-dynasty, represented by 'Abd al-Malik b.Salih, in Syria, was also destroyed, when he was arrested in 187 (803).[11]

Another development of Harun's reign which was probably the result of Barmakid influence was the policy of increasing the *sawafi* (state lands). Detailed information is hard to come by, but this policy seems to have been pursued with especial vigour in Jazira and on the frontier. One example of this was the important estate of Balis and its villages, which the caliph sequestrated from the family of Sulayman b.'Ali; perhaps he wanted these lands because they were in the strategic area of the middle Euphrates, near Raqqa, his effective capital. He also bought up other estates in the district: 'Ain al-Rumiya, near Raqqa, and Ghabat Ibn Hubayra, near Saruj. In the frontier areas, he built a new quarter at Massissa, taking rent from the houses, and rebuilt Tarsus, 'Ain Zarba and Haruniya — the last being a small town in Cilicia, which preserves the caliph's name to the present day. It may have been he who built the canal of Saybayn, in southern Iraq, and he certainly did buy the Nahr al-Amir in Basra. Zanjan, in central Iran, became part of the Abbasid estates when the people of the area sought protection from Qasim b.al-Rashid against 'brigands and tax collectors'; in another case, the people of Shu'aybiya offered themselves to 'Ali b.al-Rashid in an effort to have their taxes reduced. Both these are very interesting examples of 'commendation' as it operated in early mediaeval Europe, with communities placing themselves under the protection of powerful individuals; it suggests that this policy of increasing the Abbasid estates could benefit both the inhabitants and their rulers.[12]

The Barmakids stood for a more moderate attitude towards the Alids. There were both political and ideological reasons for this. The Alids and their supporters may have seemed a possible counterbalance to the *abna'*, always hostile to the Barmakids. In many ways, the Barmakids were trying to continue policies begun during the reign of Mahdi, the first Abbasid to place great emphasis on the religious role of his office. The advantages of this policy were twofold. A caliph who enjoyed religious authority could be much more absolute, at least in theory, than one dependent on the consensus of the Muslim community and he could attract the support of many who now looked to the Alid family for religious leadership. Harun was, however, not entirely convinced by this policy and his own attitudes to the Alid family owed more to his brother's harshness than to his father's generosity. This meant that opponents of the Barmakids could use their attitude as a way of discrediting them with the caliph. The Barmakids were famous for their patronage of heterodox and unusual thinkers of all persuasions, and it was easy for their enemies to accuse them of dabbling in heresy. All this came to a head with the rebellion of Yahya b.'Abd Allah, the Alid, in Daylam. Yahya had fled to this mountainous area, at the southwest corner of the Caspian, in the wake of the defeat of Husayn b.'Ali's rebellion under Hadi. Daylam had escaped direct Muslim occupation and it was a natural place of refuge for someone like Yahya, trying to escape the authority of the central government. This was very disturbing for the authorities, since the Daylamites were in a very good position to cut the road along the north edge of the great Iranian desert and it would be very inconvenient if they became hostile under 'Ali leadership. Fadl b.Yahya, the Barmakid, was sent against the rebel. The bad weather prevented any active campaigning and Fadl began to negotiate. In the end the rebel surrendered, in exchange for guarantees of safety countersigned by prominent *fuqaha'* and members of the Abbasid family in the army. Yahya was taken to Baghdad and the caliph seemed pleased. Soon after, however, he was killed: an open rebuff to Fadl, and the Barmakids in general.[13]

The Barmakids' power, however, suffered from one major weakness: they could call on very little military support. The most important military leaders of the early Abbasid period had supported Hadi; they were now in disgrace and their followers, the *abna'* in Baghdad and elsewhere, could not be relied on to enforce Barmakid rule. When Fadl b.Yahya was governor of Khurasan, he raised some 50,000 new troops, probably from the *dehqan*s of the province and their followers. These were to be called the 'Abbasiya and some 20,000 of them were sent to the west. It would seem that they were placed under the command of Harthama b.A'yan. Harthama came, like the Barmakids, from Balkh. He had originally been a supporter of 'Isa b.Musa when he was heir to the throne and, according to some accounts, was instrumental in establishing Harun as caliph.[14] He was not a member of the old established Arab Khurasani élite, nor was he a member of the *abna';* of all the military leaders he was the most sympathetic to the Barmakids. In 178 (794/5), shortly after the arrival of the new troops, he was entrusted with a wide-ranging pacification of the west. He visited Palestine and then moved on to Egypt, to restore order in the Delta, and finally to Ifriqiya. In 180 (796/7), he returned to court to take over command of the *haras* (guard), a post which he seems to have held, surviving the fall of the Barmakids, until his appointment to Khurasan at the end of Harun's reign.[15] While the new troops were effective and Harthama was certainly a competent leader, they could not be everywhere at once and they were too few to control the entire caliphate. Furthermore, their recruitment alienated still more the *abna'* and the traditional military leaders.

Harun seems to have used much of his abundant leisure looking for a new place to settle. He disliked Baghdad, perhaps for personal reasons and probably because, as Shaban points out, the Barmakid domination was not popular among the *abna',* who formed the bulk of the population.[16] He seems never to have used 'Isabadh as his father and brother had but, some two years after his accession, he went to Marj al-Qal'a, in the foothills of the Zagros, intending to build there. He became ill and was dissuaded from using the site. In 174 (790/1), he built a palace at Baqirda on the Tigris, north of Mosul; here, as at Marj, it was probably the climate which appealed to him. He seems never to have used it again,[17] however, and it was not until 180 (796/7) that he finally chose Raqqa as his chief residence, probably because of its proximity to the Byzantine frontier, where he was planning great things.[18]

After the year 179 (795/6), the power of the Barmakid family began to decline and the near monopoly which the family had acquired over the main offices of state was broken. In 180 (796/7), Fadl b.Yahya was abruptly dismissed from Rayy and other governorates in central Iran and, in 183 (799), he was completely disgraced.[19] Yahya remained prominent in the administration but, in both 181 (797) and 185 (801), he retired for spells to Makka.[20] Only Ja'far retained, or even improved, his status as the caliph's closest companion.

The reason for this change was probably the Barmakids' inability to deal with increasing discontent in the empire. In 178 (794) there was a rebellion among the army in Ifriqiya. We are not very well informed about this, but it may have been a protest against Barmakid rule. The leader of the mutineers was invited to court by Yahya b.Khalid and was not only given complete immunity from punishment but was even promoted in rank. There were, also, disturbances in Palestine and among the Arab settlers in the Hawf, in Egypt. It was to solve these problems that Harthama b.A'yan and the newly arrived troops from the east were sent to North Africa. Meanwhile, a much more damaging disturbance was occurring nearer home. In Jazira, a Kharijite, Walid b.Tarif, took over much of the countryside and forced the people of the small towns to pay taxes to him. At the same time Mosul was taken over by a local leader, who prevented the collection of taxes. Attempts by the government to crush Walid failed and, for two years, large parts of this crucial area were out of control. It was then that Harun was forced to turn to the very men who had opposed his own accession and, despite strong pressure from the Barmakids, he gave the command to Yazid b.Mazyad al-Shaybani. Yazid and his tribesmen succeeded where lesser men had failed. 'Iron can only be broken by iron', a contemporary poet said. The rebel had been a serious menace and Harun was so relieved by his defeat that he made the lesser pilgrimage (*'umrah*) to Makka to give thanks for his deliverance.[21]

The events of 178-80 (794-7) showed that, even with the 20,000 men 'Abbasiya Fadl b.Yahya had sent to the west, the Barmakids and their allies were not strong enough to replace the traditional military leadership and Harun was forced to turn to these leaders to ensure the security of the empire. This was made clear when in 180 (796/7), the year that Fadl the Barmakid was dismissed, the leader of the *abna'*, 'Ali b.'Isa b.Mahan, who had been living in obscurity since the death of Hadi, was appointed to the key position of governor of Khurasan.[22]

But it was not just in the provinces and the army that Barmakid power began to decline; a serious rival emerged at court and in the administration. Fadl b.Rabi' had been given a modest position in charge of the *nafaqat* (expenses) in 172 (788/9) but, in 179 (795/6), Muhammad b.Khalid, the Barmakid, was dismissed from his post as *hajib* and was replaced by Fadl, who thus succeeded to the post his father had made so powerful under Mansur and Mahdi. From this point on, he seems to have tried to undermine Barmakid influence as much as possible.[23]

The years from 180 to 186 (796-802) mark the second phase of Harun's reign, when the caliph, more assertive and self-confident, had emerged from the shadow of the Barmakids while still allowing the family, especially Ja'far b.Yahya, great wealth and prestige. The caliph had now brought other elements into the government to balance it; at court, Fadl b.al-Rabi' had become a formidable rival, while, in the provinces, determined opponents of the family, like 'Ali b.'Isa b.Mahan in Khurasan, Yazid b.Mazyad in Armenia and 'Abd al-Malik b.Salih in Syria, exercised great power. Harun himself settled in Raqqa, coming to Baghdad only once, in 184 (800), and returning to Raqqa the next year. He seems to have acquired a positive aversion to the city by this time and, when he went on the *hajj* in 186 (802), he deliberately avoided entering it. In 181 (797/8), he performed both the religious functions of his office in the same year. Not only did he lead the Muslims against the Byzantines in person but he also led the *hajj*.[24]

The main events of the period were an insurrection and an invasion. In 180 (796/7) there was a disturbance in Syria among the 'thieving *zawaqil'*, of whom we shall hear more later. We are given no details of the disturbance and its main importance seems to be that Ja'far b.Yahya, the Barmakid, was sent to suppress this. To do this he enlisted the services of prominent Khurasani Arab leaders, among them a grandson of the great Qahtaba, and a vast army. The expedition is said to have been completely successful and the opposition entirely disarmed, but one is left with the impression that the real point of the exercise was to demonstrate that the Barmakids could organise a military expedition, especially after the fiasco against Walid b.Tarif, the Kharijite, the previous year. Most of Tabari's account of the incident is devoted to a poem in praise of the Barmakids and the long and fulsome speech Ja'far made to the caliph on his return.[25]

The invasion was a more serious threat to the state. The Khazars had been quiet since the reign of Mansur, probably because the Khazar-Byzantine alliance had temporarily broken down, but in 183 (799), there was a renewed incursion. The reason for this is said to have been that the Khazar Khaqan's daughter was being brought as a bride for Fadl b.Yahya, the Barmakid, (another testimony to the continuing influence of the family) but died *en route*. Her attendants reported to her father that she had been treacherously murdered and he planned a large-scale incursion. He invaded through the pass at Darband and captured a vast number of Muslims and Christians. The governor fled and the caliph turned once again to Yazid b.Mazyad, who, with support from the Arab Khurasani leader, Khuzayma b.Khazim, drove the invaders back. It was the last time the Khazars were to attack the northern frontier and the last phase of a struggle which had lasted, off and on, since the first arrival of the Arabs in Armenia.[26] This victory consolidated the power of Yazid b.Mazyad in the area. According to Ya'qubi, he had been responsible for bringing in and settling much of the Arab population of the area and this probably accounts, in part, for his family's continuing influence there. Yazid seems to have taken refuge in Armenia on the accession of Harun, but was expelled in 172 (788/9). Reappointed at the time of the Khazar invasion, he remained governor until his death in 185 (801).[27] For many of his contemporaries, and the poets he patronised lavishly, he was the ideal of the Arab tribal leader: brave, generous and an experienced and capable soldier. His family remained powerful in the area; he was succeeded by his son, Khalid, who was the ancestor of the Sharvan Shahs who ruled the area of Sharvan until the arrival of the Turks in the fifth (eleventh) century.[28]

The last phase of Harun's reign, from 186 (802), saw a dramatic change in the form of the government. These years were dominated by three important developments; the arrangement of the succession, the fall of the Barmakids and the intensification of the Byzantine war.

Though the caliph, now in his mid-thirties, was still young by modern standards, there was no guarantee that he would not die as suddenly as his brother. The question of the succession was given added urgency by a polarisation within the governing class between the Barmakids and their allies, and those who had regained prominence in recent years, Fadl b.al-Rabi' and the military leaders. Three candidates for the succession emerged from among Harun's sons. Muhammad, who took the title of Amin, was of Abbasid descent on both sides, his mother, Zubayda, being a grand-daughter of Mansur. He is portrayed by hostile sources as a slow and stupid child but, as early as 175 (791/2), when he was only five years old, he was proclaimed heir apparent.[29] Many senior members of the Abbasid family are said to have objected to this, both on account of his extreme youth and because they themselves hoped to succeed, in the event of the caliph's untimely death; however, the nomination was supported and pushed through by his tutor, Fadl b.Yahya, the Barmakid, who would benefit greatly if his young protégé were to succeed. In 180 (796), he was left in charge of Baghdad when his father moved to Raqqa,[30] and, apart from the *hajj* in 186 (802), there is no record of his having left the city before his accession. Early on, then, he became closely identified with Baghdad and its inhabitants, the *abna'*, and this must have been strengthened by the eclipse of his tutor, Fadl.

'Abd Allah, called Ma'mun, was born the same year as his brother; a picturesque legend describes Harun hearing of his own succession and his son's birth on the same night. His mother is said to have been Marajil, a daughter of Ustadhsis, the Khurasani rebel, a connection which may have helped his future links with the province. His adoption as heir did not come until 182 (798/9), when he was appointed as heir to his brother, at the instigation of his Barmakid tutor, Ja'far b.Yahya. He was also given formal charge of Khurasan as far west as Hamadhan, although he did not visit the province for another ten years and real power was in the hands of 'Ali b.'Isa b.Mahan.[31] His nomination may have been the Barmakid response to the increasing identification of Amin with the interests of the *abna'* and he remained closely connected with the Barmakids, especially with Ja'far, the one member of the family who retained his influence to the end.

This arrangement gave rise to a number of important questions. What would the relations between the two brothers be, assuming they were still both alive at their father's death? Could Amin, once he had become caliph, alter the succession to make his brother a latter-day 'Isa b.Musa? Could Amin send agents into Ma'mun's territory and could he collect troops and taxes from there? In an effort to overcome these difficulties and to regulate the mechanics of succession in a peaceful way, Harun went on the *hajj* in 186 (802). In the mosque at Makka, with great solemnity and in the presence of almost all the important men in the Abbasid state, he obliged each of his sons to sign a document, which laid down, in as much detail as was practical, their mutual obligations. Amin was to enjoy the title of caliph and rule in Iraq and much of the west, while his brother and eventual successor, Ma'mun, was to enjoy autonomy in the eastern provinces.[32] Contemporaries are said to have been amazed that Harun's own experience, not to mention his father's, had not taught him the futility of such binding agreements.[33] It is difficult not to agree with their sentiments. Why then did he do it? There are a number of possible explanations, all of which may have contributed to his decision.

One factor was the vast size of the empire and the difficulty of keeping in touch with all the provinces. Mansur had, to some extent, sought to counter this by giving very considerable power to provincial governors but, under his successors, the government had become more centralised. Simply on the grounds of administrative efficiency, it must have seemed desirable to have more than one centre of government.

Then there was the problem of Khurasan. From the time of the Abbasid Revolution there had been tension between those who felt that the province, as the home of the Abbasid movement, should have a special status, and the central government. One way of solving this problem had been found when Mahdi acted as his father's viceroy in Rayy, between 141 and 151 (758-68). This had given the Khurasanis a degree of local government, while, at the same time, keeping them within the control of the ruling dynasty. Harun probably wanted to repeat this — to provide a measure of decentralisation without destroying the overall unity of the empire as represented in the Abbasid family.

But Harun was also trying to solve some of the tensions which had arisen within the governing class. He must have been aware that no one candidate for the throne could secure the allegiance of all the main groups. He was trying to avoid a civil war between the supporters of Amin's candidacy (the *abna'* and the Baghdadis) and the supporters of Ma'mun (the Barmakids and their allies). By defining the sphere of influence of each party, he might be able to avoid conflict. This hypothesis is supported by the curious episode of Qasim's place in the succession. There are three versions of the text of the Makka agreements; of which only one, the version given by Tabari, includes the somewhat limited provision made for this third son, which suggests that it may have been an afterthought. Qasim himself was not on the *hajj* but with his protector, 'Abd al-Malik b.Salih, in Syria. The intention of this agreement was that Qasim should in turn succeed Ma'mun.[34] In the meantime, he was to be given very similar privileges and immunities in the area of northern Syria and the Byzantine frontier to those Ma'mun was to enjoy in Khurasan. As Ma'mun was the candidate of the Barmakids, so Qasim was the candidate of 'Abd al-Malik b.Salih and his Syrian supporters.

Harun's vision seems to have been one of family rule, in which the unity of the Muslim world would be secured by having the various areas ruled by different members of the same family. Saffah had achieved something of the sort when he had appointed his relatives to extensive governorates in the west and it had been intended that Harun himself should be governor of the west under the general control of his brother Hadi; Mutawwakil tried to devise a similar plan, with even more catastrophic results, when he arranged his own succession. The idea of family rule, rather than the dictatorship of one autocratic individual, went back to pre-Islamic Arab traditions. It was not an absurd vision by any means and Harun, no doubt, hoped that the formal and detailed pacts he had drawn up would remove the potential causes of conflict. In the event the forces of disintegration proved too strong, but perhaps that only shows how right the caliph had been to try to contain them.

The provisions of the agreement deal with the details which could cause conflict. The area allotted to Ma'mun is defined as stretching from the western borders of the province of Rayy to the farthest reaches of Khurasan. This includes Sistan and, probably, Kirman. Fars is not mentioned, while Sind seems to have been attached to Amin's portion. Nor is there mention of who was to receive the tribute of the princes of Tabaristan and Daylam but these were probably included with Rayy in Ma'mun's area. This constituted a 'Greater Khurasan', almost identical with the area controlled earlier by Abu Muslim and Mahdi and, in the next century, by the Tahirids.

After specifying that Ma'mun should have control over the army, taxation and post in Khurasan, Amin goes on to promise the following: that he will not interfere with any of his brother's property in the west, nor will he take any action against his followers or servants; he will not judge the disputes of the Khurasanis, nor give any aid to rebels against his brother's authority. The document ends with a series of guarantees: if Amin alters the conditions in any way, then all oaths of allegiance to him are void and all his subjects are to support his brother, while he himself is obliged to renounce all his wives and property and make fifty pilgrimages to Makka. The conditions signed by Ma'mun were much less onerous and mostly consisted of a reiteration of his brother's obligations to him. However, he did promise, in rather general terms, to help and advise his brother, not to help any of his enemies and to send troops if he were attacked. He also agreed that, if Amin were to insist that one of his own sons should succeed Ma'mun, then he would not interfere with this arrangement. Finally there were the same penalty clauses as those signed by his brother but rather less stringent.

The conditions meant that Ma'mun was, effectively, sovereign ruler in his own area, as the vital controls over taxation and the army were in his hands. Furthermore, it is clear that taxes collected from Khurasan were to be spent in the province, thus putting an end to a grievance which went back to Umayyad times. Control over the *barid* (post) was also important, since it meant that his brother was almost completely out of touch with events in Khurasan and with those people in the province who might have been sympathetic with his point of view. The provision that Ma'mun should offer his brother military help should also be noted; it was almost the only obligation he owed him and Amin was to sieze on it as an opportunity to put Ma'mun in the wrong.

The pacts were duly signed and given maximum publicity. The texts were displayed in the Ka'aba for all to see, while the provisions were duly circulated to the provinces: public opinion in the Muslim community was to be the ultimate sanction. The court then returned to Iraq.

It was immediately after his return, on the last day of Muharram 187 (28 January 803), that Harun ordered the arrest of all the leading members of the Barmakid family. He acted swiftly and without warning and there was no possibility of escape. Yahya and his son Fadl were imprisoned, while the unfortunate Ja'far was executed without even being allowed to plead his case before the caliph. His corpse was sent to Baghdad where it was dismembered and displayed — to the delight, no doubt, of his enemies among the *abna'*.[35]

No event in early Abbasid history has provoked so much discussion and wonder. Contemporary observers and later historians were impressed by the sudden, secret ruthlessness with which the caliph acted against the family, who were not only the wealthiest and most powerful in the empire but were also responsible for so much of his own success. Explanations can be divided into three categories: the personal, the random and the political.

The personal explanations need not detain us long. According to a very ancient story, Harun used to enjoy the company of his sister 'Abbasa and that of Ja'far, the Barmakid, above all others. So that they could all be together without offending Islamic custom, he arranged that 'Abbasa and Ja'far should be married but that this marriage should be no more than a formality. However, the couple went beyond the limits laid down by the caliph, the marriage was consummated and children born. These were sent secretly to Makka, but Harun discovered their existence on the pilgrimage of 186 (802) and immediately executed the two lovers. There are many inherent improbabilities in this story and it was dismissed long ago by the great historian, Ibn Khaldun, but, whatever the truth of the matter, such personal explanations cannot account entirely for such a great political upheaval.[36]

The random explanation was the one adopted by the executioner himself, Masrur al-Khadim, who suggested cynically that all the reasons usually advanced were nonsense and that the whole event was the result of boredom and envy on the part of the caliph. Ya'qubi concurs, suggesting that Harun himself did not know the reasons for his actions, and Sourdel has some sympathy for this point of view.[37]

But explanations which postulate that rulers act in an arbitrary and irrational fashion and that attempts to understand their actions are useless can never satisfy the historian entirely. Harun's career suggests that he was not the sort of man to make so radical a change simply to gratify a whim. We must examine possible political factors.

The first of these is that Harun had become more politically self-confident and had outgrown the tutelage of the Barmakids. He was prepared to accept their control when he was an inexperienced young man, newly confronted with the problems of government. He looked to Yahya b.Khalid as the young Queen Victoria looked to Lord Melbourne, as a father figure, a pilot who could guide him through the shoals and currents of political life. His career shows him becoming more self-confident and more independent as the years went on. He began to look to other advisers, like Fadl b.al-Rabi', and became resentful of Barmakid dominance, whose influence had begun to decline before the fatal blow fell. This is certainly part of the truth but it does not explain why Harun acted so ruthlessly and dramatically, nor the timing of his move.

Contemporaries wondered whether the Alid sympathies of the Barmakids played a part in their disgrace. This is plausible. From the beginning of his reign, Harun had favoured a hard line against the Alids whereas the Barmakids tended to prefer compromise, in the spirit of Mahdi's policy. Ten years before the fall of the family, Fadl b.Yahya had incurred the caliph's displeasure by making an agreement with Yahya b.'Abd Allah in Daylam, and there was a story circulating in Bahgdad that either Fadl or Ja'far had taken it upon himself to release Yahya against the caliph's wishes. Certainly we know that attitudes on this subject had long been a point of difference between Harun and the Barmakids and it may well have played a part in discrediting them. But again the timing is wrong; they were not disgraced for a decade after Yahya b.'Abd Allah was dead, nor was there any considerable Alid threat to the Abbasid position at this time.[38]

Of course, the Barmakids had many enemies and pressure from them, no doubt, encouraged Harun in his course of action. The most prominent of these was Fadl b.al-Rabi', who was increasingly influential in government and was to take over many of the functions of the disgraced family after their fall. There was also another leading *mawla*, Sindi b.Shahik, who had been an associate of Hadi and was later, like Rabi', to be a leading supporter of Amin. He was in charge of security at Baghdad at this time and was ordered to display Ja'far's body to the people.[39] Then, of course, there were the *abna'* of the city; the sending of Ja'far's corpse to their home town can only be seen as a gesture to win their favour.[40] There can be no doubt that Harun acted, in part at least, to placate the anti-Barmakid group.

It seems logical, as well to link the fall of the Barmakids with the succession arrangements. These had just been completed in Makka and the Barmakids had played a prominent part in drawing them up. The *abna'* would not have been pleased to see Khurasan pass firmly under the control of Ma'mun. It is possible that Harun realised that, with the Barmakids in their leading position in the state, it was unlikely that Amin would be able to succeed to the position designed for him. The family which had dominated the entire caliphate would hardly be content to see their protégé confined to Khurasan. If the succession was to work as planned, then the influence of the family had to be destroyed or, at least, vastly reduced and it is significant that Ja'far, the only member of the family executed, was the one in closest contact with Ma'mun.

There is some circumstantial evidence to support this, in the arrest of 'Abd al-Malik b.Salih in the same year. As has been explained above, 'Abd al-Malik had put forward a candidate of his own, Qasim, who had been given extensive powers in the frontier regions. 'Abd al-Malik was imprisoned, on the charge of aspiring to the caliphate, on the basis of evidence produced by his own son; he was also, more realistically, accused of making trouble between Harun's sons.[41] It seems that he was removed from the political scene for the same reason as the Barmakids: that Qasim, supported by a backer as powerful and experienced as 'Abd al-Malik, would make life impossible for Amin when he became caliph. The parallel does not seem far-fetched and it can hardly be coincidence that the political power of the chief supporters of Ma'mun and Qasim was destroyed so soon after the succession arrangements were made. Harun probably sought to replace the existing leaders of powerful factions with his own sons. Thus the *kuttab* and the *dehqan*s of Khurasan could now look to Ma'mun for leadership rather than to the Barmakids; the Qaysi Arabs of northern Syria would look to Qasim, not to 'Abd al-Malik. Thus the three brothers, working in harmony, could secure the unity of the empire. This is not the whole story, but it does explain the decisiveness and the timing of Harun's action.

Harun continued to rule for some six years after the dramatic events of 186-7 (802-3); this period is usually regarded as something of an anticlimax, but there is no reason to suppose that contemporaries saw it that way. The main preoccupations of these years were the affairs of

Khurasan and the struggle against the Byzantines; Harun took an active role in dealing with both of these. The problems of Khurasan are dealt with in more detail in another chapter but must be touched on briefly here. In 180 (796/7), against the emphatic advice of Yahya b.Khalid, Harun had appointed the leader of the *abna'*, 'Ali b.'Isa b.Mahan, as governor of the province. 'Ali pursued a policy of squeezing the *dehqan*s and *ashraf* of the province for what they were worth. The sufferers naturally complained and the Barmakids, being of the same class themselves, supported them. Harun refused to take action, partly because of the extravagant gifts 'Ali continued to send him, but also, no doubt, because he thought that a reduction in the wealth and power of the Khurasani magnates might be no bad thing. In 189 (805), Harun set out for Rayy to examine the affairs of the province for himself — the first time a reigning caliph had ever visited Iran. He held court for much of the year in the city of his birth and regulated many minor matters. The governor of Armenia, Khuzayma b.Khazim, came with gifts, new treaties were made with the princes of the mountainous areas to the north of the city and he appointed the experienced military leader, 'Abd Allah b.Malik,[42] to a vast governorship which included most of northern and western Iran. He also used the visit as an opportunity to publicise the rights of his son, Ma'mun, and his place in the succession. About Khurasan itself he did nothing. 'Ali b.'Isa came to pay court, loaded with gifts, and his position was confirmed by the caliph, who returned to Baghdad at the end of the year.

The problem was only postponed. The next year, Rafi' b.Layth began his rebellion in Samarqand and he seems to have attracted widespread support from the *dehqan*s. 'Ali b.'Isa was unable to crush him. The caliph, happy to support his policy as long as it worked, saw that the situation was becoming very dangerous and, rather than risking an all-out war in the province, he dismissed the governor and replaced him by Harthama b.A'yan, himself a Khurasani magnate and a much more acceptable figure. The rebellion continued but, with 'Ali out of the way, it attracted less support.

The other preoccupation was the war against the Byzantines. Harun had received his early training on the frontier and had always taken a much more direct personal interest in what went on than his predecessors had done. Besides taking part in raids, he concerned himself with the administration of the area. Behind the actual *thughur* (frontier provinces) he established a new province, the 'Awasim, whose resources were to be devoted to frontier warfare, and he built up Raqqa, at least partly as a rear base for expeditions.

Shaban has argued that much of Harun's reign and policies can best be interpreted as preparation for an involvement in these campaigns.[43] While this is, perhaps, overstating the case, there can be no doubt that he devoted an increasing amount of time and energy to the situation. In 190 (806) he mounted the largest and most spectacular of his raids. Tabari claims that he assembled as many as 135,000 regular troops, excluding volunteers and camp followers, and, while the figures must be treated with caution, this was clearly a very large-scale venture. A number of different attacks were launched on frontier fortresses, while Humayd b.Ma'yuf al-Hamdani, who had been put in charge on the Syrian coast, led a naval attack on Cyprus. The caliph himself captured Heracleia and, after taking the inhabitants prisoner, returned in triumph.[44] But the results of all this activity were very slight; a few fortresses were captured north of the Taurus passes, but no attempt was made to occupy Heracleia on a permanent basis or to push further into Byzantine lands. The next year, Harun moved up to Hadath, while Harthama b.A'yan and 30,000 Khurasanis were sent on raiding expeditions. More evidence of his intentions was given when he ordered that churches in the frontier provinces should be destroyed because the Christians were thought to be acting as a fifth column for the enemy.[45] But, again, no permanent gains were made. The next year, 192 (808), Harun was involved in his great expedition to Khurasan and the disturbances after his death in 193 (809) gave the Greeks an opportunity to take the offensive once more.

What significance should be attached to this show of strength on the frontier? Certainly, it was an impressive demonstration of the power of the Abbasid state and a reaffirmation of the caliph's role as leader of the Muslim community. But it is impossible to see it as a serious attempt to conquer the Byzantine Empire or even to make any long-term territorial gains. The frontier fortresses were of value because they guarded the Muslim provinces from Byzantine raiders and served as a base for forays in other directions. The purpose was mostly propaganda for internal consumption. Leading the summer expedition was a mark of the caliph's position as leader of the community, much like leading the *hajj* (and Harun, it should be noted, led the *hajj* more times than any other Abbasid caliph). Looked at in this light, it is difficult to see it as the object and purpose of all his policies; it was rather an important part of them, designed to protect Muslim settlement and enhance his own prestige as defender of Islam.

The last few years of Harun's reign allowed new personalities to occupy the positions vacated by the Barmakids. Fadl b.al-Rabi' and his followers came to dominate the administration, along with Isma'il b.Subayh al-Harrani, the Syrian who had served Hadi as *wazir* but who had been pushed into the background by the Barmakids.[46] Fadl may not have been as able an administrator as Yahya b.Khalid (though it should be noted that the stories of unopened mail piling up come from a strongly pro-Barmakid source)[47] but he was placed in a very strong position at the centre of affairs. Harthama b.A'yan, commander of the guard and then governor of Khurasan, remained one of the caliph's right-hand men and his most trusted army commander. Ja'far's position as tutor to Ma'mun was taken by a Barmakid protégé, Fadl b.Sahl, who used his position to build up his influence with the young prince. Finally, in the wings there waited two figures who were at that time under arrest but who could be expected to play a major role if permitted: 'Ali b.'Isa b.Mahan, arrested after his removal from Khurasan, and 'Abd al-Malik b.Salih.

It was against this background that Harun planned his new expedition to the east. Rafi' b.Layth was still in rebellion, despite Harthama's military successes, and the avowed object of the caliph's journey was to put an end to this. The caliph left Raqqa for Baghdad in Rabi' II, 192 (March 808). He made his arrangements in the west; Qasim was left in charge of the areas assigned to him on the frontiers and the old and experienced Khurasani leader, Khuzayma b.Khazim, was appointed as his guardian. As Harun passed through Baghdad, he left Amin once more in control so that he could take over easily, if anything happened to his father. The caliph was only in his late forties but his hair was already grey and he may have known he was dying. There is certainly a story to that effect recounted by Tabari and it is suggested also by the careful preparations that seem to have been made for this eventuality. Fadl b.Sahl insisted that Ma'mun should be on the expedition, so as to be in his province, and Fadl b.Rabi' made careful plans to secure his own interests and those of his master.[48]

The journey through Iran took several months. By Safar 193 (November/December 808) the caliph had reached Jurjan, where he was met by a vast caravan of 1,500 camels carrying all the treasure which had been confiscated from 'Ali b.'Isa b.Mahan on his deposition. By the time he left Jurjan, the caliph was clearly a sick man and he stopped at the estate of one Junayd b.'Abd al-Rahman, at Sanabadh near Tus. From here he sent on his son, Ma'mun, to Marw, accompanied by most of the leading military figures in his army, including 'Abd Allah b.Malik, Asad b.Yazid b.Mazyad and 'Abbas b.Ja'far b.Muhammad b.al-Ash'ath. Only Fadl b.Rabi', Isma'il b.Subayh (his secretary) and his personal servants remained at Tus with the dying caliph. Harun grew steadily weaker and died at the beginning of Jumada II, 193 (March 809). He was buried in the tomb he had ordered to be dug for him at the house where he died.[49]

Notes

1. Tabari, *Ta'rikh*, vol. 3, p. 764.
2. Ibid., vol. 3, p. 603.
3. Ibid., vol. 3, p. 603.
4. Ibid., vol. 3, p. 606; Sourdel, *Vizirat Abbaside*, vol. 1, pp. 134-44, gives details of all the offices the family held.
5. Jahshiyari, *Wuzara'*, pp. 229-30; Sourdel, *Vizirat Abbaside*, vol. 1, pp. 196-7.
6. Jahshiyari, *Wuzara'*, p. 186; Sourdel, *Vizirat Abbaside*, vol. 1, pp. 147, 151.
7. Tabari, *Ta'rikh*, vol. 3, pp. 610-11, 647; Sourdel, *Vizirat Abbaside*, vol. 1, pp. 147, 151.
8. See below, p. 181.
9. Sourdel, *Vizirat Abbaside*, vol. 1, pp. 144-9.
10. Tabari, *Ta'rikh*, vol. 3, pp. 607-8.
11. Ibid., vol. 3, pp. 688-9.
12. Baladhuri, *Futuh*, pp. 178-9, 199-203, 214, 445, 456; Ibn al-Faqih, *Buldan*, p. 282.
13. Tabari, *Ta'rikh*, vol. 3, pp. 612-20; Jahshiyari, *Wuzara'*, pp. 189-90; Sourdel, *Vizirat Abbaside*, vol. 1, pp. 144-5, 164-7.
14. Tabari, *Ta'rikh*, vol. 3, pp. 371, 600.
15. Ibid., vol. 3, pp. 629-30, 645; Ya'qubi, *Ta'rikh*, vol. 2, pp. 496-7; Kindi, *Wulat*, p. 136.
16. Shaban, *Islamic History*, vol. 2, p. 37.
17. Tabari, *Ta'rikh*, vol. 3, pp. 606-7, 610.
18. Ibid., vol. 3, p. 645.
19. Ibid., vol. 3, p. 645; Jahshiyari, *Wuzara'*, p. 227; Sourdel, *Vizirat Abbaside*, vol. 1, pp. 146-7.
20. Tabari, *Ta'rikh*, vol. 3, pp. 646-51.
21. Ibid., vol. 3, pp. 631-8; Ya'qubi, *Ta'rikh*, vol. 2, p. 496; Azdi, *Ta'rikh*, pp. 279-83; Isfahani, *Aghani*, vol. 12, pp. 94-9; Ibn al-Athir, *Ta'rikh*, vol. 6, p. 96.
22. Hamza Isfahani, *Ta'rikh*, p. 143; Gardizi, *Zayn*, fo. 79a.
23. Tabari, *Ta'rikh*, vol. 3, p. 638; Sourdel, *Vizirat Abbaside*, vol. 1, p. 138.
24. Tabari, *Ta'rikh*, vol. 3, pp. 646, 649, 651.
25. Ibid., vol. 3, pp. 639-44.
26. Ibid., vol. 3, pp. 648.
27. Ibid., vol. 3, pp. 607, 650; Ya'qubi, *Ta'rikh*, vol. 2, pp. 515-19.
28. Tabari, *Ta'rikh*, vol. 3, p. 650; Minorsky, *Shirvan and Darband*, pp. 22 ff.
29. Tabari, *Ta'rikh*, vol. 3, pp. 610-12; Jahshiyari, *Wuzara'*, p. 193; Sourdel, *Vizirat Abbaside*, vol. 1, pp. 147-8.
30. Tabari, *Ta'rikh*, vol. 3, p. 646.
31. Ibid., vol. 3, p. 647; Jahshiyari, *Wuzara'*, p. 211; *'Uyun wa'l-Hada'iq*, p. 344; Sadighi, *Mouvements*, p. 161.
32. There are three versions of the text of the documents: Tabari, *Ta'rikh*,

vol. 3, pp. 655-66; Ya'qubi, *Ta'rikh*, vol. 2, pp. 502-8; and Azraqi, *Akhbar*, pp. 161-8.

33. Ibn al-Athir, *Ta'rikh*, vol. 6, p. 117.
34. Tabari, *Ta'rikh*, vol. 3, pp. 652-3.
35. For full bibliography on the fall of the Barmakids, see Sourdel, *Vizirat Abbaside*, vol. 1, pp. 156-81.
36. Tabari, *Ta'rikh*, vol. 3, pp. 676-7; Abbott, *Queens*, pp. 195-6; Sourdel, *Vizirat Abbaside*, vol. 1, p. 167.
37. Jahshiyari, *Wuzara'*, p. 254; Ya'qubi, *Ta'rikh*, vol. 2, p. 510.
38. Sourdel, *Vizirat Abbaside*, vol. 1, pp. 164-6.
39. Jahshiyari, *Wuzara'*, pp. 236-7.
40. Shaban, *Islamic History*, vol. 2, p. 39.
41. Tabari, *Ta'rikh*, vol. 3, pp. 688-94; Jahshiyari, *Wuzara'*, pp. 262-3.
42. Tabari, *Ta'rikh*, vol. 3, pp. 702-6.
43. Shaban, *Islamic History*, vol. 2, p. 38.
44. Tabari, *Ta'rikh*, vol. 3, pp. 709-11.
45. Ibid., vol. 3, p. 712.
46. Sourdel, *Vizirat Abbaside*, vol. 1, pp. 183-8.
47. Jahshiyari, *Wuzara'*, p. 265.
48. Tabari, *Ta'rikh*, vol. 3, pp. 730-2.
49. Ibid., vol. 3, pp. 733-4, 735-9; Ya'qubi, *Ta'rikh*, vol. 2, p. 521.

8 THE GREAT CIVIL WAR: I

The death of Harun left both his sons in a difficult position. On the one hand, Amin was already in charge in Baghdad and had no difficulty in assuming the title of caliph but many of those who might be expected to support him, like Fadl b.al-Rabi' or 'Abd Allah b.Malik, were with Harun or Ma'mun, far to the east. Ma'mun was equally in control of Marw, where his brother was proclaimed caliph and he himself acknowledged as heir, but he was still faced by the rebellion of Rafi' b.al-Layth, in Samarqand, and his army, though large, was of doubtful loyalty.

As soon as he heard the news of his father's death, Amin began to take measures to weaken his brother's position. Before his father's death he had sent a secret letter for his brother, Salih, who was with the caliph's party. This said that, if Harun died, Salih was to appoint loyal men, like 'Abd Allah b.Malik and Yazid b.Mazyad's son, Asad, to lead the army under the general control of Fadl b.al-Rabi' and that the army should then return to Baghdad, bringing the treasure with it. This would leave Ma'mun defenceless and unable to assert his authority in Khurasan.[1] As we have seen, however, these arrangements were overtaken by events because the army was already at Marw under Ma'mun's command. Fadl and the treasure were still with Harun and they, with a small escort, hastily returned to Baghdad. Here he rapidly established his position as Amin's chief adviser.[2] The treasure, too, was a source of friction. Clearly, 'Ali b.'Isa b.Mahan, now released from prison, wanted to see it in Baghdad but this treasure was equally highly regarded in Khurasan; not only was it needed to fight the war against Rafi' but much of it had been extorted from those very *dehqan*s who were to emerge as Ma'mun's main supporters. So, while the Makka agreements had not been literally infringed, Amin had made his aggressive intentions clear.

The period from the caliph's death, in Rabi' II, 193 (January 809), and the outbreak of open hostilities, at the beginning of 195 (October 810), was dominated by two developments. The first was the negotiations between the two brothers, intended partly to find a solution to their differences but rather more for each to put the other side in the wrong; the second was the growing power and influence of militants in each

135

camp, at the expense of those who wanted to avoid civil war.

Soon after his accession, it seems Amin decided to replace Ma'mun and Qasim as heirs by his own son, Musa, a move obviously encouraged by his more militant supporters. Qasim was soon removed from his position in the Syrian frontier area, as his main supporter, 'Abd al-Malik b.Salih, was still under arrest, and was replaced, in all his offices, by Khuzayma b.Khazim. A high-powered delegation was sent to Marw to persuade Ma'mun that he should come to Baghdad, since his brother needed his advice. Ma'mun, for his part, kept up the diplomatic tone of the exchange, explaining that he was unable to come, since Khurasan was threatened by enemies and, under the terms of the Makka agreements, he could not leave his post.[3] Thereafter, there were no more embassies but there was a series of letters between the two brothers, which are quoted in full by the historian Tabari.[4] In the first of these, Amin asked for some border provinces to be handed over, since he had a larger army and needed the revenue, and also that he should be able to keep an agent of his own in the east, to keep him informed. Both these seemed fairly minor concessions and, confronted by many other problems, Ma'mun nearly agreed. Only firm pressure from his most militant adviser, Fadl b.Sahl, persuaded him to refuse the demands, on the grounds that he could not break the agreement and needed the resources to defend his own frontier in the east. Amin then repeated his first demands, saying that it had only been intended that Ma'mun should have sufficient revenue to defend Khurasan and that the rest should be sent to the treasury; this, too, was an attempt to reopen a contentious issue and undermine Ma'mun's autonomy. Of course, he refused, and the tone of the exchange becomes more bitter; in reply, Amin bluntly accused his brother of causing trouble. Finally, Ma'mun pleaded poverty and asked that his family and wealth in Baghdad should be sent to the east. He can hardly have expected that his brother would give up such valuable hostages and the demand was probably made to put Amin in the wrong. As expected, he refused and negotiations were broken off. It is clear that Amin's demands were all contraventions of the Makka agreements but it should also be emphasised that strict adherence to these agreements would have put Amin in a very weak position *vis-à-vis* his brother.

It was at this point that Ma'mun proclaimed himself *imam*. No Abbasid caliph had officially used this title before, and he himself refrained from taking the title of caliph at this time. It was probably a deliberately ambiguous gesture, to announce his defiance of his brother without providing an excuse for attack. It also shows that Ma'mun was pursuing the policy, begun by Mahdi and continued by the Barmakids, of developing the religious nature of Abbasid authority and seeking a reconciliation with the Alids and their supporters.

At the same time, he cut off the *barid* on which Amin depended for information from the east. This was a source of great irritation to Amin and throughout this period Ma'mun's intelligence system was much better than his brother's. He had agents in influential positions in Baghdad and could write letters fairly freely to army leaders there. On the other hand, he closed the frontiers of Khurasan, except to a few merchants and, of course, his own agents. This made it very difficult for Amin to contact those in the east who might be loyal to him. Fadl b.al-Rabi' did have a circular smuggled in by a woman but its effectiveness was limited compared with Ma'mun's propaganda in Baghdad.[5]

Meanwhile, in Baghdad, militants were gaining ground. Fadl b.al-Rabi' urged Amin to remove his brother from the succession as 'Isa b.Musa had been removed before. He is said to have been afraid that, if Ma'mun became caliph, he would be killed. He was supported in this by another senior palace servant, the *mawla,* Sindi b.Shahik, and by the man who had been secretary to both Hadi and Harun, Isma'il b.Subayh al-Harrani. They were joined in their demands by 'Ali b.'Isa b.Mahan. 'Ali had been released on the death of Harun and he immediately became Amin's chief military adviser. His main object was to recover his position in Khurasan, even if it meant leading his followers among the *abna'* in an invasion of the province. This meant that he was more aggressive than Fadl. While the latter would probably have been content to see Ma'mun removed from the succession, 'Ali would not be satisfied unless he was dismissed from Khurasan as well. Not everyone in Baghdad supported this militant line. Khuzayma b.Khazim and his brother, 'Abd Allah, leaders of one of the most distinguished military families, urged caution, pointing out that, if he encouraged his soldiers to break their oaths, he would be the next to be betrayed.[6] It is unlikely that they were alone in their objections and it is significant that none of the old-established military leaders are found fighting alongside 'Ali b.'Isa. This disunity was to prove a major weakness in Amin's war effort.

At Marw, as well, militant counsels were gaining ground. It was at this time that Fadl b.Sahl emerged as Ma'mun's chief adviser. He has already been noted as a protégé of the Barmakids and, after their fall, he had become tutor to the young prince. Like them he was attached to the old Iranian ways; he lamented the decline of the *dehqan*s and, even after his late conversion to Islam, his enemies continued to refer to him as a Magian. At the height of his glory he had himself carried in a chair like Chosroes and was accused of wanting to restore the old Persian kings.[7] But this was more than a sentimental attachment; Fadl's plan was that Ma'mun should counter his brother's aggressive moves by turning for support to the *dehqan*s of eastern Iran. The first move was obviously to make peace with Rafi' b.Layth, because he could not afford a war on two fronts and because Rafi' and his followers might prove useful allies. In Muharram 194 (October/November 809) Rafi' surrendered to Harthama b.Ayan and Ma'mun and was very generously treated.[8] It is likely that a number of his followers joined Ma'mun's army, since they shared a common hostility to 'Ali b.'Isa b.Mahan, and it is interesting that the agreement was negotiated by members of the *dehqan* Samanid family, who were to be so important in the later history of the area.[9] Later, when Amin began his military preparations Ma'mun was in despair and felt that he had no alternative but to go to Baghdad or flee to the Turks; Khurasan had been ravaged before he arrived and the frontier princes, and *khaqan* of Tibet, the *jabghu* of the Turks and the kings of Kabul and Utrar, who had supported Rafi', were still restive. Fadl suggested that he make peace with these very princes and recall his troops from the frontier to oppose his brother. If things went badly, he could still flee to the Turks. The reluctant Ma'mun was persuaded and instructed him to go ahead with the plan.[10]

Fadl's policy was opposed by most of the senior army commanders and troops who had been sent to Marw by Harun. Men like 'Abd Allah b.Malik had no wish to see a civil war and their sympathies probably lay with the Baghdadis and Amin anyway. The same was true of the rank and file. When Fadl tried to attract support among them by reminding them of the part their ancestors had played in the original Abbasid Revolution, the reaction was very lukewarm.[11] As a result Ma'mun never trusted them; 'Abd Allah b.Malik was never given the posts to which his seniority and experience would normally have entitled him and others, like 'Abd Allah b.Humayd b.Qahtaba and Asad b.Yazid b.Mazyad, both scions of notable military families, slipped away to join Amin's forces.[12]

Before the end of the year 194 (October 810), both sides had begun to take up military positions. Amin sent 'Isma b.Hammad, whose father had led the troops who arrested Ja'far, the Barmakid, to blockade Khurasan,[13] while Ma'mun sought to strengthen his hold over the frontier city of Rayy by sending an almost unknown landowner from Bushang, near Harat, with a few thousand men. The landowner's name was Tahir b.al-Husayn and his appointment to so crucial a post at this time was to affect the history of the whole Islamic world for the next fifty years.[14] Recent research[15] has shown that Tahir's family were of Arab origin but that, during the late Umayyad and early Abbasid period, they had settled in Bushang and become, in effect, hereditary governors of the small town. They became thoroughly Iranianised and had many connections among the *dehqan*s of the area. Tahir's father had fallen foul of 'Ali b.'Isa b.Mahan during his persecution of the *dehqan*s, so it was natural for Fadl b.Sahl to recruit him to the cause. The appointment to Rayy was a doubtful honour but a great opportunity; his own father, for one, thought that he was being foolhardy and many at Ma'mun's court must have felt that he had little chance against the forces of Amin.

At the beginning of the next year, the breach became final. In Safar 195 (November 810), Amin had his son, Musa, proclaimed heir, despite his youth, and Ma'mun's name was no longer mentioned in the prayers. Two months later, in Rabi' II (January 811), 'Ali b.'Isa b.Mahan was appointed as governor of all the eastern provinces.[16] While this was, no doubt, a popular move in Baghdad, it had the opposite effect in Marw. Nothing could unite the disaffected Khurasanis behind Ma'mun more effectively than the thought of 'Ali b.'Isa as governor, but the ruling group in Baghdad seems to have been so confident of victory that this did not concern them. In the spring of that year – 195 (811) – a great expedition was planned under 'Ali's leadership to take control in the east and, on 15 Jumada II (15 March), 'Ali led some 40,000 men out of Baghdad and camped at Nahrbin, on the Khurasan road. Never, it was said, had a larger or better-equipped army been seen in the city. 'Ali was confident of victory and he carried with him silver chains to fetter the unfortunate Ma'mun after his capture.[17] He led his mighty army up the road through the Zagros towards Ma'mun's most westerly outpost at Rayy.

The two armies which met near the city in Sha'ban 195 (May 811) were very different. In addition to the large number of the *abna'* 'Ali commanded, he had been joined on his journey through Iran by a large number of volunteers, scornfully dismissed by Tahir as 'nomad Arabs and mountain brigands', from the area of Jibal. These were led by Abu Dulaf al-Qasim b.'Isa al-'Ijli. The 'Ijlis were the most important tribal group to have settled in western Iran and Abu Dulaf himself was an important landowner in the area southeast of Hamadhan. No doubt, they joined 'Ali now in hope of rich booty, but they probably followed Abu Dulaf, as they had followed another 'Ijli, Jahwar b.Marrar, against the rebel Sunbadh, sixty years before, because they feared that the Iranians would drive them from their lands.[18] But 'Ali's large army had one serious weakness: the absence of any general of standing and experience except the leader himself. It has already been pointed out that many of the established military leaders had been lukewarm towards the campaign and none had chosen to join it. This weakness was to be a crucial factor in turning the defeat at Rayy into a rout.

Tahir's army was very much smaller; estimates vary from 3,800 to 5,000.[19] His commanders were either connected with him personally or were members of the Khurasani *dehqan* class. His *sahib al-shurta*, for example, was Ahmad b.Hisham, whose father, like Tahir's, had been one of the *dehqans* persecuted by 'Ali b.'Isa, while 'Abbas, the son of the Bukhara Khuda, or local prince of Bukhara, led a contingent of the army.[20] There is no mention of any of the established military figures whom Harun had sent to join his son.

Faced by the approach of this massive army, Tahir had two possible courses of action. His advisers suggested that he should fortify himself in Rayy and await reinforcements. Tahir overruled them; he did not trust the people of Rayy and some sources say they even locked the city gates against him. He decided to meet 'Ali's army in the open country. Just before the battle began, in order to increase the morale of his men, he had Ma'mun proclaimed caliph, the first time such a gesture had been made.

Accounts of the battle are confused[21] but the outcome is clear. 'Ali b.'Isa b.Mahan was killed early in the fighting, after which his army disintegrated and fled. It was at this point that the lack of an experienced second-in-command was so apparent; attempts by 'Ali's son, Yahya, to rally remnants of the army failed, the irregulars dispersed to their mountain homes and the *abna'* retreated down the road to Hamadhan. The result had transformed Tahir's position. Overnight, he became Ma'mun's leading general and the commander of his victorious army; the rest of his life was spent trying to preserve the position he had won against jealous rivals.

The news reached Marw in only three days. For Ma'mun it was not a moment too soon. Opposition to him and the policies of Fadl b.Sahl was still strong, especially among the military leaders, and his opponents were ready to take advantage of 'Ali's expected victory. The news from Rayy transformed the position; Fadl b.Sahl's policy had been vindicated completely and his enemies were reduced to silence. Ma'mun was proclaimed caliph in all the mosques of Khurasan.[22]

Good news travels faster than bad and it was not until two months later, in the middle of Shawwal (10 July 811), that news of the disaster reached Baghdad. Amin was, typically, amusing himself fishing. 'Damn you!', he said to the messenger, 'Go away! Kawthar has caught two fish and I have got nothing yet.'[23] Other people in Baghdad were less complacent. Anxious rumours spread among the common people; the military were demanding more pay, capitalising on the government's need of them, and were only calmed when 'Abd Allah b.Khazim was authorised to satisfy them. A disturbing sign for the future was the violence between the *abna'* and Arab elements in the army.[24]

After his victory, Tahir, acting apparently on his own initiative, began to pursue the enemy across the Iranian plateau and through the passes and gorges of the Zagros mountains to Iraq. He moved quickly, to give his opponents no time to regroup, and to cross the mountains before the winter snows closed the road. The first obstacle on his road was the ancient city of Hamadhan, which 'Abd al-Rahman b.Jabala had taken over with twenty thousand veteran *abna'*. Tahir invested the city for a month but it was pressure from the townspeople, who were, as at Rayy, reluctant to become involved on either side, which forced 'Abd al-Rahman to surrender; by the end of August (Dhu'l Qa'ada) the city was in Tahir's hands. 'Abd al-Rahman was taken prisoner but, as the army was negotiating the steep and winding road over the pass at Asadabadh, he escaped and made a surprise attack on Tahir; it was only with difficulty that he was beaten off and killed.[25] Thereafter, the road was open to the forces from the east, the small garrison at Qasr al-Lusus fled and Tahir reached the area of Hulwan, right on the edge of the Zagros. Here, in the little village of Shalashan, in an area where the climate was mild and the fodder plentiful, Tahir fortified himself and awaited developments.[26] In four months, he had destroyed two large armies and broken the confidence of the *abna'*. Amin's supporters in Iran had either fled or been dispersed but Tahir knew that he could not undertake the much more difficult war in Iraq without reinforcements. The opposition would be fighting for their survival on their own territory and the canals, rivers and palm forests of Iraq would be much less suitable for his cavalry than the open plains of Iran.

While Tahir wintered behind his fortifications at Shalashan, he could watch with satisfaction the internecine feuds which destroyed the opposition. The leadership was in disarray. The caliph Amin had commanded little respect in the days of his prosperity and now, when things were going badly, he failed to show any signs of leadership at all. Furthermore, his most prominent advisers and the men most responsible for the war were no longer on the scene; 'Ali b.'Isa was dead and Fadl b.al-Rabi', discredited by the failure of his policy, went into hiding, around the beginning of 196 (autumn 811). The absence of any firm leadership at this stage allowed factional disputes to rage unhindered. The main cause of dissension was the privileged position of the *abna'*. The disasters of the previous year had proved that they were unable to withstand the forces of Ma'mun and that they would have to look for allies. These could be found among Arabs who were already supporters of the regime, like the followers of the Mazyadid family, and among the Arabs of Syria who could be expected to resist any further invaders from the east. There was, however, a price to be paid for their co-operation and the price was that the *abna'* should be prepared to relinquish their privileged position and allow these other groups a share in political leadership and policy making. This they were not prepared to do, and the failure of these groups in the west to work together was a decisive factor in the success of the Ma'munids.

This rivalry now began to assert itself. Early in 196 (autumn 811), Fadl b.al-Rabi', as one of his last acts before disappearing, had prepared a joint expedition of 20,000 *abna'* and the same number of Arabs, to attack Tahir. Members of the most distinguished families were selected to lead the two contingents; the commander of the *abna'* was a grandson of the great Qahtaba, 'Abd Allah b.Humayd, while a member of the family of Ma'n b.Za'ida was to lead the Arabs. Trouble began early: Asad b.Yazid b.Mazyad, the Arab leader, refused to march until his men were given a year's pay and a thousand horses, alleging that they had been discriminated against. Furthermore, he wanted to see the war ruthlessly pursued, he would not be responsible for the fate of captured cities and he wanted those members of Ma'mun's family who were in the west to be used as hostages. It was probably the last of these demands that led the caliph to dismiss him as a 'mad beduin' and have him imprisoned, but he could not forgo the support of so powerful a family. Asad's uncle, Ahmad, was sent for and agreed to lead the force.[27] The two groups were completely incompatible. It was, after all, Ma'n b.Za'ida who had boasted of killing Qahtaba at the time of the Abbasid Revolution but, as always, there was more to the dispute than the jealousies of leaders. The force marched as far as Khaniqin but never met the enemy. Tahir sent agents to complete the work and the army broke up in dissension and bitterness as the old suspicions and resentments between Arab and *abna'* came to the fore once more.[28]

At the same time, an attempt was made to find other allies in Syria. The leader of the Syrian branch of the Abbasid family, 'Abd al-Malik b.Salih, had been imprisoned by Harun at the time of the fall of the Barmakids. He was released after the old caliph's death and was now sent to Syria to raise troops. The response was impressive; men from all over Syria, both from the Kalbites of Hims and Damascus and the Qaysites of the north, now known as Zawaqil,[29] flocked to Raqqa to meet their old leader. But here, again, the jealousy of the *abna'* prevented any common action; a large number of them, under the command of 'Ali b.'Isa's son, Husayn, had previously been sent to quell disturbances in Syria and were now ensconced in Harun's garrison town at Raqqa. Inevitably, there were tensions that dated back to the Battle of the Zab and the defeat of 'Abd Allah b.'Ali, but all might have been well had not 'Abd al-Malik himself fallen gravely ill. A stolen horse provided the excuse for violence; the Kalbites melted away, leaving the Qaysite Zawaqil and the *abna'* to settle old scores. Meanwhile 'Abd al-Malik lay dying and with him died any hope that Amin and his supporters might find useful allies in the west.[30]

The *abna'* seem to have had the better of the fighting and the Zawaqil retired, to terrorise the countryside of northern Syria, while Husayn led his *abna'* back to Baghdad, to make his presence felt in the capital.

At the same time as Amin's support in the west was crumbling, Tahir received important reinforcements. Ma'mun sent Harthama b.A'yan with thirty thousand troops to prosecute the war in Iraq. Harthama had been for many years Harun's most trusted army commander and was a man of vast experience, and it was intended that he should take over command from Tahir and bring the whole Iraqi campaign firmly under the control of Marw.[31] Tahir was detached from the main body of the army, which remained at Hulwan, and sent to Ahwaz, which he captured after a short but bitter struggle. Thereafter resistance rapidly collapsed. From Ahwaz he sent his agents to all the provinces around the Gulf, while he himself moved up the road to Wasit. Everywhere the demoralised agents of Amin deserted their posts or fled; Wasit itself fell without resistance, on 3 Rajab 196 (20 March 812). Shortly after, Kufa surrendered to a small detachment of Tahir's men, while the governor of Basra, Mansur b.al-Mahdi, not a man lacking ability or energy, surrendered his city by post.[32] There were pro-Ma'munid coups in Mosul[33] and Egypt,[34] while, on 27 Rajab (13 April), the governor of the Hijaz, Dawud b.'Isa b.Musa, declared for Ma'mun and prayers were said, in the name of the new caliph, in the holy cities of Makka and Madina.[35] By the end of the month (16 April 812), only Baghdad, Syria, where there was anarchy, and Ifriqiya, which ceased to be an integral part of the empire at this time, had failed to acknowledge the new ruler. The reason for the sudden collapse is clear; the confusion and lack of any firm direction of leadership in Baghdad, along with the

apparently irresistible advance of Tahir, meant that few local
governors had any enthusiasm for making war. It seemed as if Ma'mun
had won a swift and decisive victory.

In Baghdad all was confusion. Power still rested with the *abna'* but,
with the death of 'Ali b.'Isa, there was no one man with enough influence
and experience to keep control. His son, Husayn, returned with his
followers from Raqqa just after news of the fall of Wasit had arrived.
He decided that his best course of action was to try to bring the city
over to Ma'mun and so win the favour of the new regime for himself
and his followers. But he had reckoned without the rivalries which
divided the people of Baghdad. The family of 'Ali b.'Isa drew most of
their support from the *abna'* of the East Bank. 'Ali himself had first
emerged as a supporter of Mahdi and it was natural that most of his
followers came from Mahdi's suburb of Rusafa. The *abna'* of the West
Bank, however, especially those settled in the Harbiya quarter, were
reluctant to accept this leadership without question and they rallied
around the figure of Muhammad b.Abi Khalid. Muhammad came from
a family which had been prominent in the army since the days of the
Abbasid Revolution and he and his family now became the effective
leaders of the West Bankers.[36]

On his return to the city, Husayn had been summoned to meet the
caliph in the middle of the night; suspicious and very angry, he refused,
saying that he was not a boon companion or a singer to be ordered
around in this fashion. The next day, 11 Rajab 196 (29 March 812), he
assembled his men on the East Bank and crossed the river to the Khurasan
gate of the old city and the Khuld Palace, defeating on the way some
Arab troops sent by Amin to restrain them. The caliph himself was
arrested by a parallel coup within the palace and Husayn and his men
formally renounced their allegiance, Husayn explaining that Amin had
betrayed them to the Zawaqil and they could no longer trust him. For
two days the Harbiya accepted the situation but then things began to
go wrong. The *abna'* of the West Bank gathered by the Syrian gate and
Muhammad b.Abi Khalid and other respected leaders urged them not
to accept Husayn's leadership and to release Amin, who had never done
them any harm. After some fighting, the men of the Harbiya succeeded
in releasing Amin, while Husayn was killed, trying to escape to join
forces with Tahir. On 16 Rajab, the next Friday (2 April), the oath of
allegiance to Amin was renewed. The entire coup and counter-coup had
taken less than a week.[37] It demonstrated yet again, however, the deep
divisions among Amin's supporters and his own inability to heal the
splits. It had another consequence, which was to be very important in

the future: after his release, Amin distributed arms to the common people of Baghdad, whom he sought to use as allies against rebellious elements among the military.[38]

Amin was now back in control in Baghdad but the pressing problem of defeating the enemy remained unsolved. As the summer wore on, Tahir moved inexorably towards Baghdad, taking Mada'in and, finally, in Shawwal (June/July) approaching the southern outskirts of the city, where he camped on the Nahr Sarsar.[39] The situation looked very grim for Amin but Tahir, too, had his problems. It seems that his political masters kept him very short of money and some of his men actually deserted to join Amin. Amin, for his part, was looking around for more support; he began to recruit the people of Baghdad in large numbers, opening his treasury and distributing arms and payments; his new commanders were paraded before him and given five hundred *dirhams* and scent for their beards, from which they were known as the 'perfume generals'. Meanwhile, the Harbiya regulars received nothing and felt their position threatened. But Amin, despite the advice of his counsellors, who pointed out how it was the Harbiya who had saved him from Husayn, was determined to break with them and rely on his new recruits. The Harbiya leaders, predictably, deserted to Tahir.[40] Men like Muhammad b.Abi Khalid fought for Tahir throughout the siege, while the Harbiya quarter itself was in the besiegers' hands.

The siege of Baghdad can be said to have begun on 12 Dhu'l-Hijja 196 (25 August 812), when Tahir encamped at the garden by the Anbar Gate,[41] which was to be his headquarters until the final surrender over a year later. There were three besieging armies: Tahir, with his recent recruits from the Harbiya, was encamped to the west and north of the Round City; Harthama b.A'yan had arrived from Hulwan and blockaded the East Bank, while a third general, Zuhayr b.al-Musayyab, set up camp at the south end of the East Bank settlements. He does not seem to have had very many troops but commanded the siege engines, which did vast damage in the city. He also commanded the river to the south. Meanwhile, the market area of Karkh, to the south of the Round City, was effectively neutral.

The defenders were less well organised. There were, of course, the caliph and his immediate courtiers and some senior members of the Abbasid governing class, whose allegiance to the cause seems to have been a bit half-hearted, like Khuzayma b.Khazim. But the overwhelming majority of the defenders came from the people of the city, whom Amin had begun arming earlier in the year. The chroniclers have a number of names for these people, which mean, roughly, mob, scum, plebs; in addition, they are also referred to as 'naked ones' because they had no armour.[42] These people also speak to us directly through their poetry, most of it anonymous. This poetry laments the destruction of Baghdad and its fall from recent prosperity, and expresses anger and sadness at the destruction caused by fire and siege engines, and the plight of women and families unprotected in the ruins. But, sometimes, the poems are defiant as well. The authors glory in the fact that they are not *sharif* and come from no famous desert tribe, that all the armour they have is wool, with palm leaves for helmets, and yet they can still defeat their opponents.[43] Their enemies stressed that they were not men of substance. The prosperous merchants of Karkh wrote to Tahir to disassociate themselves from the mob, explaining that the latter had no houses in Karkh but stayed in mosques and baths. They were nothing but vagabonds and escaped prisoners and the merchants among them merely street-vendors trading in trifles, a social distinction still apparent in any Middle Eastern *suq* to this day.[44] As one might expect, their leaders were not found among the regular army commanders and the two most important, Hatim b.al-Saqr, on the East Bank, and Hasan al-Harsh, on the West, were complete unknowns.

This, then, was a radical movement of the most disadvantaged groups in the city, determined to assert themselves at the expense of the now discredited *abna'*, who had formed a large part of the city's population, and the richer merchants. In times of financial stringency, later in the siege, the houses of the prosperous were raided for funds.[45] They seem to have had no clear ideological position, though they abused their enemies as heathens and certainly considered themselves as good Muslims.[46] The fact that the movement is comparatively well-documented gives us a unique glimpse of the social stresses produced by the rapid growth of the city. In a situation not unlike the Paris Commune of 1871, the failure of the traditional military class gave an opportunity for popular elements, hitherto of little importance, to make their mark on the political scene.

The siege lasted over a year. The details that have come down to us suggest that the fighting was bitter but spasmodic. The main areas of conflict were the western suburbs, around the Kunasa and Darb al-Hijara, where fighting was almost continuous, the area of the palace of Salih b.al-Rashid and the East Bank. In Jumada II (late February 813), the commander defending the palace of Salih for Amin deserted to Tahir and Tahir tried to make use of the opportunity provided to cut communications between East and West Banks. The fighting was extremely fierce but the attack failed and the victory was a great boost for the defenders' morale; a poem went the rounds saying that God was giving them victory in place of defeat. On the East Bank, too, the defenders showed their mettle. Some time after the battle at Qasr Salih, they drove all the attackers from the Shammasiya quarter and even captured Harthama in person. Unfortunately, they did not recognise their captive and released him after cutting off his hand. Even so, his forces fled in confusion to Hulwan and the situation was only saved by Tahir, who, acting with his usual energy and determination, ordered a temporary bridge to be built across the Tigris and sent his men to restore the situation.[47]

As the year wore on, the situation of the defenders became more desperate. After the battle at Qasr Salih, Tahir ordered that the markets at Karkh be closed, and supplies coming from Jazira, Wasit or Basra were all diverted to his camp.[48] Inside the city, Amin was forced to resort to desperate measures, authorising the plunder of private houses to raise money, and he is said to have abandoned himself to drink. Nonetheless, it was not until the beginning of the next year, 198 (September 813), that Tahir made a major breakthrough. It was not so much military as diplomatic. He persuaded some of the richer and most influential citizens, who were not happy with the turn of events in the city, to defect. Among them was the veteran military leader, Khuzayma b.Khazim, now old and almost blind, whose house dominated the eastern end of the main bridge across the river. On the night of 21 Muharram (Wednesday, 21 September) he cut the bridge and so destroyed communications between the two banks. The commander of the East Bank, Hasan al-Harsh, was stuck on the West and the East surrendered, with little resistance, to Harthama's men.[49] The next day, Tahir launched a new attack on the West Bank. The defenders were driven back into the Round City and the Khuld Palace.[50] It was only a matter of time before they surrendered.

The boldest of Amin's advisers, new men like Hatim b.al-Saqr, urged him to make a break for Syria and rally support there. Tahir was informed of this and was clearly worried, so he played the game which had been successful before. He wrote to Amin's more prosperous courtiers, men like Sulayman b.al-Mansur and the *mawla,* Sindi b.Shahik, threatening them with the loss of all their estates if they did not frustrate the scheme. Once again, Amin, with his unerring instinct, made the wrong decision. He rejected the advice which might have saved his life and a remnant of his power, and decided to surrender.[51] But which of the leaders of the besiegers was to have the honour of taking the caliph captive? Amin was adamant that he should surrender to Harthama, an old servant of the family and a man likely to respect the life of a member of the Abbasid house; he might even be able to effect a reconciliation between the defeated caliph and his brother. Tahir was deeply suspicious of any such cosy arrangements, which might exclude him from the position of influence he felt himself entitled to. A compromise formula was worked out at a meeting in Khuzayma's house, probably on Saturday, between Harthama, Tahir and Amin's advisers, Sulayman b.al-Mansur and Sindi b.Shahik; Amin was to surrender to Harthama, while the symbols of office (the staff, ring and mantle of the Prophet) were to be handed over to Tahir.[52]

But Tahir's suspicions remained and he decided to take action. On the night of Sunday, 25 Muharram (25 September), Amin went down to the river bank where a small boat was waiting with Harthama, who greeted him as lord and master. But no sooner had the boat set off for the East Bank when it was set upon and capsized by Tahir's men. No doubt, it was intended that all should be drowned but both Harthama and Amin swam ashore. The ex-caliph, now completely alone, was picked up by Tahir's men and taken half-naked to a house on the West Bank. Here he met his *sahib al-mazalim,* Ahmad b.Sallam, whose powerful and moving account[53] of the last moments of his master's life is one of the high points of the historical writing of the period. Simply and eloquently, he describes how the caliph succeeded in escaping from the river but was arrested and taken to a house where Ahmad himself was confined. He goes on to say how he tried to comfort the lonely and terrified caliph, who behaved with more dignity, faced with death, than he had in the days of his power, refusing to put any of the blame for his misfortunes on the shoulders of his advisers. Around midnight, a group of Iranians with their swords drawn came to the house; Amin attempted to defend himself with a cushion but he was no match for the armed men. It was all soon over; his severed head was taken to Tahir, who sent it on, with the regalia, to Marw. Ahmad was allowed to go at dawn when his ransom money was brought by his steward.

It was a tragic day for the Abbasid caliphate. No member of the family had been publicly killed or executed since the revolution. Now that inviolability had gone. If it could happen once, it could happen again and the prestige of the caliphs had been seriously damaged. But more than the charisma of the sovereign had been injured. The state, so carefully built up by Mansur and nurtured by his son and grandsons, had torn itself apart. The old system had gone for ever; it remained to be seen whether a new one could be put in its place.

Notes

1. Tabari, *Ta'rikh,* vol. 3, pp. 768-71.
2. Ibid., vol. 3, p. 772; Sourdel, *Vizirat Abbaside,* vol. 1, p. 189.
3. Tabari, *Ta'rikh,* vol. 3, pp. 778-9, 810-14; Dinawari, *Akhbar,* p. 390; Gabrieli, *Successione,* pp. 17-20.
4. Tabari, *Ta'rikh,* vol. 3, pp. 782-7.
5. Ibid., vol. 3, pp. 777, 779, 788-90, 793.
6. Ibid., vol. 3, p. 809.
7. Jahshiyari, *Wuzara',* pp. 231-2, 316-18.
8. Tabari, *Ta'rikh,* vol. 3, p. 777; Ya'qubi, *Ta'rikh,* vol. 2, p. 529.
9. Narshakhi, *Bukhara,* p. 76.
10. Tabari, *Ta'rikh,* vol. 3, pp. 815-16; Gabrieli, *Successione,* pp. 18-19; Dunlop, *Arab Relations with Tibet,* pp. 310-11.
11. Tabari, *Ta'rikh,* vol. 3, pp. 773-4; Jahshiyari, *Wuzara',* p. 278.
12. Tabari, *Ta'rikh,* vol. 3, p. 790. Asad was in Marw at the death of Harun (Tabari, *Ta'rikh,* vol. 3, p. 734), but, two years later, he was with Amin (ibid., vol. 3, p. 833).
13. Tabari, *Ta'rikh,* vol. 3, pp. 678, 794, 817; Ya'qubi, *Ta'rikh,* vol. 2, p. 530.
14. Tabari, *Ta'rikh,* vol. 3, p. 794; Jahshiyari, *Wuzara',* pp. 290-3.
15. M. Kaabi, 'Les Origines des Tahirides' in *Arabica,* vol. 19 (1972), pp. 145-64.
16. Tabari, *Ta'rikh,* vol. 3, pp. 796, 817.
17. Ibid., vol. 3, pp. 796-7; Gabrieli, *Successione,* p. 27.
18. Tabari, *Ta'rikh,* vol. 3, pp. 119-20, 797, 812; Ibn al-Faqih, *Buldan,* p. 261; Ibn al-Athir, *Ta'rikh,* vol. 6, p. 291.
19. Tabari, *Ta'rikh,* vol. 3, p. 797; Ya'qubi, *Ta'rikh,* vol. 2, p. 530.
20. Tabari, *Ta'rikh,* vol. 3, pp. 799-801, 856.
21. The main accounts of the battle are Tabari, *Ta'rikh,* vol. 3, pp. 799-801, 822-5; Ya'qubi, *Ta'rikh,* vol. 2, pp. 530-1; Dinawari, *Akhbar,* p. 393.
22. Tabari, *Ta'rikh,* vol. 3, p. 825; Jahshiyari, *Wuzara'; Fragments,* ed. M. Awad, p. 39.
23. Tabari, *Ta'rikh,* vol. 3, p. 803.
24. Ibid., vol. 3, p. 826. No doubt some of the *abna'* were of Arab origin but they thought of themselves as a group apart from the Syrians and other western Arabs.
25. Ibid., vol. 3, pp. 827-32; Dinawari, *Akhbar,* p. 394.
26. Tabari, *Ta'rikh,* vol. 3, p. 834.
27. Ibid., vol. 3, pp. 833-9; Gabrieli, *Successione,* pp. 31-2.
28. Tabari, *Ta'rikh,* vol. 3, p. 840.
29. Ayalon, *Military Reforms of al-Mu'tasim,* pp. 18-20; Shaban, *Islamic History,* vol. 2, p. 29. The term seems to originate from the way they tied their turbans.
30. Tabari, *Ta'rikh,* vol. 3, pp. 841-5.
31. Ibid., vol. 3, pp. 840-1.
32. Ibid., vol. 3, pp. 855-7; Ya'qubi, *Ta'rikh,* vol. 2, p. 534.
33. Azdi, *Ta'rikh,* p. 325.
34. For events in Egypt, see Kindi, *Wulat,* pp. 147-53.
35. Tabari, *Ta'rikh,* vol. 3, pp. 860-4.
36. See above, p. 105.
37. Tabari, *Ta'rikh,* vol. 3, pp. 846-51.
38. Ibid., vol. 3, p. 846.
39. Ibid., vol. 3, pp. 858-60.
40. Ibid., vol. 3, pp. 865-7; Gabrieli, *Successione,* pp. 38-9.

41. Tabari, *Ta'rikh*, vol. 3, p. 868; Gabrieli, *Successione*, p. 41.

42. *sufla, suqa, fussaq, lusus, 'ayyarun, ghawgha'* and *awbash* are among the terms used. See Gabrieli, *Successione*, p. 44.

43. See especially, Tabari, *Ta'rikh*, vol. 3, pp. 883-7.

44. Ibid., vol. 3, pp. 899-900.

45. Ibid., vol. 3, pp. 892-3.

46. Ibid., vol. 3, p. 882.

47. Ibid., vol. 3, pp. 880-2, 896-7.

48. Ibid., vol. 3, pp. 890-1.

49. Ibid., vol. 3, pp. 903-4.

50. Ibid., vol. 3, p. 906.

51. Ibid., vol. 3, pp. 911-16.

52. Ibid., vol. 3, p. 916.

53. Ibid., vol. 3, pp. 919-23; Gabrieli, *Successione*, pp. 48-53.

9 THE GREAT CIVIL WAR: II

The death of Amin ended the first phase of the long struggle. There was no doubt now who was caliph and Ma'mun was generally acknowledged. The new ruler, however, was in distant Marw and it was from there, not from the old Abbasid capital at Baghdad, that he intended to rule. This decision led to strife which was to prolong the civil war for another six grim years. Four main parties were involved in the struggles which ensued. There was the government in Marw, now effectively controlled by Fadl b.Sahl. Fadl was determined that the caliph should stay in Khurasan, where he could be managed and where he would be completely in the power of his *wazir* and the Khurasani magnates allied to him. His objective during the fighting was to secure the obedience of Iraq to the Marw government and, to this end, he sent his brother, Hasan, to take control there. The main drawback to this scheme was that Hasan had very few reliable troops and no effective power base. The second party consisted of Tahir and his followers. It has already been pointed out how suspicious he was of attempts to oust him and deprive him of the fruits of his victory. The appointment of Hasan intensified this fear. He was still kept short of money and, only a few days after the triumphant end to the siege, he was faced by a mutiny of his own troops demanding their pay, and was forced to rely on members of the *abna'* who advanced him the necessary cash.[1] During the siege many of the leaders of the *abna'*, like Muhammad b.Abi Khalid, had worked with Tahir[2] and they continued to look to him for leadership, so beginning the Tahirid association with Baghdad which was to last for the next half-century. On Hasan's arrival in Iraq, Tahir was sent to Raqqa, supposedly to restore order in Syria,[3] in fact, to remove him from the centre of affairs. There he remained, occupying himself with building and reading philosophy,[4] while keeping an eye on events in Iraq. He made no effort to subdue Syria or lend Hasan any military support in his efforts to control Baghdad, but he preserved his position and prestige intact until the fall of the Sahlids enabled him to become reconciled to Ma'mun.

Then there was Harthama. He was less determined; he began by lending his prestige and his great military experience to the Sahlid cause but he was too powerful and too independent to be a useful instrument and was treacherously done to death by them. Finally, there were the people of Iraq: notably, the *abna'* of Baghdad but also the people of the Sawad. They were defeated but by no means impotent and the economic disruption caused by the way seems to have made it easy for would-be rebels to find support. They objected, not to Ma'mun himself, but to the Sahlids and their policy of government from Marw, since government from Marw meant that Iraq, and especially Baghdad, would become impoverished and provincial. It was these competing interests which kept the civil war alive for the next three years.

After the fall of Baghdad and the death of Amin, the rest of 198 (up to August 814) was comparatively peaceful and it was not until the arrival of Hasan b.Sahl, early the next year (autumn 814), that serious fighting began. In Jumada I (December 814/January 815), Tahir was sent to Raqqa while Harthama set out for Khurasan. Thus did Hasan intend to clear the field of his rivals. The departure of the two experienced generals was the signal for trouble. Hasan brought with him two Khurasanis, his cousin, 'Ali b.Abi Sa'id, and a prominent magnate, 'Ali b.Hisham. 'Ali b.Hisham's father, like Tahir's, had been among the *ashraf* of Khurasan persecuted by 'Ali b.'Isa b.Mahan. Neither of these seems to have been in the west before, yet 'Ali b.Abi Sa'id was given charge of the taxation, while 'Ali b.Hisham was made governor of Baghdad.[5]

The trouble began in Kufa. It took the form of an Alid uprising. There were many factors involved in the rebellion: the desire of Alid supporters to take advantage of the weakness of the government and the disruption caused by the long war; the fact that the leader, Abu'l-Saraya, was himself an unemployed soldier, dismissed from Harthama's army, and there must have been many more in the same position; but the most important grievance seems to have been dissatisfaction with the Sahlid government and the widespread feeling that Ma'mun was no more than a puppet in the hands of this upstart family.

Muhammad b.Ibrahim, the Alid, known as Ibn Tabataba, rebelled in Kufa on 10 Jumada II, 199 (27 January 815), with Abu'l-Saraya as his military commander and leading adviser.[6] The success of the rebels was spectacular; on 1 Rajab (25 February), Hasan's leading general still in the field, Zuhayr b.al-Musayyab, was soundly defeated and the rebels extended their control over most of the Sawad, to Basra in the south and as far as Kutha in the north, though the rebels were in no position to risk a direct attack on Baghdad. This success revealed just how flimsy Sahlid power really was. A Persian commentator says that Hasan understood administration[7] but not war and never led his troops into battle himself. He was forced to rely in this crisis on elements of the *abna'* and other ex-supporters of Amin but, not only was their loyalty to the new regime doubtful, but they could not command sufficient men to oppose the rebels effectively. Hasan badly needed military support. He could have asked Tahir but he would have made his own terms and left no room for the Sahlids in Iraq. Then there was Harthama, who had just set out for Khurasan but was still at Hulwan. He was resentful at being deprived of command in Iraq and was very reluctant to help Hasan out, but eventually Hasan sent Sindi b.Shahik and Salih, the *sahib al-musalla,* both court officials of long standing, who knew Harthama well from the old days, and they persuaded him to change his mind.[8] It is striking to see Sindi, so recently one of Amin's inner circle, now attached to Hasan.

Once Harthama had committed himself, the rebel successes ended. He was a very experienced soldier and could attract the support of many in Iraq who would not serve under the leadership of Hasan. In Ramadhan 199 (April/May 815) Abu'l-Saraya had taken Mada'in and advanced as far as the Sarsar Canal. Harthama launched a two-pronged campaign. He himself, with Mansur b.al-Mahdi, now emerging as the leading member of the Abbasid family in Iraq, attacked across the Sarsar Canal, gradually driving Abu'l-Saraya back towards Kufa, while 'Ali b.Abi Sa'id, with a motley army of ex-supporters of Amin, moved down the east bank of the Tigris, taking first Mada'in and then Wasit. In Dhu'l-Qa'ada (June/July) Abu'l-Saraya was decisively defeated outside Kufa and the leading citizens of the town took advantage of the situation to remove his supporters and make terms with Harthama. Abu'l-Saraya fled towards Basra, which was still in Alid hands, but he never reached there. On the way he was met by the governor of Ahwaz, a supporter of Tahir, who told him that he would not oppose him if he left the province peacefully, but the rebel leader, optimistic as ever, decided to fight and was defeated and wounded. Basra was soon retaken by 'Ali b.Abi Sa'id. After this, he decided to make for his Jaziran homeland (he was a Shaybani tribesman) but was caught at Jalula' and brought to Hasan. On 10 Rabi' I, 200 (19 October 815), he was executed.

The rebellion had been defeated but it had shown clearly the weakness of Hasan's position and that he could not govern Iraq without finding reliable supporters in the country. It had also revealed how deep the split between Hasan and Tahir had become and how much support an Alid pretender could command in Iraq, a lesson not lost on the Sahlids. Otherwise, Hasan seems to have learned nothing; even before

Abu'l-Saraya was dead, his insensitivity to local feeling had landed him in still more serious trouble.

After the final defeat of Abu'l-Saraya, Hasan deprived himself of his two main army commanders. He quarrelled with his cousin, 'Ali b.Abi Sa'id, for reasons unknown, and 'Ali was summoned back to Marw. At the same time, Harthama set out once again for Khurasan. He intended to awaken Ma'mun to the real state of affairs in Iraq and expose the lies the Sahlids had been telling to protect their position. He also hoped to persuade Ma'mun to come to Baghdad, since he realised that, until this happened, there could be no lasting peace. The Sahlids saw this as a real threat to their position. Their power depended on keeping the caliph in Marw and hiding from him the extent of their failure in the west. Fadl b.Sahl tried persuasion; Harthama was offered the governorship of either Syria or the Hijaz. The offer was less than generous; if he chose Syria he would have to fight, not only the numerous rebels who controlled the country, but probably Tahir as well, while the Hijaz at this time would be little more than an honourable exile. He refused and continued on his way. Fadl b.Sahl then demonstrated the ruthlessness and power over the caliph which was the secret of his success. Amazingly, he persuaded Ma'mun that Harthama had actually been in league with Abu'l-Saraya and was only coming to Khurasan to make trouble. By the time the veteran general reached Marw in Dhu'l-Qa'ada 199 (June 816), the caliph's mind had been well and truly poisoned. Harthama was hardly given a hearing before being thrown in prison, where he 'died' a few days later.[9]

This cynical ruthlessness may have preserved Fadl's position in Marw but it did nothing to help his brother in Iraq. Indeed, the disappearance of Harthama was the immediate cause of the rebellion which finally caused the downfall of the family. Since the end of the siege, Baghdad, now reduced to the rank of a provincial city, had been effectively ruled by the leaders of the *abna'*, especially Muhammad b.Abi Khalid in co-operation with 'Ali b.Hisham. This convenient arrangement was somewhat strained for two reasons; the *abna'* could not accept, as a permanent feature, rule from Marw and the consequent decline of their city, Baghdad, and 'Ali was unable to pay their salaries regularly. The *abna'* were dependent on their salaries and, by the end of the year 200 (spring 816), many of them must have been suffering considerable hardship; the court had moved away, it can hardly be imagined that trade was thriving and the government was unable or unwilling to pay even the reduced wages they had agreed to serve for. There were sporadic disturbances, which led on occasion to severe fighting, but the old jealousies between East and West Banks prevented a common effort. News of Harthama's death arrived at the end of the year (29 July) and this persuaded them that Hasan could not be trusted at all. All the *abna'* united under the leadership of Muhammad b.Abi Khalid and drove 'Ali b.Hisham out of the city.[10]

The Baghdadis were fighting to save their city from decline and to save their own status and prosperity. This common purpose united disparate factions in the city. The sons of 'Ali b.'Isa b.Mahan agreed to serve under Muhammad's leadership and members of old Khurasani Arab families played an important role; grandsons of Qahtaba and Abu Muslim's old friend, Malik b.al-Haytham, were prominent. The veteran Khuzayma b.Khazim was there and so was the wily Mansur b.al-Mahdi, the most prominent member of the Abbasid family; finally, Fadl b.al-Rabi' emerged from his hiding place in Basra and began to play an important part in public life. It was, then, a coalition of all interests in the city. Furthermore, the Baghdadis enjoyed the tacit support of Tahir, who allowed Muhammad b.Abi Khalid's son, 'Isa, to leave Raqqa and join the rebel forces. At first, the rebels proposed to elect Mansur b.al-Mahdi as caliph; he was too cautious to accept but was persuaded to agree to be Ma'mun's deputy in the city. It was not, then, a rebellion against Ma'mun but against the Sahlids.[11]

Faced by this new emergency, Hasan's position was weaker than ever. Harthama was gone while Tahir was hostile and did not lift a finger to help. Hasan suffered from three major disadvantages. The first was that he was forced to follow policies decided in Marw; communications were slow and, as we shall see, this sometimes meant that orders were out of date. Fadl b.Sahl was constantly anxious lest the true state of affairs in Iraq should be revealed to Ma'mun, who seems to have believed that all was peaceful. Hasan's second handicap was his own personality: he seems to have been a very difficult man to get on with. He quarrelled constantly with his army commanders, many of whom were driven to desertion by his suspicious nature. After the civil war, Hasan was forced by mental illness to retire into private life and it may be that he had been mentally unbalanced for some time before. Above all, however, he had no real power base and no reliable support in Iraq, except 'Ali b.Hisham, himself an outsider. So he blundered along, recruiting troops where he could find them, constantly reacting to events, never controlling them.

When the fighting broke out at the beginning of 201 (August 816), Hasan and 'Ali b.Hisham were unable to offer any serious resistance to the Baghdadis. Muhammad b.Abi Khalid pursued them down the east bank of the Tigris as far as Wasit, while his son Harun took Kufa. Zuhayr b.al-Musayyab was captured and later executed.[12] At Wasit, Hasan decided to resist. Most of his army was composed of men like 'Isa al-Juludi and Sa'id b.Sajur, who had been with Amin throughout the siege of Baghdad but, about this time, a new general arrived from Khurasan — Humayd b.'Abd al-Hamid al-Tusi.[13] Half a century before, his father, a relation of Qahtaba, had been a leading figure in the Abbasid Revolution, but he had made the mistake of joining the rebellion of 'Abd Allah b.'Ali and his career was brought to an abrupt close.[14] However, his family seem to have remained influential in their native Tus. Why his son, Humayd, was chosen to help Hasan in Iraq is not clear, nor can we be certain that he brought more troops with him, but, from the time of his arrival in the west, he became Hasan's leading military commander. These disparate groups enabled Hasan to meet the Baghdadis in the field. On 23 Rabi' I (18 October 816) a battle was fought outside Wasit. An autumn dust-storm confounded the Baghdadis, who were driven back along the Tigris as far as Jarjaraya. Even more serious than the military reverse was the fact that Muhammad b.Abi Khalid received wounds from which he died some two weeks later.[15] Muhammad seems to have been the only leader in Baghdad with the experience and prestige to unite the people of the city. After he was gone, the divisions began to reappear and the fortunes of the Baghdadis to decline.

This was not, however, immediately apparent. His son, 'Isa, took over the leadership of the army, while Mansur b.al-Mahdi, although still refusing the caliphate, controlled affairs inside the city. Sporadic fighting continued all the winter Rabi'-Shawwal 201 (October 816-May 817), in the once prosperous areas between Jarjaraya and Mada'in, on the east bank of the Tigris. 'Isa b.Muhammad commanded a huge army, estimated at 125,000 men, but was unable or unwilling to launch a major offensive; he toyed with the idea of making terms with Hasan but he demanded an agreement in writing from Ma'mun. Since this would have meant revealing to the caliph the true state of affairs in Iraq, the Sahlids refused and the war dragged on.[16]

During the spring of 817 (Sha'ban-Shawwal 201), the position of the Baghdadis worsened considerably. This was due, not to Hasan's military success, but rather to deteriorating conditions within the city. The vast numbers of soldiers commanded by 'Isa b.Muhammad seem to have been more a rabble than an organised army, recruited, presumably, from disbanded soldiers, out-of-work artisans and peasants whose lands had been ravaged. They supported themselves largely by pillage and banditry and, towards the end of Sha'ban (March), a group of them pillaged the little town of Qatrabbul, outside the city, and openly sold the goods in the markets. For six years the city had been the scene of constant violence and destruction and there grew up two groups of what might be called 'home guard', or vigilantes. The first of these was formed by a man called Khalid al-Daryush, in the western quarters of the city, near the Anbar gate. It consisted mostly of humble men and disclaimed all political objectives. The other group was more ambitious. Founded by a Khurasani from the Harbiya quarter, Sahl b.Salama al-Ansari, it was a movement of moral and political regeneration. His followers were enjoined to live according to the Qur'an and the Sunna and their names were registered in a *diwan*. While he had no overt political aspirations, he arranged that his followers would swear an oath of allegiance to him.[17] It was essentially a property owners' movement but it attracted enough to threaten the position of 'Isa b.Muhammad and Mansur, who were heavily dependent on these brigands. Faced by this loss of control in Baghdad, Mansur hurried back from Mada'in but 'Isa again wrote to Hasan, asking for terms; these were given and they were not ungenerous. The Baghdadis were to be paid six months' salary, and the administration of the city and the Sawad was to be divided between 'Isa b.Muhammad and a cousin of Hasan. On 13 Shawwal (4 May 817), 'Isa returned to Baghdad, where he announced the terms of the truce; Sahl b.Salama was arrested and 'Isa set about restoring order. There was some trouble among the people of the East Bank because 'Isa b.Muhammad came from a leading West Bank family, but it did not last long. By the end of the month (20 May 817), Baghdad and all Iraq were at last at peace under Sahlid rule.[18]

No sooner was this fragile peace established than it was shattered by the news from Marw. On 2 Ramadhan (25 March 817), just before resistance in Baghdad collapsed, Ma'mun, in his distant capital, publicly adopted 'Ali b.Musa b.Ja'far, the Alid, called al-Rida, as his heir. 'Ali al-Rida seems to have had no previous political experience and had, up to this point, lived the life of an obscure traditionist in the Hijaz. He was now in his fifties and some twenty years older than the man whose heir he was to be. 'Ali was also given the caliph's daughter in marriage, the first person outside the Abbasid family to be so honoured.[19] This passing of the caliphate from the Abbasid to the Alid family was a dramatic move but it is not a complete break with previous policy. Abbasid propaganda at the time of the revolution had justified their claim, not on the grounds that they were Abbasids but because they were members of the house of the Prophet, Hashimites. 'Ali al-Rida was chosen as heir, not because he was an Alid but because Ma'mun had considered all the Hashimites and found him the most suitable. Recognition of 'Ali, therefore, did not necessarily imply recognition of the hereditary right of the Alid imams. It was rather an affirmation of the unity of the family of the Prophet: Alids and Abbasids were both Hashimites and should work together to lead the community. This was an extension of the policy of reconciliation with the Alids, which had begun under Mahdi and had been continued by the Barmakids. Fadl b.Sahl, author of the scheme, had been a pupil of the Barmakids and it was natural that he should develop their ideas. Ma'mun had already shown his interest in the religious aspects of his office when he had proclaimed himself imam and he had attracted support from Shi'i groups in Khurasan.

It was a move designed to attract support for Ma'mun's cause and to provide legitimacy for his rule.[20] In the long term, it could heal the damaging split between Alids and Abbasids and so strengthen the Muslim state. In the short term, it could attract new support to Ma'mun's war effort. Nowhere was this support more desperately needed than in Iraq. It has been stressed that the Sahlid position in Iraq was weak because they lacked any effective popular support. At the beginning of Ramadhan, when 'Ali was adopted as heir, this was painfully apparent; the Baghdadis were in open rebellion and Hasan's troops were faced with an army of 125,000 men, led by the experienced 'Isa b.Muhammad. There was, however, one group in Iraq who had shown themselves militant, numerous and distinctly hostile to the Baghdadis; these were the supporters of the Alids, especially in Kufa, who had rallied with such enthusiasm to the cause of Abu'l-Saraya. If these martial energies could be harnessed to the Sahlid cause, then all their problems would be over, and it may be that this was one of the reasons for choosing 'Ali. But it took three months for the news to reach Baghdad, by which time the rebellion in the city had collapsed and a scheme which was intended to put an end to the fighting merely succeeded in prolonging it.

In Marw, the move produced considerable opposition from opponents of the Sahlids, notably from such veterans of the early Islamic state as 'Abd Allah b.Malik, who was 'whipped like a small boy' for his pains.[21] In Baghdad the move proved disastrous. If Fadl had set out to disrupt the newly established peace, he could hardly have done so more effectively. Not only were the Baghdadis, as a whole, hostile to Alid pretensions, as had been convincingly shown when they turned out in force against Abu'l-Saraya, but leading members of the

Abbasid family saw this as a direct threat to their position and prestige. The news of the new appointment arrived in Baghdad on 5 Dhu'l-Hijja (25 June 817) and for a time there was confusion; some were prepared to accept the new arrangement, with the six-month salary bonus that 'Isa b.Muhammad was offering them, to try to sell the scheme, but, gradually, opposition hardened under the leadership of Mansur and Ibrahim, both sons of Mahdi. On the first Friday of the new year, 202 (24 July 817), the people of Baghdad swore allegiance to Ibrahim b.al-Mahdi, not as deputy to Ma'mun, but as caliph in his own right.[22] Ibrahim was a political lightweight compared with his brother Mansur, who refused the nomination. His main claim to fame, hitherto, had been as a singer and poet at the court of Amin and he had kept that unhappy caliph company during the darkest hours of the siege. He seems to have had little previous political experience and he himself admitted to being wise in other people's affairs and foolish in his own.[23] His leading supporters were to be found among those who had most to lose from the Alid succession. These naturally included the members of the Abbasid family and, besides Mansur b.al-Mahdi, we find two sons of Hadi, 'Abbas and Ishaq, as governors of the east and west sides of the city. Abbasid *mawali* were also prominent, among them Salih, the *sahib al-musalla,* and Sindi b.Shahik, both palace officials of long standing. When 'Isa b.Muhammad saw the way things were going in the capital, he, too, threw his weight behind the new regime and became its military leader. Despite the shortage of money (the troops had to be given drafts on the surrounding countryside, through shortage of cash) the Baghdadis seemed set, once again, for a long war.[24] For the first time since the death of Amin, there were now two rival caliphs but, while Ibrahim certainly intended to press his claims, many of his supporters seemed to have considered his caliphate more as a bargaining counter, to persuade Ma'mun to drop the Alid succession and return to Baghdad.

Meanwhile, Hasan b.Sahl, in Wasit, had to prepare to meet this new challenge but, with his usual maladroitness, he made his own position worse. His army, based on Qasr Ibn Hubayra, was now composed of two groups, the Khurasanis, led by Humayd b.'Abd al-Hamid, and the ex-supporters of Amin under Sa'id b.Sajur and Abu'l-Butt. The latter were discontented, either because they disliked the Alid succession or because they resented Humayd, and they wrote to the Baghdadis, agreeing to come over to their side. At the same time, they wrote to Hasan accusing Humayd of just such a treachery. Hasan chose to believe them and summoned Humayd to Wasit to explain himself. The results were predictable; in Rabi' II (October/November 817) the rebel commanders deserted *en bloc* to the enemy and Hasan's army was greatly weakened.[25]

This problem might not have been so serious if large numbers of Alid supporters had joined the Ma'munid cause, as had been hoped. This does not seem to have happened. In an effort to win support in the traditional stronghold of the Alids, 'Ali al-Rida's brother, 'Abbas, was appointed governor of Kufa.[26] Some joined him, but many other Alid supporters were reluctant to do so. They were suspicious of an arrangement which allowed the still youthful Abbasid caliph to enjoy power in his lifetime, when he could rearrange the succession yet again if he chose. And it went deeper than this. The whole strength of the Alids' appeal was that they represented a radical alternative to the existing power structure, whereas 'Ali was seen to be an ally of the existing ruling class.

The decisive battles of the war were fought between the turncoat commanders and 'Abbas b.Musa, for the control of Kufa. Abu'l-Butt and Sa'id b.Sajur, now fighting for the Baghdadis, marched on the town. 'Abbas gathered his supporters, including Abu'l-Saraya's brother, Abu 'Abd Allah, who presumably attracted some of his brother's supporters. On 2 Jumada II, 202 (16 December 217), there was a battle outside the city and the Alids were worsted. Driven back to Kufa, they were faced with a rebellion which revealed clearly the social factors in such Alid rebellions. The Alid soldiers were mostly drawn from the *ghawgha'*, *'amma* (lower classes) of Kufa society and much property was destroyed by looting and burning. The most properous citizens and the members of the Abbasid family in the city (mostly descendants of 'Isa b.Musa) opened negotiations with the attackers. Resistance crumbled, the Alids melted away and a leading upper-class Kufan, Fadl b.al-Ash'ath al-Kindi, was made governor in the name of Ibrahim b.al-Mahdi.[27]

Though it may not have been apparent at the time, the fall of Kufa was the end of the road for Sahlid policy. The idea of appealing to the Alids in Iraq, against the Baghdadis, had been something of a desperate gamble. Now it had failed; there had not been enough Alid supporters even to defend Kufa, let alone attack Baghdad. From then on, the fighting between Hasan and the Baghdadis was a desultory and confusing anticlimax. The real struggles were taking place in Baghdad and Marw.

Ironically, since it meant his own undoing, it was 'Ali b.Musa himself who finally persuaded Ma'mun, where Harthama had failed, that all was not well in Iraq, that the Sahlids had deceived him and that his reliance on them was a mistake. Apparently Ma'mun did not know that there was still war between the Baghdadis and Hasan, nor that his own family so strongly resented his appointment of 'Ali as heir that they had elected Ibrahim to the caliphate. 'Ali produced a number of prominent witnesses, opponents of the Sahlids, who confirmed his story and spoke of the injustice done to Harthama and Tahir.[28] Thus informed, the caliph took action with surprising firmness. It was probably in Jumada II, 202 (December 817/January 818) that Ma'mun decided to leave Marw and come west. Such a move was fatal to Sahlid power; Fadl took pains to punish some of those who had informed the caliph and, in doing so, he signed his own death warrant. If he could not accept the change gracefully, then he would have to go. At the beginning of Sha'ban (mid-February 818) he was murdered in his bath at Sarakhs.[29] Ma'mun did not want to break completely with the family, since this could lead to problems in Iraq, and he punished severely the unfortunates who had carried out his orders. The caliph moved west with slow deliberation. Six months later, he had only reached Tus. Here it was that 'Ali b.Musa died from eating poisoned grapes, in Sha'ban 203 (September/October 818).[30] If the caliph was not himself responsible, the death was very convenient for him. It would have been very difficult for him to reach an accommodation with the Baghdadis while his Alid heir was still alive. Immediately after 'Ali's death, he wrote a conciliatory letter to the Baghdadis but they were still suspicious and he received a dusty answer.

The decisions taken in Marw, the progressive elimination of Fadl b.Sahl and 'Ali b.Musa al-Rida, made the resistance in Baghdad increasingly half-hearted. The only person who really believed in Ibrahim's caliphate was Ibrahim himself, who acted with determination to preserve his dignity and position, in the face of gathering opposition within the city. Among the leaders, the disputes were concerned largely with the control of the city after peace was made. The war continued in a desultory way; Hasan was still based in Wasit and his generals, Humayd b.Abd al-Hamid and 'Ali b.Hisham, made little effort to advance until events in Baghdad had swung in their favour.

While Ibrahim tried to keep the war going, 'Isa b.Muhammad tried to reach an agreement with the enemy which would leave him in control in Baghdad. He negotiated, not with Hasan, but with his generals, Humayd and 'Ali b.Hisham, who were much more acceptable figures. At the end of Shawwal 203 (29 April 819), he announced publicly that he had made an agreement with Humayd.[31] The old Baghdad rivalries were not yet dead; the people of the East Bank resented the domination of the West Banker, 'Isa b.Muhammad, while Ibrahim saw this as a direct threat to his shadowy caliphate. 'Isa was lured to Ibrahim's palace, imprisoned and beaten, so it was left to his deputy on the West Bank, 'Abbas, to welcome Humayd's troops on 3 Dhu'l-Qa'ada 203 (2 May 819). He promised a salary, 50 *dirhams*, later increased to 60 *dirhams*, to the soldiers of the West Bank. This, it should be noted, was much lower than the 80 *dirhams* which had been the standard payment before the civil war, but, at least, it was a livelihood and some of them had been prepared to accept less. Even after the fall of the West Bank, Ibrahim continued to resist, but his leading military supporters were more concerned with who should get the credit for betraying him to the enemy than with fighting a real war. But Ibrahim forestalled them all. On the night of 16 Dhu'l-Hijja (13 June 819), he went into hiding and, when Humayd arrived, his palace was empty. This meant an effective end of the fighting, with the city in the control of Humayd in the name of Ma'mun.[32]

Ma'mun, meanwhile, continued his slow progress west. By the end of 203 (June 819), he had reached Hamadhan. As he approached Baghdad, he was met by his family and the generals and leaders of the people of the city. He was also greeted by another important figure in the state, Tahir, who had been in contact with him during his journey west and now came in person from Raqqa to welcome him. At sunrise, on 14 Safar 204 (10 August 819), Ma'mun entered the city of his fathers. The long civil war was over.[33]

Notes

1. Tabari, *Ta'rikh*, vol. 3, pp. 934-6.
2. Ibid., vol. 3, p. 883.
3. Ibid., vol. 3, pp. 975-6.
4. Michael the Syrian, *Chronique*, vol. 3, p. 36.
5. Tabari, *Ta'rikh*, vol. 3, pp. 975-6, 998.
6. For the rebellion, see ibid., vol. 3, pp. 976-86; Isfahani, *Maqatil*, pp. 523-59; Ya'qubi, *Ta'rikh*, vol. 2, pp. 542-3; Gabrieli, *Al-Ma'mun e gli Alida*; Arioli, *La Rivolta di Abu Saraya*.
7. Balaami, *Chronique*, vol. 4, p. 499.
8. Tabari, *Ta'rikh*, vol. 3, p. 979.
9. Ibid., vol. 3, pp. 996-8.
10. I have simplified the complex events of these few days for the sake of clarity; for the full details, see ibid., vol. 3, pp. 999-1000.
11. Ibid., vol. 3, p. 1002.
12. Ibid., vol. 3, pp. 1002-3.
13. The exact time of his arrival is not clear; he is first mentioned a month later (ibid., vol. 3, p. 1005) but it may have been his arrival which allowed Hasan to defeat the Baghdadis at Wasit.

14. Tabari, *Ta'rikh,* vol. 3, pp. 15, 28, 38, 53, 93; Baladhuri, *Ansab,* fo. 576.

15. Tabari, *Ta'rikh,* vol. 3, pp. 1003-4.

16. Ibid., vol. 3, pp. 1005-8.

17. Ibid., vol. 3, pp. 1008-12; cf. I. Lapidus, *The Separation of State and Religion,* which seems to exaggerate the importance of this movement.

18. Tabari, *Ta'rikh,* vol. 3, pp. 1111-12.

19. Ibid., vol. 3, pp. 1012-3; Ya'qubi, *Ta'rikh,* vol. 2, p. 545; Gabrieli, *Ma'mun e gli Alidi,* pp. 29-47, and "Ali al-Rida' in EI (2).

20. D. Sourdel, *La Politique Religieuse du Calife 'Abbaside al-Ma'mun,* discusses the general, long-term considerations involved in the move.

21. Jahshiyari, *Wuzara',* pp. 312-15.

22. Tabari, *Ta'rikh,* vol. 3, pp. 1013-14.

23. Ibn Tayfur, *Kitab Baghdad,* p. 199.

24. Tabari, *Ta'rikh,* vol. 3, p. 1016.

25. Ibid., vol. 3, pp. 1018-19.

26. Ibid., vol. 3, p. 1019.

27. Ibid., vol. 3, pp. 1020-2. Fadl b.al-Ash'ath was a first cousin of the famous philosopher, Ya'qub b.Ishaq al-Kindi and a direct descendant of the celebrated Ash'ath b.Qays.

28. Tabari, *Ta'rikh,* vol. 3, pp. 1025-6.

29. Ibid., vol. 3, pp. 1027-8; Ya'qubi, *Ta'rikh,* vol. 2, p. 549.

30. Tabari, *Ta'rikh,* vol. 3, p. 1030.

31. Ibid., vol. 3, pp. 1030-1.

32. For the complex manoeuvrings of this time, see ibid., vol. 3, pp. 1030-6.

33. Ibid., vol. 3, pp. 1016-17.

10 MA'MUN: AN AGE OF TRANSITION

The new caliph is something of an enigma. He was now in his mid-thirties but had had very little chance to show his political hand. His character is difficult to assess. He certainly had intellectual interests and it was he and his court who encouraged and patronised the translation of Greek works into Arabic. As a politician he was cautious and shrewd, working by negotiation and compromise rather than by force, but he seems to have had no long-term political vision and ruled by a series of *ad hoc* expedients.

The end of the civil war, which looks at first sight to have been a victory for Ma'mun, was in many ways a compromise. In order to achieve peace in Iraq, he had been forced to sacrifice his chief adviser, Fadl b.Sahl, and two of his main policies: the rule of the empire from Marw and the adoption of an Alid heir. The civil war had not been won by overwhelming military force; concessions made by the new caliph and divisions among his enemies, as well as a general war-weariness, had all played their part. There was no equivalent to the Khurasanis of the Abbasid Revolution – a reliable military force which could crush any resistance. The long years of civil war had shown that Ma'mun's chief supporters, the *dehqan*s of eastern Iran, were unable to supply the manpower to assert the caliph's authority effectively. Furthermore, the government seems to have been faced with severe economic problems. Many provinces like Syria and Egypt were outside government control and contributed no taxation at all. The yield from the war-ravaged Sawad must have been much reduced. Even in Iran, which had not suffered so badly, Ma'mun had reduced the sums of taxation demanded. This financial weakness meant that the government lacked sufficient funds to recruit a powerful and effective army. 'He who lacks money, lacks men', Mansur had said: Ma'mun continued to lack both.

There were no reprisals against the leaders of the opposition, after Ma'mun had entered Baghdad, and even Ibrahim b.al-Mahdi was eventually restored to the caliph's favour. Nonetheless, the pillars of the early Abbasid state had been brought down. The Abbasid family, though still rich and respected, lost much of their political power. They were almost completely excluded from provincial governorates. There is a complete and striking contrast between the court of Mansur, where the family of the caliph were always giving advice or being appointed to govern provinces and lead armies, and the court of Mu'tasim, where only their heir apparent was of any importance at all. The Khurasani Arab families, whose ancestors had led the original revolution, disappeared almost completely from the stage. So did the Muhallabi family, while the family of Ma'n b.Za'ida withdrew to the remote Caucasus, where they made themselves an independent hereditary principality, which survived for many centuries. The *abna'* lost their élite position among the military. Many of them did continue to serve, however, under the leadership of 'Isa b.Muhammad b.Abi Khalid, until 206 (821/2) when he was worsted by Babak, and under the Tahirids. The *mawali,* too, disappeared as an important political group. Fadl b.Rabi' was reconciled to the new caliph but he is described by one source as the remnant of *mawali* and he had no successor. Only the *kuttab,* led by such followers of the Barmakids as Ahmad b.Ali Khalid and Fadl b.Marwan, succeeded in retaining and even improving their status.

More surprising, perhaps, is the complete eclipse of those who had fought the war in Iraq on Ma'mun's behalf. Hasan b.Sahl was removed from the scene by illness and, despite his fabulous wedding to the caliph's daughter, Buran, he remained in affluent but powerless retirement until his death in the reign of Mutawwakil.[1] Neither he nor his brother seems to have had any children who achieved prominence in public life. His faithful lieutenant, 'Ali b.Hisham, was also left in obscurity, at least until 214 (829/30), when he was appointed to Jibal. There he disgraced himself, apparently by oppressing the people, and was removed from office and killed by one of Ma'mun's new men, 'Ujayf b.'Anbasa.[2] Humayd b.'Abd al-Hamid was never given another government appointment and, when he died in 210 (825/6), it was rumoured that the caliph had poisoned him.[3]

Ma'mun built up his power on two important foundations: the Tahirid family and his own brother, Abu Ishaq, later known as Mu'tasim. Tahir had remained undamaged by the failures of the Sahlids; indeed, it could be argued that he and the caliph had both been victims of their schemes. From the time of Ma'mun's arrival in the city until the end of 205 (May/June 821) he was in Baghdad. Here his principal role seems to have been that of mediator between the Baghdadis and the caliph. He was instrumental in persuading Ma'mun to abandon the green of the Alids as the colour of court dress and return to the traditional black of the Abbasids.[4] He arranged the reconciliation between the caliph and his friend, Fadl b.al-Rabi', and, as effective governor of Baghdad, appointed Fadl's nominees to important positions. He arranged that other members of the opposition should be restored to their positions in the *diwan*.[5] In this way, the foundations of Tahirid power in Baghdad were laid. At the end of 205 (820), he was appointed to Khurasan at the suggestion of the *wazir*, Ahmad b.Abi Khalid[6] (who may have been the brother of his old associate, Muhammad b.Abi Khalid). He did not arrive in the province until the next year – Rabi' II, 206 (September 821) – and only ruled for fourteen months before his death in Jumada II, 207 (October/November 822).[7] It was not an easy year. He himself complained that he found it very difficult to reconcile his duty to the caliph with obligations to old friends, who expected to be rewarded.[8] The circumstances of his death are mysterious. He is said to have omitted the caliph's name from the *khutba* and, since this was treated as a sign of rebellion, he was poisoned; however, it is hard to see what Tahir could have gained from rebellion at this stage in his career and the government did not object to his son Talha taking over his position. It was the most successful solution the Abbasids ever found to the problem of governing the province. The Tahirids sent the caliph large sums in taxation, probably more than when the area was under tighter control from Baghdad,[9] and they kept the peace. Tahir had extensive connections with both the *abna'* and the *dehqan*s of Khurasan and it may have been these contacts, along with the enfeeblement of the *abna'* after the civil war, that enabled the family to maintain order. It is striking witness to the success of this arrangement that there was no major disturbance there from the time of Tahir's appointment until after the death of Mutawwakil, in 247 (861).

The Tahirids were not just rulers of Khurasan. When Tahir left for Khurasan, he did not abandon his responsibilities in Baghdad but handed them over to his son, 'Abd Allah, still only in his mid-twenties. The next year, 'Abd Allah was appointed to lead the wars against the rebels of Syria and Egypt, both of which he eventually brought to a triumphant conclusion. In 211 (826), he was confirmed as governor of Egypt, Syria and Jazira, a post he held until his brother's death, two years later, led to his transfer to Khurasan.[10] These western provinces then passed out of Tahirid hands, but the family retained control of Baghdad. On his departure for the war in the west, 'Abd Allah left his cousin, Ishaq b.Ibrahim, in charge of the city and the *shurta*, offices he retained for almost thirty years, until his death in 235 (July 850).[11] Both as ruler of Baghdad, especially after the transfer of government to

Samarra, and as spokesman for its people, he was one of the great figures of the state. It would be wrong, then, to think of the Tahirids as the first of the independent dynasts; they were partners in the Abbasid state and it was a partnership which, though not without strains, served the dynasty well.

The caliph's other main source of strength was his brother, Abu Ishaq. His rise to prominence was very recent. He had been only fifteen years old at the outbreak of the civil war and, though he probably supported Amin to the end, he did not play an important role. By the year 200 (816), he had made his peace with the Sahlids and Hasan sent him with military forces to prevent the *hajj* from being molested.[12] The adoption of 'Ali al-Rida as heir forced him, along with the rest of his family, into opposition once more. He swore allegiance to Ibrahim b.al-Mahdi and in 202 (817/8) he was sent to combat one, Mahdi b.Alwan, who had rebelled in the countryside around Baghdad in response to the depredations of the soldiery.[13] It is in connection with this disturbance that we find the first mention of the Turkish slaves who were to form the basis of his power. As early as 199 (814/5), he purchased Itakh, a Khazar[14] who had been a cook with his previous owner, and he continued to buy slaves during the subsequent years, forming them into a small but efficient military unit. Most of those who later became famous were bought in Iraq from their previous owners; Ashinas, who distinguished himself in the campaign of 202,[15] had been recently bought from Nu'aym b.Khazim, Wasif had been a slave of the family of Nu'man,[16] Sima al-Dimashqi of Fadl b.Sahl.[17] He also established a connection with the Samanid family, effective lords of much of the Samarqand area, and arranged that they should supply him with slaves direct from Turkestan.[18] By the end of Ma'mun's reign, these Turkish troops numbered three or four thousand,[19] not a big army by the standards of the day, but well trained and efficient. He was the only member of the Abbasid family to have a body of troops at his disposal and he soon made himself indispensable to the new regime. He was able to fill the gap left in the west when 'Abd Allah b.Tahir was appointed to Khurasan, in 213 (828/9), and was made governor of Syria and Egypt.[20] By the later years of his brother's reign, he was, without doubt, the most powerful man in the west, after the caliph himself.

The main challenge facing the new government was the restoration of law and order in the provinces. The caliph was now firmly established in Baghdad, and Iraq, after the long years of civil war, was now moderately peaceful. But there were many other areas where the collapse of central government had allowed local magnates to take over power and local tensions to erupt into open warfare. In Egypt, after a long series of struggles, the country was uneasily peaceful, divided between 'Ali al-Jarawi in the north and the leader of the local *abna'* garrison, 'Ubayd Allah b.al-Sarri, in Fustat. Syria was controlled by numerous rebels of local origin; Ya'qubi describes a sort of 'Guelf-Ghibelline' situation, with each area having its pro-Amin and pro-Ma'mun party but where these labels merely disguised and dignified local feuds.[21] Nasr b.Shabath, leader of the Zawaqil in Raqqa, in 196 (812), was the most prominent and dangerous of these rebels but had no real authority or control over the others. Finally, in mountainous Azerbayjan, there was the anti-Arab, anti-Muslim movement, led by Babak. All these enemies had to be suppressed if the government was to recover its credibility and its sources of revenue. But these intentions were hampered by a continuing shortage of reliable troops and the necessity of making bargains with allies and rebels alike, in order to achieve anything.

The most pressing threat that the government faced was the opposition of Nasr b.Shabath al-'Uqayli. Nasr came from the same tribe of 'Uqayl which had produced Ishaq b.Muslim in the early days of Abbasid rule and he appeared in the same area, northern Syria, around the great bend of the Euphrates. Like Ishaq, he came from Armenia hoping to take advantage of disturbances which broke out in Jazira after the death of Harun.[22] He and his followers began to establish a series of protection rackets in northern Syria; on one occasion, they were paid 5,000 *zuze* (*dinar*s) to leave Edessa unharmed, and monasteries seem to have been especially vulnerable to his depredations.[23] In 196 (812), he came to Raqqa with the rest of the Zawaqil and clearly emerged as their leader during the subsequent fighting. Thereafter, he and his followers settled themselves around Saruj and Kaysum, while other local Arab leaders took over the cities of northern Syria. These Qaysis' principal concern was to expel the Iranian *abna'*.[24] Though they were descended from the supporters of Marwan b.Muhammad and Nasr himself acknowledged that they were the 'army of the Banu Umayya', he disclaimed any hostility to the Abbasids, as such, and refused to proclaim either an Alid or an Umayyad pretender. His only quarrel with the dynasty was the way in which they had given Iranians *'ajam* (precedence) in the army over the Arabs.[25] As we have seen, this was a widespread grievance and it had been an important factor in the break-up of Amin's army during the civil war.

The military efforts of the rebels concentrated on driving the *abna'* out of their fortress at Raqqa but, apart from this, they did not act as a unit, each local chief being effectively independent; Nasr was simply the most aggressive and successful of them. When Tahir arrived early in 199 (813), after his expulsion from Iraq by the Sahlids, he made no effort to subdue the area and there was a time, after the proclamation of Ibrahim b.al-Mahdi as caliph in Baghdad, when he even reached an accommodation with them. When Ma'mun finally reached Baghdad and was reconciled with Tahir, the war was begun again in earnest. After a brief interval, 'Abd Allah b.Tahir was sent to command the forces against the rebels. Nasr, for his part, considered seeking an alliance with the Byzantines but was deterred by fear of the wrath of his co-religionists, although he did take measure to win the support of Christians in his own area.[26] Even after 'Abd Allah's arrival, the government forces were unable or unwilling to launch a major campaign and made several attempts to win Nasr over; Ma'mun himself entered into correspondence with the rebel. But Nasr was adamant and it was not until his city of Kaysum was besieged by the enemy, in 209 (824/5), that he agreed to accept terms.[26] These do not seem to have been very harsh; his family were allowed to keep their property in Syria and, while he and his immediate supporters were taken to Baghdad, there is no evidence that they were badly treated.

Having finally restored order in Syria, 'Abd Allah moved on to Egypt. Egypt had been the scene of much fighting during the civil war, little of it related to the conflict in the rest of the caliphate. By 206 (821/2), this fighting had left the country divided. 'Ubayd Allah b.al-Sarri b.al-Hakam, whose father had led the *abna'* garrison to declare for Ma'mun, controlled Fustat and the south while the north and the Delta were in the hand of 'Ali al-Jarawi, except for the city of Alexandria, which was in the hands of exiles from Andalus, recently expelled by the Umayyad Amir. Apart from the latter, all these groups acknowledged Ma'mun as caliph but his first attempts to assert real power were unsuccessful. In 207 (822), Khalid b.Yazid b.Mazyad, the Shaybani leader, arrived with an army and the title of 'governor'. Khalid was trapped on unfamiliar terrain by 'Ubayd Allah and forced to leave the country,[27] his mission unaccomplished. Ma'mun then settled for the expedient of appointing 'Ubayd Allah and 'Ali as governors to the areas they effectively controlled.[28] The two leaders were bitter rivals; as 'Abd Allah b.Tahir approached, 'Ali hastened to join him, offering his services and acting as his naval commander. 'Ubayd Allah decided to resist but was out-manoeuvred and obliged to ask for terms.[29] As in the case of Nasr, these were not very severe. 'Ubayd Allah had to leave the country and go to Baghdad but he was paid the not inconsiderable sum of 10,000 *dinar*s for his pains and he survived as a prosperous exile, until he died in Samarra, in 251 (865).[30] After this, it proved comparatively easy to drive the Andalusis out of their stronghold. They sailed away and eventually took over Crete, whence they continued their depredations at the expense of the Byzantines. Having completed this pacification, 'Abd Allah returned to Baghdad, where he was given a triumphant reception by the caliph and his brother, Abu Ishaq, at the end of 211, or the beginning 212 (827).[31] His campaigns had been a complete success. With little loss of life, he had restored the provinces to caliphal control. His reputation for honesty and justice had made the imposition of this control much more palatable to local populations than might be imagined. At the same time, it should be recognised that there was a large element of compromise in all these arrangements; the rebel leaders were generously treated, the local populations were conciliated. It was as much the achievement of a sensitive politician as of a great general, and this illustrates again the comparative military weakness of Ma'mun's government.

The problem of Babak was much more intractable. Azerbayjan was one of those areas of the caliphate where Arab settlement had been very scattered. The initial Arab conquest seems to have been little more than the establishment of a few fortified posts in strategic areas of the plains; Bardha'a, Ardabil and Maragha, the capital at the time of Babak's campaign, were among these. With the people of the highlands, the Arab invaders made a series of treaties which allowed the local people almost complete independence, in return for the payment of a small tribute. During the course of the early Abbasid period, this easy-going arrangement began to break down. More and more Arabs from the Mosul area came to settle the plains and to prospect for minerals in the mountain areas. Typical of these Arab entrepreneurs was 'Ali b.Sadaqa al-Azdi.[32] He had begun as a brigand in the province and caused so much trouble that Harun, just before his death, had sent a military expedition to crush him. Like many later expeditions, this one was trapped in the mountains and defeated. The uncertainty following the caliph's death had prevented any further punitive raids and had allowed 'Ali to expand his influence in the province. On his death, his son, Zurayq, continued his father's work; he took estates and castles from the people of Marand and the ruler of Arran, but it seems to have been the mineral resources of the province which he was especially interested in — the gold, lead, iron, mercury, and arsenic.[33] He recruited to his cause a large number of fellow adventurers (30,000, one source says),[34] eager to make their fortunes. This activity provoked opposition in two quarters. In Mosul, governed at this stage by Zurayq's brother-in-law, Sayyid b.Anas al-Azdi, his growing power and his depredations on the Mosul countryside were regarded with apprehension. Secondly, the local inhabitants of the mountain areas, who found their traditional homelands under increasing pressure from the influx of outsiders, took up arms to defend themselves.

The local resistance seems to have been fiercest in the area of the Jabal Budhdh (Qara Dagh) between Marand and Ardabil,[35] which seems to have been a centre of mineral prospecting. In this area, a religio-political group called the Khurramiya[36] had been formed to resist outside pressures. It was probably at the end of Harun's reign that the leader of the Khurramiya in the Qara Dagh, Javidhan b.Sahl, engaged the services of a young bastard, from a village near Maymand, called Babak, whom he employed to manage his property in the area. The young Babak must have proved his abilities in many ways. Not only did he begin an affair with Javidhan's wife, but when his master was killed in battle, he took over the leadership of the movement, claiming that Javidhan's spirit had passed to him. It was in 201 (816/7), that Babak was first recorded as leading the Khurramiya against the Muslims.[37]

After Ma'mun had established his position, one of his first concerns was to take action against this group. A military expedition under the veteran Yahya b.Mu'adh was defeated in 204 (819/20), and an expedition under 'Isa b.Muhammad b.Abi Khalid, despatched the next year, fared no better.[38] Faced with a shortage of reliable troops and more pressing problems elsewhere, the government seems to have been prepared to abandon the enterprise for a while, when an offer arrived from Zurayq b.'Ali.

Zurayq saw his opportunity in the government's difficulties; he made contact with one of Ma'mun's *kuttab,* Ahmad b.al-Junayd, who in turn passed on a message to his master that Zurayq would be prepared to carry on the war against Babak if he were given the governorate of Armenia and Azerbayjan.[39] It is a measure of the weakness of the caliphate that his terms were agreed to. Ahmad b.al-Junayd, not wishing to be left out of what promised to be a very profitable venture, also arranged to go, in return for a partnership in tax-gathering in the area. Having received his commission, Zurayq set about gathering an army. There was no shortage of volunteers from Azerbayjan and from Mosul, and it is said that 50,000 men gathered in Ardabil in 205 (autumn 820). Since the local resources could not support so many for the winter, he decided to march north through the mountains, to winter in Bardha'a. Meanwhile, Ahmad b.al-Junayd, accompanied by a small military force and a large number of merchants, had arrived at Ardabil and, against the advice of his military commanders, decided to press on through the mountains. Disaster was inevitable; Babak's horsemen fell on the expedition, Ahmad was captured and the merchants pillaged.[40] In the spring of 205 (821), Zurayq allowed his army to melt away, while he himself returned to his home in Azerbayjan without waiting to be dismissed by the caliph. He was not a man to give up easily and the explanation of this apparent feebleness must be that he had already got all he wanted. Certainly, he had collected a year's taxes and it may well be that he had reached a secret agreement with Babak about mineral rights. After this, they seem to have lived in peaceful coexistence in the province.

There was little the government could do but accept the new circumstances. For the next six years, Zurayq's energies were devoted to the feud with his brother-in-law, the governor of Mosul, because the governor, Sayyid b.Anas, had taken over all the property of Zurayq's family near the city.[41] Several times the dispute resulted in open warfare around the plains of the Upper Zab. Of Babak we hear nothing and must presume that he enjoyed his independence undisturbed. In 211 (826/7), however, the governor of Mosul was killed during one of these periodic clashes and the caliph decided to take action. The campaign against Nasr b.Shabath was over and there may have been more troops to spare as a result.

The leadership of the campaign was entrusted to Muhammad, the son of Humayd al-Tusi,[42] who had been Hasan b.Sahl's leading general in Iraq. It is interesting to see that he, like Zurayq, organised his expedition on a contract basis, and he agreed to raise and pay the army out of his own private funds. Clearly, the take-over of Azerbayjan seemed a good business proposition; when the army reached Baradan, he paid out 1,000,000 *dirham*s of his own money. He had been appointed as governor of Mosul. Here he could collect resources and recruits from those who wished to avenge Sayyid's death. Many local Arabs came to join him, including the dead man's son, Muhammad, and it was these, rather than Muhammad b.Humayd himself, who decisively defeated Zurayq when the two armies met on the Upper Zab in 212 (827).[43] Zurayq fled to the hills, whence he wrote to make terms with Muhammad b.Humayd and was then despatched, like other rebels before him, to Baghdad. The victor was rewarded for his boldness and financial outlay; he was given all Zurayq's property, including his castles and fortresses as an *iqta'*. Muhammad then immediately regranted the land to Zurayq's family.[44]

Having achieved his primary objective, the removal of Zurayq, Muhammad then pressed on with the much more difficult task of attacking Babak. In the autumn of 827 (Sha'ban 212), he was in Azerbayjan, where his first task was to make trouble. To this end, he invited all the notables of the province to come to advise him on the conduct of the war. Twenty-six leading men, each one of whom owned a town or a mountain, were assembled. Then, acting on secret orders from the caliph, he had them bound and rushed through the mountains to Dinawar, far to the south, where they were kept under arrest by the governor.[45] The next year, 213 (828), Muhammad began operations against Babak.[46] His approach was thorough and professional; he was careful to bring in supplies, to build fortresses and leave garrisons at every stage on his route. He also collected more recruits. Here he had the advantage that Babak was not a Muslim; hence, volunteers arrived to fight the Holy War from all over western Iran and the Gulf provinces. Then he moved from Maragha to the north, through the pass at Ahar into the heart of Babak's country. He moved slowly, leaving fortified supply bases as he went and, by Safar 213 (April/May 828), he confronted Babak and his forces. Muhammad had some members of his own family, but most of his forces were composed of local Arabs from Azerbayjan, and Mosul and the volunteers. The battle was hard-fought; Muhammad's irregulars put up a good fight but they were out-manoeuvred in a mountain valley, and the enemy were all too ready for them. Babak himself commanded the Khurramiya, the Muslims were routed and Muhammad himself killed, fighting bravely.[47]

The defeat and death of Muhammad b.Humayd meant the end of any attempt by Ma'mun's government to subdue Babak, and the area seems to have relapsed into anarchy until Mu'tasim began to take determined measures. But the whole affair is of interest for a number of reasons. It shows once again how limited Islamic penetration was in some areas, particularly mountain areas nominally included in the caliphate, and how these areas could retain their autonomy long after the 'conquest'. It also shows the military weakness of Ma'mun's government, and the failure to raise a reliable standing army, like the Khurasaniya and *abna'* of previous generations. To get round this problem, Ma'mun began to adopt the expedient of making bargains with military leaders. Both Zurayq and Muhammad b.Humayd raised their own armies at their own expense to fight Babak. They were very different men — Zurayq was a rogue and a fraud while Muhammad was a conscientious and determined soldier, related to the great Qahtaba family — but they had a common objective. They both hoped to raise and lead armies to take over this potentially very valuable province. Here, they could have established themselves and their followers as rich, almost independent princes. These 'private enterprise' military expeditions were a far cry from the organised campaigns of early Abbasid times, and they boded ill for the future of the caliphate. The most important change was not so much in recruitment of leadership (the Khurasaniya seem to have been led by the *quwwad* who recruited them) but in the matter of payment. Early Abbasid armies were paid by the administration from revenue raised by taxation; in the Azerbayjan campaigns, by contrast, the leaders were entrusted with a province to exploit as they wished. The government had lost direct control over taxation and salaries and with it a large measure of its authority.

The years from 212 to 214 (827-8) mark a turning point in Ma'mun's reign. From the time of his arrival in Baghdad, his main concerns had been the suppression of internal rebellion and the reassertion of control over the provinces. This process was now at an end; Syria and Egypt had been restored to the central government, while Ifriqiya and Azerbayjan had been effectively abandoned. In 213 (828), 'Abd Allah b.Tahir went to take over Khurasan, and his vast governorate in the west (Syria, Jazira and Egypt) passed to the caliph's brother, Abu Ishaq al-Mu'tasim. Under the caliph, power was effectively in the hands of a triumvirate, 'Abd Allah b.Tahir, Mu'tasim and, as junior partner, the Tahirid ruler of Baghdad, Ishaq b.Ibrahim. This consolidation of control by Mu'tasim and the Tahirids marks the beginning of another era. The period of transition was drawing to a close and the surviving elements from the early Abbasid caliphate were being replaced by the dynamic, centralising army and administration which were to characterise the next thirty years.

Notes

1. Tabari, *Ta'rikh,* vol. 3, pp. 1030, 1081-5, 1406.
2. Ibid., vol. 3, pp. 1101, 1107-9.
3. Ibid., vol. 3, p. 1085; Muhammad b.Habib, *Kitab al-Muhabbar,* ed. I. Lichtenstädter (Hyderabad, 1949), pp. 199-200.
4. Tabari, *Ta'rikh,* vol. 3, p. 1037.
5. Ibn Tayfur, *Kitab Baghdad,* pp. 23-4.
6. Tabari, *Ta'rikh,* vol. 3, pp. 1041-3; Ibn Tayfur, *Kitab Baghdad,* p. 31; Gardizi, *Zayn,* fo. 82a.
7. For the circumstances of Tahir's death, see Tabari, *Ta'rikh,* vol. 3, pp. 1063-6; Ibn Tayfur, *Kitab Baghdad,* p. 117; Shabushti, *Kitab al-Diyarat,* ed. G. Awad (Baghdad, 1966), pp. 147-8; D. Sourdel, *Les Circonstances du Mort de Tahir.*

8. Ibn Tayfur, *Kitab Baghdad*, pp. 113-15.

9. Ibn Khurdadhbih, *Masalik*, p. 39.

10. Tabari, *Ta'rikh*, vol. 3, pp. 1045-6, 1093-4, 1096; Shabushti, *Diyarat*, pp. 133, 137-8.

11. Tabari, *Ta'rikh*, vol. 3, pp. 1062, 1403; Ibn Tayfur, *Kitab Baghdad*, p. 166.

12. Tabari, *Ta'rikh*, vol. 3, p. 995.

13. Ibid., vol. 3, p. 1017.

14. Ibid., vol. 3, p. 1383.

15. Jahshiyari, *Wuzara'*, p. 313.

16. Ya'qubi, *Buldan*, p. 256.

17. Ibid., p. 256.

18. Ibid., p. 255.

19. Ibid., p. 256; Kindi, *Wulat*, p. 188.

20. Tabari, *Ta'rikh*, vol. 3, p. 1100.

21. Ya'qubi, *Ta'rikh*, vol. 2, p. 534.

22. Michael the Syrian, *Chronicle*, vol. 3, p. 22; Ibn al-Athir, *Ta'rikh*, vol. 6, p. 208, for his origins and the beginning of his rebellion.

23. Michael the Syrian, *Chronicle*, vol. 3, pp. 22-3.

24. Ibid., vol. 3, p. 27.

25. Ibid., vol. 3, pp. 36-7, 60.

26. Tabari, *Ta'rikh*, vol. 3, p. 1067; Michael the Syrian, *Chronicle*, vol. 3, p. 54.

27. Kindi, *Wulat*, pp. 173-6.

28. Ibid., pp. 176-7.

29. Tabari, *Ta'rikh*, vol. 3, pp. 1093-8; Kindi, *Wulat*, pp. 180-4.

30. Kindi, *Wulat*, p. 182.

31. Tabari, *Ta'rikh*, vol. 3, p. 1098.

32. For 'Ali's career and the early activities of Zurayq, as recounted by a hostile source, see Azdi, *Ta'rikh*, p. 358.

33. Ibid., p. 354.

34. Ibid., p. 358.

35. See M. Rekaya, *Mise au point sur Theophobe et l'Alliance de Babak*.

36. For the Khurramiya in general, see Sadighi, *Mouvements*, pp. 229-80. For Babak's origins and early career, see Ibn al-Nadim, *Fihrist*, p. 343.

37. Tabari, *Ta'rikh*, vol. 3, p. 1015.

38. Ibid., vol. 3, pp. 1039, 1044, 1045.

39. For Zurayq's offer and the subsequent campaign, Azdi, *Ta'rikh*, pp. 356-7.

40. There is some disagreement about the date of Ibn al-Junayd's campaign; Azdi, *Ta'rikh*, p. 357, says it was 205 (820/1); Tabari, *Ta'rikh*, vol. 3, p. 1072, has 209 (823/4). I am inclined to accept the more detailed account in Azdi.

41. Azdi, *Ta'rikh*, p. 372.

42. Ibid., pp. 373-4.

43. Tabari, *Ta'rikh*, vol. 3, p. 1099; Azdi, *Ta'rikh*, pp. 378-9.

44. Azdi, *Ta'rikh*, pp. 379-81.

45. Ibid., pp. 381-2.

46. Ibid., pp. 383-4.

47. For Muhammad's expedition against Babak and his final defeat, see the detailed account in Azdi, *Ta'rikh*, pp. 386-91.

11 PATTERNS OF PROVINCIAL POWER

The provinces at the fringes of the Islamic world presented the Abbasids with special problems of government and, in order to examine these problems, two such areas, Khurasan, to the northeast, and Ifriqiya, to the west, will now be considered. Both these provinces shared some of the same problems. There was a frontier which was liable to attack, for example. In both cases, this frontier was not a simple line drawn on the map but a complex 'internal frontier', dividing those areas which were under government control from those which were not. Khurasan and Ifriqiya both had native populations jealous of their independence and determined to preserve their old customs and social organisation. These populations were very different in character; the mountain principalities of Khurasan had little in common with the more egalitarian society of the Berber tribes of Ifriqiya, except that, in both cases, the government had to reach some sort of working arrangement with them. These factors limited both the choice of governors and the power they were able to exercise. In Khurasan, the governor had to be acceptable to the local Abbasid garrison, without, if possible, alienating the native magnates of the province. In Ifriqiya, as well, he had to be able to defeat or win over the Berbers, while at the same time retaining the loyalty of the local *jund* (militia), always concerned to retain its privileged status. This meant that the choice of governors was limited to those with roots and contacts in the province, or those who could recruit sufficient followers to make their power a reality. Once in the area, the governor had to follow a narrow and difficult path. If he were, like 'Abd al-Jabbar al-Azdi, in Khurasan, too responsive to local pressures, he would find himself in rebellion against the caliph; if, on the other hand, he attempted to enforce government policy with complete disregard for local interests, he would, like Muhammad al-'Akki, in Ifriqiya, find himself out of a job. In addition, he had to keep a watchful eye on the 'internal frontier'; 'Ali b.'Isa b.Mahan, for example, kept the favour of the local *abna'* and of the caliph, but ultimately failed because he alienated too many of the local magnates. Of course, there were great differences between the provinces, too. Events in Khurasan spilled over into the rest of the caliphate and the politics of the province were intimately bound up with those of the caliphate as a whole. In Ifriqiya, by contrast, the tendency was always to separatism: that the province would go its own way, completely independent of the caliphate. These developments reached their logical conclusion after the death of Harun, when the Khurasanis, for the second time in a century, overturned the whole structure of the caliphate, while the people of Ifriqiya, under the leadership of the Aghlabid family, became completely independent. Despite these differences, however, there are enough similarities to make the comparison illuminating and to shed some light on the problems of Abbasid provincial government.

Khurasan

Khurasan, the enormous and complex province at the northeastern frontier of the caliphate, had a unique place in Abbasid history. It was here that the Abbasid movement had been created, and events in Khurasan always had a a quite disproportionate effect in the rest of the empire. A local disturbance in Egypt, for example, would pose problems for the local governor but was unlikely to excite much attention elsewhere. A major disturbance in Khurasan had repercussions throughout the Abbasid caliphate. This was partly a result of its size, partly because it was the third most important source of revenue for the government (after the Sawad and Egypt), but mainly because the province was the homeland and the recruiting ground for much of the armed forces of the caliphate. It is remarkable how the Khurasaniya who had settled in Baghdad and other areas in the west, nonetheless remained very conscious of and concerned about what went on in their native province.

Diversity was the most striking feature of the province. Most obviously, this diversity was geographical. The area was vast; as the crow flies, it was a thousand miles from Rayy to Samarqand. The landscape was enormously varied but could be divided into three important types. There were the large oases and river valleys, the Zarafshan, the Marw oasis, Khwarazm, in the Oxus delta, and the great cities of Nishapur and Rayy, with their highly developed *qanat* systems. Here, cultivation and population were densely concentrated. Then there were the mountain areas: the massive Hindu Kush, to the south of the Oxus, the mountains of Kish and Khuttal, between Oxus and Zarafshan, and distant Farghana to the east of Samarqand. Finally, there were the deserts, especially the Kara Kum and Kizil Kum sands, which border the lower Oxus and serve to isolate and divide the inhabited areas.

These vastly differing landscapes naturally produced different social and political structures. In the large oasis cities, government was strongest. The Arabs had settled here; in Marw, most of all, but in Balkh, Harat, Nishapur and Samarqand, as well. Local Iranian rulers had largely lost their authority in these towns, although the Bukhara-Khuda was still a figure to be reckoned with in Bukhara. The Iranian upper class seem, however, to have retained much of their wealth and social status. The people of the seven hundred castles, whom Narshakhi records living in the Bukhara oasis, were in this position.[1]

The mountain areas were different. As so often happens, the old order lingered on in the mountains when it had disappeared in the plains. In the small valley-kingdoms of the upper Oxus, Ushrusana, in the mountains above the Farghana valley, and the remoter parts of Badhghis, ruling families, like the Afshins and the ancestors of the Tahirids, retained control over their own areas with a minimum of interference from the Abbasid governors. This is still more true of Khwarazm, which, unlike the other oasis areas, had remained largely unaffected by Arab penetration. Many of these areas were dominated by poor, pastoral economies. A striking contrast with the cities of the plains is revealed by taxation records; Harat produced 1,159,000 *dirham*s and Nishapur, 4,108,900 *dirham*s, compared with 50,000 from Ushrusana, 48,500 from Saghaniyan and a mere 5,000 from distant Bamyan. Gharshistan produced 2,000 sheep, in addition to the 100,000 *dirham*s it owed in cash.[2] But these areas were rich in men and local rulers could provide troops. They were valuable allies but jealous of their independence and privileges, and potentially dangerous.

The local rulers of Khurasan played a vital role in the history of the early Abbasid caliphate. Arab geographers give lists of them, along with their titles (*shah, ikhshid, khaqan*), but tell us disappointingly little about their rule. The best idea of what it meant to be the ruler of one of these principalities comes from the account of the 'trial' of the ruler of Ushrusana, Afshin, who was a prominent military leader at the court of Mu'tasim. His accusers sought to show that he was an apostate from Islam and so worthy of the death penalty, and they stressed pre-Muslim elements in his rule. He had punished men for attempting to spread Islam in his area because, as late as the third (ninth) century, he had an agreement with the kings of Soghdia that conversion to Islam should be discouraged. Not only did he keep pre-Islamic religious books, but he allowed his subjects to address him as a god. Here we have a clear picture of a semi-divine ruler preserving old Iranian traditions and determined, along with his fellow princes, to keep outside influences at bay. These rulers are known in the sources by a variety of terms but, following Shaban's usage, they will be referred to as *dehqans* in this study.

These social and geographical divisions naturally led to political tensions, and it was these tensions which produced both the Abbasid Revolution and the civil war. Unfortunately, we are very badly informed about the political life of the province during this period. No detailed local histories have survived from the early Abbasid age and we must try to reconstruct the pattern of events from scattered and often confused notices in general chronicles or later local histories. Much of what follows is necessarily somewhat speculative, but the affairs of Khurasan are so crucial that some effort must be made to put them in perspective, however limited the sources. The caliphs faced three main problems in the province; the choice and status of the governor, local rebellions and relations with the *dehqans* and the question of the eastern frontier. All these concerns are closely bound up together, but it might be helpful to begin by discussing them individually.

The extent of the governorate varied from time to time. Under Abu Muslim, the governor of Khurasan ruled much of Iran, including Fars but not Hamadhan or Azerbayjan and not Sind. After his fall, the area seems to have been much reduced from this Greater Khurasan, but it still stretched from the city of Rayy to the far northeastern frontier. The governors of the lands beyond the Oxus were always dependent on the governors of Khurasan, but the situation in Sistan is less clear; Abu Muslim certainly appointed governors here, but Ma'n b.Za'ida, in 151 (768), was appointed directly by the caliph.[3] From the time of Mahdi, however, appointments seem to have been made by the governor of Khurasan, who had responsibility for the province. The centre of government was usually at Marw, up until the civil war, except for the ten years when Mahdi ruled from Rayy — 141-51 (758-68). Mahdi seems to have had overall responsibility for affairs in the east, while appointing governors to act in his name in Khurasan itself.

From the fall of Abu Muslim until the reign of Harun, the governor was always chosen from among the leading Khurasani Arab families, who had served the Abbasid movement from the beginning, and this usually, but not always, ensured their loyalty. A case in point is that of 'Abd al-Jabbar b.'Abd al-Rahman al-Azdi. He had a record of service in the Abbasid movement before the revolution and rose to be *sahib al-shurta* to both Saffah and Mansur, afterwards. Given his record,

Mansur must have felt that he could be trusted when he appointed him as governor in 140 (757/8). Quite what went wrong is not clear, but, within the year, he was in open rebellion. He seems to have decided to put himself at the head of those people in the province who wanted to reduce the power of the Abbasid caliph in the area. Certainly, there was a dispute about taxation, reviving an old Umayyad controversy about whether the taxation raised in the province should be spent there, or whether it should be sent to the capital. Then there was a further disagreement about the army; in order to test his loyalty, Mansur ordered that 'Abd al-Jabbar should send troops to help him against the Byzantines. 'Abd al-Jabbar refused, saying that the Turks on his eastern frontiers were restless and he could not spare the men. Thereupon, the caliph offered to send troops to help the hard-pressed governor but this offer was rejected on the grounds that the harvest had been bad and such a large army could not be fed. All this was more than verbal sparring; it raised fundamental issues about the status of the province. Mansur saw Khurasan as a province like any other: its revenues were to be spent by the central government and its troops were to be regarded as part of the main army, to be sent where the caliph ordered. 'Abd al-Jabbar, however, supported those who felt that Khurasan should have a privileged, almost independent status.[4]

The rebellion was defeated with considerable bloodshed and the caliph decided to try a new approach to the problem. He sent his son, Mahdi, to Rayy to act as viceroy of the east.[5] He, in his turn, appointed Arab Khurasani military leaders as his representatives in Marw. This allowed a measure, so to speak, of devolution. Power no longer rested in distant Baghdad but much closer, in Rayy, and Khurasan achieved something of a special status, without this threatening the overall unity of the empire. The arrangement worked well; it benefited Mahdi, in that he gained experience and contacts among the Khurasanis, and it seems to have satisfied the aspirations of most of the inhabitants. After Mahdi returned to Baghdad permanently, this arrangement was discontinued. He was replaced by a governor chosen from one of the most distinguished Arab families of the area, Humayd b.Qahtaba, who was responsible directly to Baghdad.[6] Once again, Khurasan became a province directly dependent on the capital and ruled by Arab-Khurasani soldiers, but neither Humayd nor his successors succumbed to the temptation to assert their independence and there were no further rebellions by provincial governors.

With one short interval, the pattern continued until 177 (793/4), when Harun decided, or was persuaded, to break with established practice and appoint Fadl b.Yahya, the Barmakid, as governor. The Barmakids came from a completely different class from their predecessors in the office; they were Iranians, unlike any previous governor, and they were *dehqans*. During this short tenure of office, Fadl decided to work with the *dehqans*. This is most apparent in the military expeditions he launched. He attacked Kabul and was joined by the princes and *dehqans* of Tukharistan, among them the ruler of Bamyan, whom Fadl had restored to his throne. He also made an expedition to Ushrusana and came to an agreement with the king, Kharakharah, who had never consented to see any governor before. Fadl was determined to make a favourable impression on the province. Chroniclers comment on his building projects and the frontier forts he constructed, while the local historian of Bukhara mentions his contribution to the mosque there. In addition, he raised another 50,000 Iranian troops in the province, to be known as the *'Abbasiya,* 20,000 of whom were sent to Baghdad, while 30,000 remained in Khurasan.[7] The balance of probability is that they were recruited from among the *dehqans* and their followers, to form an army to support the Barmakids, now at the height of their power, and as a counter-balance to the traditional Khurasaniya, many of whom were hostile to the family and all they stood for. It is likely that most of the troops who remained in Khurasan were disbanded by 'Ali b.'Isa, when he was governor, but many of them may later have joined the armies of Rafi' b.al-Layth and Ma'mun.

Fadl's departure in 179 (795/6) was followed by a year of indecision, which ended with another radical move, the appointment of 'Ali 'Isa b.Mahan. Enough has already been said of 'Ali, elsewhere in this book, to show what a complete reversal of previous policy this was.[8] Disappointingly, we know nothing of the circumstances which led to such a turn-round but it is likely that it was a response to pressure from the Khurasaniya in Baghdad, concerned about Barmakid power in the province, and it coincided with the first attempts of Harun to reduce the power of the family throughout the caliphate.

'Ali's governorate is difficult to assess. In most of the sources, he is portrayed as a greedy and violent tyrant[9] and modern writers on the subject, like Bartold and Mottahedah, have tended to accept this uncritically.[10] But it must be remembered that the histories on which we depend were all written after the civil war, when 'Ali was killed and his policies discredited. Furthermore, the historical image was formed at a time when Khurasan was ruled by the *dehqan* families of the Tahirids and the Samanids and we can hardly, in these circumstances, expect the unadorned truth.

'Ali began a policy of attacking the power and position of the *dehqan*s. Tabari speaks of his oppressing the highest people of Khurasan and the nobles, while, according to Jahshiyari, 'he killed the most prominent people of Khurasan and its kings'; he makes an explicit contrast between Fadl b.Yahya's pro-magnate policy and 'Ali's, which, though it brought in more revenue, was alienating the most important men in the area. Tabari, with his usual eye for the relevant detail, gives us two examples of leading men in the province who were threatened with death by 'Ali, supposedly for plotting against him. One of these was Husayn b.Mus'ab, the ruler of Bushang, who fled to Harun at Makka, where he was given the caliph's protection; the other was Hisham b.Farkhusraw, a landowner from Marw, who was forced to escape the governor's anger by feigning paralysis; small wonder his son, 'Ali, wept for the Barmakids.[11] Both examples were of great importance for the future. Husayn's son, Tahir, and Hisham's son, 'Ali, were among Ma'mun's earliest and most militant supporters.

'Ali's firm power base in the army enabled him to survive both pressure for his dismissal in Baghdad and opposition in Khurasan. Until their fall from power in 187 (803), the Barmakids tried to persuade Harun to dismiss him, but the caliph refused to listen.[12] 'Ali sent him huge gifts from the wealth he had confiscated and, on two occasions, in 183 (799), and again in 189 (805), he met the caliph in person to justify his conduct.[13] In the end, it was not intrigue in Baghdad but disturbances in Khurasan which led to his dismissal. As long as the province was peaceful, Harun seems to have been prepared to overlook the excesses of 'Ali's conduct, but, in 190 (805/6), a serious revolt broke out in Samarqand, led by Rafi' b.Layth, grandson of Nasr b.Sayyar, the last Umayyad governor of Khurasan.[14] Strange as it may seem, the power and influence of this family had not been entirely destroyed by the revolution. Nasr's son, Layth, had helped Abbasid forces to put down the rebellion of Muqanna' during the reign of Mahdi and Rafi' himself had a palace in Samarqand.[15] With such a background, he was likely to incur the hostility of 'Ali and, in 190 (806), he attempted to arrest him for adultery. Rafi' defied the governor and was supported by the people of Samarqand, who proclaimed him their leader. Immediately, the rebellion became a focus of resistance and, from all the principalities of Transoxania, those who were opposed to 'Ali's government flocked to join Rafi'.[16] Many of these came from the independent principalities, and we find *dehqan*s, like the ruler of Shash and 'Ujayf b.'Anbasa, playing an important role in military operations.[17] With all this support the rebellion was very successful; 'Ali's attempts to suppress it failed and his own son 'Isa was killed by the rebels. His failure convinced the caliph that there could not be peace as long as 'Ali was governor but the problem was to remove him from office without causing bloodshed. To do this, Harun sent his most trusted military adviser, Harthama b.A'yan, ostensibly to help 'Ali to crush the rebellion. Once in the province, he sent agents into the various districts and made contact with such opposition leaders as Tahir b.al-Husayn. When he was securely established in Marw, he produced to the unsuspecting 'Ali the letters from the caliph which appointed him to the governorship. 'Ali was sent to Baghdad in disgrace.[18]

The removal of 'Ali did not automatically end the rebellion but Harthama persuaded many of Rafi''s followers to desert and 'Ujayf b.'Anbasa and the people of Shash and Farghana came over to the Abbasid side. Harthama was able to take the war to Samarqand and Rafi' had ceased to be a threat to the whole province.[19] Nonetheless, the area was still very disturbed. Not only was Rafi' still holding out, but the long-term political future of the area was undecided. The most important question was this: was Khurasan to be ruled by military leaders like 'Ali b.'Isa, or by men like the Barmakids or Harthama himself, who had close links with the traditional local aristocracy, the *dehqans*? It was with the aim of solving this problem that Harun decided to do what no previous caliph had done and visit the province himself, but he died *en route* and his death left all the problems unresolved.

The second major problem the government faced in Khurasan was that of sporadic rebellion among sections of the non-Arab population. In many cases, these uprisings are said to have been religious, the leader having claimed to be a prophet, but it must be remembered that many people in this part of the world considered their ruler divine, a point which comes out clearly in the trial of Afshin, in the reign of Mu'tasim. Afshin was a Muslim with no pretensions to religious leadership, as far as we can see, and yet his own people in Ushrusana revered him as God.[20] Although these rebellions may have had religious overtones, they were, at the same time, protests against the encroachment of Arabs and other Muslims on traditional ways of life and long-cherished independence. It would be a mistake to see them, in most cases, as independence movements by those already under Abbasid rule; it was rather a local response to attempts to extend the authority of the government to areas it had not previously reached.

The first of these conflicts was the 'rebellion' of Ustadhsis in 150 (767). Ustadhsis had been an independent ruler in remote and mountainous Badhghis since at least 147 (764) and possibly much earlier. In some sources, he is said to have claimed to be a prophet or to have been a follower of the Zoroastrian reformer, Bihafarid, and Tabari describes the army sent against him as 'the Muslims', implying that the rebels were not. A Christian Arab source, who is probably well-informed, says that the rebellion was in protest against Arab attempts to take over control of the local silver mines, which contributed much of the prosperity of the area.[21]

The 'rebels' naturally came into conflict with the nearest Arab settlement at Marwrudh, where they defeated the local militia. It was not until Mansur sent Syrian and Khurasani reinforcements, under Khazim b.Khuzayma, that the situation was brought under control. There was a hard-fought battle at an un-named site on the road from Nishapur to Harat and the insurgents were compelled to flee back to their native mountains. As was customary, the chroniclers portray this as an Abbasid victory; in fact, it looks as if some sort of compromise was reached. Ustadhsis and his followers surrendered but were allowed to go free, all 30,000 of them, and they were given presents of clothing. Ya'qubi says that their leader was sent to Baghdad and executed, but there is no confirmation of this. There is an important sequel to this story. According to some sources, Ustadhsis was the father of Marajil, the mother of Ma'mun.[22] Such a move may have been designed to secure the loyalty of the people of Badhghis and, if Ma'mun did have a native Badhghisi leader for a grandfather, it would go some way to explain why he was so successful at making contacts among the native aristocracy of Khurasan.

In 160 (776/7), there occurred the rebellion of Yusuf al-Barm. This is a very obscure incident but it seems to have been centred in Bukhara and, according to Ya'qubi, it was a religious revival movement. The rebel leader, a non-Arab, attracted support from Soghdia and Farghana, as well, but was defeated by Yazid b.Mazyad and taken to Baghdad for execution. None of the sources gives us very much information about this incident, but it seems to have lacked the anti-Islamic flavour of many of the disturbances in the province at this time.[23]

The second major disturbance of this type occurred in a completely different area, the mountains of Kish, to the south of Bukhara. Kish was an independent kingdom in the time of the early Abbasids but the leader of the rebellion was an outsider, originally named Hashim or Hakim but called Muqanna' because he veiled his face, even from his followers. His father is said to have come from Balkh and he himself served under Abu Muslim and was closely associated with the ill-fated

'Abd Jabbar al-Azdi. After the failure of his rebellion, Hashim was arrested and taken to Baghdad. When he was released, now thoroughly dissatisfied with the Abbasid regime, he began to preach his claims to prophecy in Marw. The Marwis do not seem to have been over-impressed by his curious mixture of extreme Shi'i beliefs and anti-Muslim enthusiasm, which was hardly surprising, as Marw was the main centre of Arab settlement in the area. But he did send out missionaries and these found a much more ready response in the largely Iranian areas of Kish, Sughd and some of the villages of Bukhara. Muqanna' himself left Marw and settled in a fortress he built in the mountains of Kish, a land barely penetrated by the Arabs and where there is no record at all that they settled.[24]

The first fighting occurred in Bukhara. The son of the local prince, the Bukhara-Khuda, had been won over by Muqanna''s teaching and, though there is no evidence that he played an active part in the rebellion, he, nonetheless, hoped that it would free him from Arab rule. In 159 (775/6), supporters of Muqanna' massacred the Muslims in one of the villages of the Bukhara oasis but the governor, Husayn b.Mu'adh, prevented them from taking over the city for four months, until reinforcements arrived from Samarqand. Bukhara was now safe but it was the turn of Samarqand next; this came under attack from Muqanna' and Khaqan, of the Kharluq Turks, with whom he was in alliance, and the city fell. This was the low point of the war for the Arabs, but, in 161 (778), there was a change of command and the new governor of Khurasan, Mu'adh b.Muslim, began to take more effective action, clearing the roads of Turkish brigands and, with the help of Sa'id al-Harashi, the under-governor of Harat, launching an attack on the fortress of Kish itself. It was Sa'id who finally forced Muqanna' to commit suicide in his mountain stronghold, probably in 163 (780).

The rebellion was now at an end, though whether the Arabs took over Kish is impossible to tell; the probability is that they were content with a return to the *status quo*, with Arab rule secure in the cities and the settled plains. The son of the Bukhara-Khuda found that his attempt to throw off Abbasid rule was his undoing and, three years after the end of the rebellion, he was killed by the Arabs in his palace in the city. The family continued to be important, however, and we find one of his descendants fighting for Ma'mun. Muqanna''s memory remained alive in Khurasan for many years after his death, and Narshakhi mentions a sect in existence, in his own day, who still believed he was a true prophet.

The rebellion of Muqanna' was, perhaps, the most serious threat to

Abbasid rule in the province. After it was crushed there was a number of sporadic outbreaks of discontent, which seem to have intensified after 180 (796), when 'Ali b.'Isa was appointed as governor. In Nasa, to the northwest of the province, a certain Abu'l-Khasib defied 'Ali, off and on, for four years, before being killed in 186 (802),[25] while Sistan slipped entirely from Abbasid control. From about 182 (798), this province had been effectively in the hands of one Hamza b.Adharak, a Khariji leader of Iranian extraction, who had even taken the capital, Zaranj, and prevented 'Ali from appointing governors. Hamza carried his raids, with devastating ferocity, into southern areas of Khurasan, around Harat and Badhghis, and all attempts to crush him failed.[26] Although both these movements were confined to rural areas and never took over any of the larger cities of the province, they prevented the collection of taxes and led to a progressive weakening of 'Ali's control over the area. They show, too, that separatist sentiment was very much alive in the remoter areas of Khurasan and local leaders seem to have found it fairly easy to rouse support for an anti-Abbasid cause. When this has been said, however, it must be remembered that the Abbasids were very effective in retaining control over the most important areas. Rayy, Nishapur, Marw, Harat and Balkh were always under government control, while their hold on Bukhara and Samarqand only faltered briefly at the time of the rebellion of Muqanna'; with these centres under their authority, the Abbasids could afford some degree of complacency about disaffection in the more remote areas.

The northeastern frontier of the caliphate in Khurasan was very difficult to define. In the case of the Byzantine frontier, for example, there was an area under Muslim control and another under Christian control, with a no-man's-land in between. There were some fairly remote areas, like Balkh or Samarqand, which were firmly under government control, while places like Badhghis and Kish, though much closer to the centre of the caliphate, were not. In addition, there were nomadic Turkish tribes, in the steppe-lands between Marw and Bukhara, which were in no real sense under Abbasid control and which could and did cut the road between these two important Muslim centres.[27] Nor is it easy to define which areas were part of the caliphate and which were not; Kabul, for example, is treated by the ninth-century geographer, Ibn Khurdadhbih, as part of the province of Khurasan whereas, in fact, there is no evidence that the Muslims actually ruled there and the area was included simply because the independent kings sometimes paid tribute. Such expansion of the caliphate as took place in this area in the early Abbasid period was more in the form of internal conquest and consolidation, rather than pushing the limits of Muslim influence further to the northeast.

From time to time, Abbasid governors launched expeditions to the east. The objectives seem to have been to secure oaths of friendship or allegiance from the local rulers and to ensure that they paid tribute, rather than to effect a lasting conquest. In 152 (769), Humayd b.Qahtaba, then governor of Khurasan, led a raid on Kabul[28] and, some time towards the end of Mansur's reign, the caliph sent his *mawla,* Layth, to invade Farghana. The king of the country, who lived in Farghana, was defeated and forced to pay a large sum in tribute to secure peace.[29] In Mahdi's reign, one Ahmad b.Asad again attacked Farghana and conquered the land as far as Kasan, at this time the royal capital. Ya'qubi gives a list of the princes who, he claims, gave allegiance to the caliph: the kings of Kabul, Tabaristan, Sughd, Tukharistan, Bamyan, Farghana, Ushrusana, the Kharluq Turks, Sistan, the Turks and, perhaps more fancifully, the kings of Tibet, Sind, China, India and the *khaqan* of the Taghuzzghuzz Turks.[30] As has already been mentioned, when Fadl b.Yahya was governor, he launched an expedition against Kabul. His general was accompanied by the kings and *dehqan*s of Tukharistan and the king of Bamyan, who had been appointed to the office by Fadl shortly before, and Fadl, as part of his conciliatory policy towards the local aristocracy, established contact with the king of Ushrusana.[31]

After the deposition of Fadl, this forward policy seems to have come to an end. 'Ali b.'Isa's relations with the local aristocracy were not happy and he was too concerned with internal security to mount major offensive operations. When the princes of the eastern frontier appear on the scene again, it is as allies of Rafi' b.Layth or supporters of Ma'mun.

The tensions within the province came to a head after the death of Harun. The rivalry between Amin and Ma'mun and Amin's close connections with the *abna'* and Baghdad gave the *dehqan*s the opportunity to reassert their position. Fadl b.Sahl linked their cause to that of the young Ma'mun and, once again, armies from Khurasan marched west to overthrow the government and kill the caliph.

Ifriqiya

The Arab conquest of North Africa had been swift but very partial. The Byzantine administration based on Carthage, which had ruled the coastal plains for a century and a half since the reconquest under Justinian, was swept aside. The coastal plains were to form the nucleus of the Muslim province of Ifriqiya, as they had of the Byzantine province. The mountain and desert areas which bordered these plains remained largely autonomous, in the control of the local Berber tribes. Fiercely independent, they resisted all attempts to reduce them to the status of docile, tax-paying subjects, like the Copts of Egypt or the native populations of Iraq. The first phase of Berber resistance was a simple war of independence waged by the tribes, either Jewish, Christian or pagan, against the Muslims, a resistance which ended, at least in Ifriqiya and the surrounding areas, with the defeat and death of the famous queen/priestess, known to the Arabs as Kahina, in about 78 (697/8).

With the defeat of these indigenous movements, the Arabs were able to exert some sovereignty over the area. Under the later Umayyads, the area was heavily taxed, paying not only money but tribute of female slaves as well, and it is worth remembering that both Mansur and the first Umayyad ruler of Spain, 'Abd al-Rahman b.Mu'awiya, had Berber mothers.[32] This period of exploitation and comparative peace was not characterised by large-scale Arab settlements. The numbers of the invaders were fairly small and many of those who took part in campaigns either returned to the east or moved on to the richer areas of Spain.[33] Settlement seems to have been confined to the newly founded cities of Qayrawan and Tunis and some scattered outposts like Tubna, the capital of the Zab region.

During the last part of Hisham's reign, however, this situation began to change; a new wave of Berber resistance began under the leadership of Arab Kharijite missionaries from the east. The Kharijites had come to form three distinct sects in the first century of Islam. The most extreme and militant of these, the Azariqa, were largely destroyed in unsuccessful rebellions against the Umayyads. The two others, the Sufriya and, above all, the moderate 'Ibadiya, were able to reconcile themselves to the dynasty. This was especially true of the 'Ibadis, who came to be a prosperous commercial community in Basra, with trading links in many different places.[34] After the death of 'Abd Malik in 86 (705), Umayyad policy towards these groups changed and they were forced to adopt a more militant attitude and to send missionaries to establish centres away from Basra, which was too closely controlled by the Umayyads for comfort.[35] Naturally, it was in remote fringe areas, like 'Uman and, above all, the Berber districts of North Africa, that they received the most enthusiastic response. It may be that their trading contacts provided an opportunity for these Basran missionaries to spread their message. Kharijism, at the end of the Umayyad period, meant many different things in different places, but one important common feature that all Kharijis shared was the refusal to pay taxes to the government; this coincided exactly with the concerns of the Berbers of Ifriqiya. Kharijism also preached the equality of all believers and held that the leadership of the community, the imamate, should be open to all, regardless of their social or racial background. This, again, appealed to Berbers, resentful at being treated as second-class citizens.

From 117 (735) onwards, Kharijite preachers, first Sufrite and then 'Ibadite, as well, began to make their appearance in Ifriqiya. They soon made many converts in the Berber areas to the south of Tripoli and the west of Tunisia and 122 (740) saw a major rebellion against Umayyad authority, led by the Sufrites.[36] The Abbasid Revolution had no direct impact in the area. Since 127 (745), the country had been held by an Arab adventurer, 'Abd al-Rahman b.Habib al-Fihri, who had no formal mandate from the Umayyad government, and the revolution left him unaffected. When Mansur became caliph, he wrote, demanding 'Abd Rahman's obedience but he, while sending some presents and offering allegiance, made it quite clear that he intended to retain his independence.[37] This led to an open quarrel with the Abbasids, who were denounced by 'Abd al-Rahman, which, in turn, led to a dispute within the governor's family. 'Abd al-Rahman was assassinated in 137 (755), and was eventually succeeded by his son Habib[38] but the dissension within the family gave the Berbers, who had been held firmly in check by 'Abd al-Rahman, the opportunity to launch a major insurrection. Once again, the leaders were Kharijis; at first, the initiative was taken by the Sufrite Warfajuma of Nafza, to the southeast of Qayrawan, who took the city itself and massacred many of the leading Arabs. But they did not hold the scene for long. The general confusion allowed the 'Ibadi tribes of Nafusa and Hawwara, to the south of Tripoli, to take to the field under the leadership of their *imam*, Abu'l-Khattab. In 140 (758), the 'Ibadiya took Qayrawan and the rest of the western Maghrib. The centre of their power remained in Tripoli, where Abu'l-Khattab established himself and Qayrawan was ruled by a close associate of his, the Persian, 'Abd al-Rahman b.Rustam.[39]

This rebellion meant that the Arab conquest of the country was almost completely undone. The new rulers were Muslims, of the Khariji persuasion, but they were Berbers owing no allegiance whatever to the caliphate. It remained, then, for the Abbasids, who had taken no part in the struggle, to reconquer the country. This was done by a massive expedition of some 40,000 Khurasani troops, led by the veteran commander, Muhammad b.al-Ash'ath. Abu'l-Khattab and his forces were decisively defeated and Ibn al-Ash'ath was installed as governor in Qayrawan. Ibn Rustam and the remains of the 'Ibadi army fled west to Tahert, where he established an independent state. The newly arrived troops were settled in the country, especially at Qayrawan, which was fortified, and Tunis and formed the nucleus of the *jund* who were to play so important a part in the affairs of the province. In addition, the new governor appointed one of his subordinates, a Khurasani of Arab origin, called Aghlab b.Salim, as governor of Tubna, in the Zab, where he could keep an eye on the Berbers of the Aurès mountains.[40]

The new governor did not have an easy task. Not only did the Berbers refuse to accept this new domination peacefully, but the *jund*, knowing that they were indispensable, were determined to preserve their status and make sure that their salaries were paid. Ibn al-Ash'ath succeeded in keeping the Berbers at bay but, for reasons which are not clear, his relations with the *jund* deteriorated. In 148 (765), he was asked to leave by the military, led by 'Isa b.Musa al-Khurasani.[41] 'Isa himself was soon replaced by Aghlab b.Salim, while Muhammad returned to the east, where he died fighting the Byzantines the next year.[42]

Despite the fact that he was drawn from their ranks and was said to be popular, Aghlab was no more successful than his predecessor in satisfying the *jund*. He had been in power for less than two years when he was forced to lead an expedition against a leader of the Sufriya, Abu Qurra, of Tlemcen, who was threatening Ifriqiya. He gathered his army, and the enemy melted away, but Aghlab was not content to let matters rest. He wanted to pursue the enemy to Tlemcen and even Tangier. His troops, however, were not so enthusiastic; the immediate peril was passed and they wished to return to their homes. His army melted away, while his capital was seized by the commander of the troops of Tunis, Hasan b.Harb al-Kindi. Aghlab was forced to abandon his ambitious project and returned to Qayrawan with a few personal adherents. There, in Sha'ban 150 (September 768), he was killed by the garrison.[43] Once again, the *jund* had shown that the country could not be ruled without their consent.

After the death of Aghlab, Mansur despatched a new governor from the east, 'Umar b.Hafs. 'Umar was the first representative of the Muhallabi family, who were to dominate the life of Ifriqiya for the next quarter of a century, to be appointed. He arrived in 151 (768), with some five hundred extra troops and, almost immediately, serious trouble began. The rebellion of this year took the form of a grand coalition of all the Khariji leaders, in an effort to destroy the Abbasid administration in the area. Ibn Idhari gives us an interesting breakdown of the rebel forces, from which we can gauge something of the relative strength of the different groups.[44] The largest of these were the Sufrites, led by Abu Qurra of Tlemcen, whom Aghlab had wished to attack at the time of his death, but they were joined by large numbers of 'Ibadis as well. These were led by Ibn Rustam of Tahert, with 15,000, Abu Hatim, who had succeeded Abu'l-Khattab in the Tripoli area, with 'a large number', 'Asim al-Sadrati, with 6,000, Miswar al-Zanati, with 10,000, and others. Against this formidable opposition, 'Umar could raise only 15,500 members of the *jund*. He was besieged at Tubna, in the Zab, but succeeded in bribing Abu Qurra's Sufri troops to go home. Having thus disposed of the largest contingent, he was able to defeat Ibn Rustam in battle and return to Qayrawan. His troubles were not yet over, however. In Qayrawan, he was besieged by the forces of Abu Hatim in overwhelming numbers. At the end of 154 (November 771), he was killed while making a sortie and the city was stormed soon after.[45] Once again, the Berbers were the undisputed masters of the province.

The man chosen to lead a new expedition to restore order in the province was, like his predecessor, a member of the Muhallabi family. Yazid b.Hatim was one of Mansur's inner circle; Ibn Idhari explains that the caliph was knowledgeable about Ifriqiya and would send only his closest supporters to the province. Yazid was a man of great personal qualities and had experience as governor of Azerbayjan and Egypt. But there were other reasons for offering him this difficult appointment. The Muhallabi family had always had close connections with commercial circles in Basra, especially with the 'Ibadiya, and it was, no doubt, intended that Yazid should try to make use of these contacts to win the 'Ibadis of North Africa over.[46]

Yazid brought with him a vast army of some 60,000 men, the largest force that had ever been sent to the west.[47] Clearly, the fifteen thousand men that 'Umar had been forced to rely on could never hope to hold the province, and reinforcements were badly needed. Recruits were found, not only from Khurasan, but from Iraq and Syria as well. Yazid had had previous experience of this sort of colonisation, having been instrumental in encouraging the settlement of Basrans in Azerbayjan when he had been governor.[48] His first task was to defeat Abu Hatim near Tripoli, which signalled the end of 'Ibadi power in Tripolitania and Ifriqiya. Some of the more militant 'Ibadis left to join Ibn Rustam at Tahert, but many remained in the eastern provinces and even in Qayrawan itself, and there can be no doubt that Yazid succeeded in reconciling them to his rule.[49] His concern for commerce was shown on his arrival in Qayrawan, when he organised the markets of the city, a move which must have pleased the commercially minded 'Ibadites.

His fifteen years of rule were a period of stability and peace. The mosque at Qayrawan was restored and beautified but otherwise we have little information about internal developments. Most of the main commands in the province, especially the governorate of the Zab, seem to have been held by members of the Muhallabi family and, when Yazid died in 171 (788), it was natural for the caliph to appoint his brother, Rawh, to succeed him.

Rawh was older than his brother, Yazid, and the sources make it clear that he was not as effective, but the prestige of the family was such that his three years of rule were largely peaceful.[50] On his death in 174 (791), his son, Qabisa, made an attempt to take over from his father but leaders of the *jund* had taken care to secure Harun's approval for the choice of another Muhallabi, Nasr b.Habib, who was able to take over without serious opposition. Nasr had been *sahib al-shurta* to Yazid in both Egypt and Ifriqiya and would thus be very well known in the army, while Rawh and his children were comparative newcomers. Rawh had left another son, Fadl, who was governor of the strategic area of the Zab at the time of his father's death, and he was not prepared to see his branch of the family pushed aside. Accordingly, he set off for Baghdad, where he was able to secure Nasr's dismissal and his own appointment from Harun, no doubt advised by the Barmakids, who must have seen this as a way of bringing the province under more direct control. Fadl was accepted in the province in 177 (793/4), but he soon made the fatal mistake of antagonising the *jund*. The trouble began in Tunis, where Fadl appointed his inexperienced nephew, Mughira, as governor, and the leaders of the garrison there, headed by 'Abd Allah b.al-Jarud, wrote to Fadl to complain of his conduct. The letter made it plain that no disloyalty was intended but Fadl chose to side with his nephew; open conflict broke out, with the result that Fadl, deserted by his soldiers, was killed, in 178 (794).[51] With his death, Muhallabi rule came to an end. They failed partly because of internal family disputes and partly because Fadl allowed himself to become alienated from the *jund,* most of whom had arrived with Yazid b.Hatim and had proved devotedly loyal to him and his immediate successors.

The government in Baghdad made no effort to appoint another Muhallabi. The family did not have the close links with Harun that they had had with Mansur and Mahdi, and the Barmakids were hostile to powerful provincial dynasties.[52] Nor did the Barmakids have the power to force their choice on the *jund*. Instead, they began negotiations with Ibn al-Jarud, sometimes also known as 'Abdawayh, and, in the end, persuaded him to go peacefully to Baghdad, where he was generously treated. Once again, the *jund* had triumphed. The Barmakids now made a sustained attempt to assert their authority over the province and, to this end, they appointed Harthama b.A'yan as governor. Harthama was the military figure most closely associated with the Barmakids, and he probably had under his command the 30,000 new troops whom Fadl b.Yahya, the Barmakid, had recruited in Khurasan and sent west. He had already pacified Palestine and, having passed through Egypt, reached Ifriqiya, with a large army, in 179 (795). However, this was not to be a new wave of immigrants like the one which had accompanied Yazid b.Hatim. Harthama pacified the country and built the famous *ribat* at Monastir, which survives to the present day, but was reluctant to stay in the province because he found the people too unruly. He asked to be withdrawn and returned to the east, where he played a prominent part in the political events of the next twenty years.[53]

The Barmakids then appointed another associate of theirs, Muhammad b.Muqatil al-'Akki, to replace him. He was a young man with no government experience and no roots in the province. Harun's government was always very concerned about taxation and he may have had orders to lower the salaries paid to the *jund*. This would account for his otherwise inexplicable attempts to reduce their wealth. Needless to say, the *jund* were bitterly hostile to this and their anger was increased when Muhammad treated the opposition with arrogant disdain. He had been governor for almost exactly two years, when, in Ramadhan 183 (October 799), he was deposed by a military uprising, led by the commander of the garrison in Tunis, Tammam b.Tamim al-Tamimi. Muhammad was allowed to retreat to Tripoli, but Tammam seems to have been unable to maintain himself in Qayrawan. He was ejected by another rebel, the son of a previous governor, Ibrahim b.al-Aghlab, who drove him out on the pretext of restoring Muhammad and legality. But Muhammad was so unpopular that Ibrahim wrote to Harun requesting the office for himself. So it was with every appearance of loyalty to the Abbasid regime that Ibrahim b.al-Aghlab became governor, in Jumada II, 184 (July 800).[54]

Ibrahim is traditionally considered the first of the independent rulers of Ifriqiya and it is true that after his accession the caliphs effectively lost the power to appoint and dismiss governors in the province. None of this, however, was apparent at the time. Ibrahim claimed to have acted in the cause of legitimacy, against the rebel Tammam, and had been duly confirmed in his position by Harun, a procedure much the same as with some of his predecessors. The basic requirements for a governor were that he be acceptable to the *jund* and that, by some means or another, he could prevent Ifriqiya being taken over by the Kharijite Berbers; anyone who could achieve this, while professing loyalty to the Abbasids, was likely to be confirmed in office.

Ibrahim's background certainly qualified him for office. His father, Aghlab, had been chosen by the *jund* to succeed Ibn al-Ash'ath, although his subsequent ambitions alienated many of them. After his death, in 150 (768), it seems that his son left for Egypt, whence he was eventually expelled. In about 174 (790), he made his way back to the Zab province and, during the upheavals which accompanied the collapse of Muhallabi rule, he made himself master of the area.[55] When Harthama arrived, Ibrahim made peace with him and it seems that the Zab was made a separate district, directly dependent on Baghdad rather than on Qayrawan. In this position, Ibrahim was able to do the caliph a service by arranging the poisoning of Idris b.'Abd Allah, the Alid, in Morocco. Ibrahim was thus in a very strong position to take advantage of the revolt of the *jund* against Muhammad al-'Akki. He came from a family long established in the army and had been in command of the most important frontier province. In addition, he had been accepted by Harthama and proved useful to Harun. He made certain of his selection by offering the caliph an attractive financial arrangement. It seems that Ifriqiya, far from being a source of revenue to Baghdad, was, in fact, a drain on the treasury and some 100,000 *dirham*s a year were forwarded from Egypt to subsidise the province. Ibrahim agreed to do without any such payments and promised to pay 40,000 *dirham*s a year to Baghdad.[56] For Harun's money-conscious administration, this offer was too good to refuse, but Ibrahim was not given any hereditary rights, nor was it envisaged that he should be anything more than a provincial governor.

Once in power, Ibrahim took measures to consolidate his hold on the country by recruiting a bodyguard of some 5,000 black slaves, loyal only to him, and building a new fortified administrative centre, called 'Abbasiya, in honour of the ruling dynasty, near Qayrawan. His relations with the *jund* were delicate. In 186 (802), they had stood by him, when his authority was threatened by a rebellion in Tunis, but, by 194 (810), relations had deteriorated. The import of a slave army and, as so often, the non-payment of salaries were the main causes of the rebellion of that year. In order to raise money for this, he was forced to appeal to the caliph Amin, who bailed him out: the Abbasids and Aghlabids still needed each other. It is interesting to note that Ibrahim was conciliatory to the defeated rebel leaders, who were merely exiled to the Zab. He could not afford to antagonise the *jund*.[57]

In 196 (812), Ibrahim died. This was the moment when the caliph could have asserted his control over the province by appointing the new governor. Circumstances, however, made this impossible. Amin was faced with the prospect of war with his brother, Ma'mun. He could not afford to alienate anyone in the west. Circumstantial evidence suggests that the caliph may have allowed Ibrahim's son, 'Abd Allah, to succeed in exchange for military support. Two years later, in 198 (813/4), we find another of Ibrahim's sons, Muhammad, among the partisans of Amin and he continued to play a minor role in the civil wars in Iraq, after the caliph's death. It may have been with him that the Ufariqa, who had a *qati'ah* on the West Bank in Baghdad, arrived in the city.[58] When 'Abd Allah, in his turn, died in 201 (817), the civil war was still at its height and the caliph Ma'mun, in distant Marw, could not possibly interfere in Ifriqiya. 'Abd Allah's brother, Ziyadat Allah, succeeded without reference to the Abbasids, and it was during his twenty-two year reign that Aghlabid authority became firmly established.[59] When Ma'mun eventually took effective control in the west, he had to accept that Ifriqiya had slipped outside the Abbasid's power. Without the civil war it might have been a different story.

The fates of the two provinces were very different. The effect of victory in the civil war and rule by the Tahirid family was to integrate Khurasan much more fully into the Islamic world. The local princes tended to abandon their isolation and their traditional status, and to seek careers in the wider Islamic world. Ifriqiya, by contrast, was to become an important Mediterranean power in its own right, and Qayrawan became the cultural and intellectual centre of Muslim North Africa. In both cases, these developments began while the areas were provinces of the Abbasid empire. In both these areas, the Abbasid caliphate was far from being a centralised, bureaucratic state, with the caliph as absolute ruler. The powers of both the caliph and his governor were severely circumscribed by local forces, and successful government was the result of negotiation and compromise, as much as the exercise of authority.

Notes

1. Narshakhi, *The History of Bukhara*, trans. R. Frye (Cambridge, Mass., 1954), pp. 62-3.

2. Ibn Khurdadhbih, *Masalik*, pp. 34-9.

3. Tabari, *Ta'rikh*, vol. 3, p. 368; Ya'qubi, *Buldan*, p. 286; C.E. Bosworth, *Sistan under the Arabs* (Rome, 1968).

4. Tabari, *Ta'rikh*, vol. 3, pp. 128, 134-5; Baladhuri, *Ansab*, fos. 640-2; Gardizi, *Zayn*, fo. 73b; S. Moscati, 'La Rivolta di Abd al-Gabbar contra il Califfo al-Mansur' in RANL, Series 8, vol. 2 (1945); Omar, *Abbasid Caliphate*, pp. 204-8.

5. Tabari, *Ta'rikh*, vol. 3, p. 134.

6. Ibid., vol. 3, pp. 369, 459.

7. Ibid., vol. 3, pp. 629, 631-7, 638; Ya'qubi, *Ta'rikh*, vol. 2, p. 492; Ya'qubi, *Buldan*, p. 290; Hamza al-Isfahani, *Ta'rikh Sini Muluk al-Ard* (Beirut, 1961), pp. 142-3; Gardizi, *Zayn*, fo. 78b; Narshakhi, *History*, p. 49. For the 'Abbasiya, see above, pp. 120-1.

8. Hamza, *Ta'rikh*, p. 143; Gardizi, *Zayn*, fo. 79a. See above p. 121.

9. See, for example, Tabari, *Ta'rikh*, vol. 3, pp. 713-18; Jahshiyari, *Wuzara'*, p. 228.

10. Barthold, *Turkestan*, p. 203; R. Mottahedeh, *The Abbasid Caliphate in Iran. Cambridge History of Iran*, vol. 4, pp. 70-1.

11. Tabari, *Ta'rikh*, vol. 3, pp. 713-18; Jahshiyari, *Wuzara'*, p. 228; Isfahani, *Aghani*, vol. 5, p. 312.

12. Tabari, *Ta'rikh*, vol. 3, p. 675; Jahshiyari, *Wuzara'*, p. 228.

13. Tabari, *Ta'rikh*, vol. 3, pp. 648-9, 704.

14. Ibid., vol. 3, pp. 707-8; Ya'qubi, *Ta'rikh*, vol. 2, p. 515.

15. Ibn al-Athir, *Ta'rikh*, vol. 6, p. 26; Gardizi, *Zayn*, fo. 75b; Yaqut, *Mu'jam*, vol. 4, p. 111.

16. Ya'qubi, *Ta'rikh*, vol. 2, p. 528.

17. Tabari, *Ta'rikh*, vol. 3, pp. 712, 732; Ya'qubi, *Buldan*, p. 113.

18. Tabari, *Ta'rikh*, vol. 3, pp. 719-27; Ya'qubi, *Ta'rikh*, vol. 2, p. 528; Hamza, *Ta'rikh*, p. 143.

19. Tabari, *Ta'rikh*, vol. 3, p. 732.

20. See the discussion of his 'trial' in E.G. Brown, *Literary History of Persia*, vol. 1, pp. 330-6.

21. Tabari, *Ta'rikh*, vol. 3, pp. 354-8; Ya'qubi, *Ta'rikh*, vol. 2, pp. 457-8; Agapius, *'Unwan*, p. 544; Gardizi, *Zayn*, fo. 74b; Sadighi, *Mouvements*, pp. 155-62.

22. Gardizi, *Zayn*, fo. 74b; Mas'udi, *Muruj al-Dhahab*, ed. C. Pellat (Beirut, 1973), vol. 4, p. 299; Sadighi, *Mouvements*, p. 161.

23. Tabari, *Ta'rikh*, vol. 3, p. 470; Ya'qubi, *Ta'rikh*, vol. 2, p. 478; Gardizi, *Zayn*, fo. 76a; Sadighi, *Mouvements*, p. 174.

24. Tabari, *Ta'rikh*, vol. 3, p. 484; Gardizi, *Zayn*, fo. 76b; Narshakhi, *History*, pp. 65-71; Sadighi, *Mouvements*, pp. 163-86; Barthold, *Turkestan*, pp. 199-200; *Cambridge History of Iran*, vol. 4, pp. 498-502.

25. Tabari, *Ta'rikh*, vol. 3, pp. 649, 650, 651.

26. Ibid., vol. 3, pp. 638, 650; Ibn al-Athir, *Ta'rikh*, vol. 6, pp. 101, 103, 114, 143.

27. Narshakhi, *History*, pp. 71-2.

28. Tabari, *Ta'rikh*, vol. 3, p. 369.

29. Ya'qubi, *Ta'rikh*, vol. 2, p. 465.

30. Ibid., vol. 2, p. 479.

31. Tabari, *Ta'rikh*, vol. 3, p. 631; Ya'qubi, *Buldan*, p. 290; Gardizi, *Zayn*, fo. 78b.

32. For this phase, see Talbi, *Emirat Aghlabide*, pp. 21-35.

33. Talbi, *Emirat Aghlabide*, pp. 21-2.

34. T. Lewicki, 'The Ibadites in Arabia and Africa' in *Cahiers d'Histoire Mondiale*, vol. 13 (1971), pp. 58-67.

35. Ibid., pp. 67-8.

36. Talbi, *Emirat Aghlabide*, pp. 37-41; Lewicki, *Ibadites*, pp. 83-7.

37. Talbi, *Emirat Aghlabide*, pp. 35-7.

38. Ibn Idhari, *Bayan*, vol. 1, pp. 67-70.

39. Ibid., vol. 1, pp. 70-1; Lewicki, *Ibadites*, p. 89.

40. Baladhuri, *Futuh*, p. 275; Ibn Idhari, *Bayan*, vol. 1, pp. 72-3; Talbi, *Emirat Aghlabide*, pp. 73-4.

41. Ibn Idhari, *Bayan*, vol. 1, pp. 72-3.

42. Tabari, *Ta'rikh*, vol. 3, p. 353.

43. Ibn Idhari, *Bayan*, vol. 1, pp. 74-5; Talbi, *Emirat Aghlabide*, pp. 74-5.

44. Ibn Idhari, *Bayan*, vol. 1, p. 75.

45. Ibid., vol. 1, pp. 75-8.

46. Lewicki, *Ibadites*, p. 68.

47. Tabari, *Ta'rikh*, vol. 3, p. 372; Ibn Idhari, *Bayan*, vol. 1, pp. 78-9; Talbi, *Emirat Aghlabide*, pp. 21, 75.

48. Ya'qubi, *Ta'rikh*, vol. 2, p. 446.

49. Lewicki, *Ibadites*, pp. 91-7.

50. Ibn Idhari, *Bayan*, vol. 1, pp. 84-5.

51. Ibid., vol. 1, pp. 85-8; Talbi, *Emirat Aghlabide*, pp. 76-80.

52. See above, pp. 117-18.

53. Ibn Idhari, *Bayan*, vol. 1, p. 89; Talbi, *Emirat Aghlabide*, pp. 80-1; G. Marcais, *L'Architecture Musulmane d'Occident* (Paris, 1954), p. 32.

54. Ibn Idhari, *Bayan*, vol. 1, pp. 89-92; Talbi, *Emirat Aghlabide*, pp. 82-7.

55. For a detailed examination of these events, see Talbi, *Emirat Aghlabide*, pp. 89-102.

56. Ibid., pp. 108-9, with references.

57. Ibid., pp. 136-54.

58. Tabari, *Ta'rikh*, vol. 3, pp. 912, 1005, 1018, 1022, 1073, 1076; Ya'qubi, *Buldan*, p. 249.

59. See Talbi, *Emirat Aghlabide*, pp. 164-216, for Ziyadat Allah's struggle against the *jund*.

12 ALID REBELLIONS IN THE EARLY ABBASID PERIOD

It was natural that the establishment of the Abbasid regime would provoke opposition. Some of this naturally came from the supporters of the Umayyads in Syria and elsewhere, and from people in both Egypt and Jazira who felt crushed by over-taxation and maladministration. But the most important focus of opposition within the Muslim community was the family of 'Ali b.Abi Talib. The Abbasid Revolution had drawn mass support from the idea that rule by the house of the Prophet would bring true Islam and the end of injustice and oppression, but there were many different groups who became rapidly disillusioned with the regime of Saffah and his successors. It was easy enough for members of the Alid family to argue that the Abbasids were not really members of the house of the Prophet at all, that only 'Ali and his descendants could really be considered as legitimate rulers and that the fight for a truly Islamic state must therefore go on.

Those who supported the claims of the Alids are usually described as Shi'ites. We are given detailed accounts of the emergence of Shi'ism in a number of sources, dating from the fourth (tenth) century on.[1] These give a picture of an orderly progression of imams, descending from 'Ali and his son Husayn, until the disappearance of the twelfth imam in the mid-third (ninth) century. On the way, different splinter groups, following different leaders and holding slightly different beliefs, split off to form sects on their own. For anyone trying to understand the Alid movements of the early Abbasid period, however, these sources suffer from two grave disadvantages. The first is that the orderly procession of generally accepted imams seems to have little reality, at least until the time of Ja'far al-Sadiq — died, 148 (765) — and is designed to prove the legitimacy of these *imams* rather than to describe an historical situation. The second disadvantage is that they, and all subsequent writers on the subject, have lived in societies where Sunnis and Shi'is formed two different communities, with their own traditions and ideology and a fairly stable membership. In the early Abbasid period, this was not true; although there were some who would support any Alid claimant, out of religious conviction, there were many

198

others who would support a particular Alid at one time and in one set of circumstances, but might equally support the Abbasids at other periods. The situation was very fluid and membership of the Shi'ite community, if such a group can be said to have existed at this early period, was very fluctuating.

So the accounts of the heresiologist have to be treated with caution, and the historian must try to escape from the limitations of hindsight and examine the problem from the earliest possible sources. There are two distinct features of Shi'ism in this period which deserve consideration. The first is the ideological one. The basic belief which separates Sunni from Shi'i is that the Shi'i believes in the necessity of a divinely guided imam to interpret the Faith, whereas the Sunni holds that the *ijma'* (consensus) of the community is the best guide. The Shi'i will then go on to argue that the family of 'Ali is the best qualified among Muslims to fulfil this role. It was during the early Abbasid period, especially under the guidance of Ja'far al-Sadiq, that these views were developed and the elaboration of the ideas of the imamate was one of the most significant contributions of the period to Islamic religious thought.[2] The second feature to be discussed is the number of Alid rebellions in this period: that is, armed uprisings against the Abbasid regime by groups who wished to see a member of the family of 'Ali as caliph. Those who joined in these rebellions were sometimes, but not always, the same as those who believed in the imamate. Ja'far al-Sadiq and his circle, for example, refused to support any such disturbances; indeed, one of Ja'far's main contributions was to differentiate between caliphate and imamate and so allow an Alid *imam* and his Shi'i followers to live at peace in a Sunni society. Correspondingly, there were others who might join an Alid uprising, not because they believed in the necessity of an *imam* but because they were dissatisfied with the Abbasids, and the Alids seemed the most viable alternative. Thus, many of the notables of Madina who supported Muhammad Nafs al-Zakiya in 145 (762) were won over by the regime and opposed Husayn b.'Ali in 169 (786). It is with this second feature that the political historian must be concerned and this chapter is devoted, not so much to ideological issues, as to investigating who joined each separate Alid uprising and why.

The Abbasid Revolution was only one of a series of armed uprisings against the Umayyad regime in the name of the family of the Prophet. Only ten years before Saffah was proclaimed caliph in the mosque at Kufa, Zayd b.'Ali had led his supporters in a brave but futile resistance to the authorities, in that very mosque. Since then, 'Abd

Allah b.Mu'awiya, though not an Alid himself, had led a rebellion which attracted widespread support among those who considered themselves members of the house of the Prophet, including Abu Ja'far, later to be the caliph Mansur. After the defeat of Ibn Mu'awiya, two different groups claimed the leadership of the family. The first was the Abbasid branch, under the leadership of Ibrahim b.Muhammad, and the second were the sons of 'Abd Allah b.al-Hasan, the Alid. During the confused period of the fall of the Umayyads, 'Abd Allah caused his son Muhammad, known as Nafs al-Zakiya (The Pure Soul) to be acknowledged as 'mahdi', a title which indicated not only that he claimed religious leadership but also that he intended to take militant action to assert his claims.[3] At the time of the revolution, Abu Salama had entered into negotiations with the Alids, with a view to offering one of them the caliphate but, in the event, Abu Muslim's agents in Kufa asserted the claims of the Abbasids and the attempt came to nothing. Muhammad did not, however, relinquish his ambitions and continued his political activity until his premature rebellion in 145 (762).[4]

Naturally, the members of the Alid family were among his most important supporters. Muhammad did not make an hereditary claim to the leadership of the family (after all, his father was still alive), but based his leadership on the Zaydi principle that anyone who was prepared to take military action to assert the rights of the family was entitled to the leadership. This view attracted widespread support among his relatives. The Hasanid branch of the family, from which he himself came, was represented among the rebels by his third cousins, Zayd and 'Ali, sons of Hasan b.Zayd b.Hasan. Two of the sons of the martyred Zayd b.'Ali, Husayn and 'Isa, joined, although their brothers, Hasan and Muhammad, remained aloof.[5] The attitude of the Husaynid branch, who were later to be considered the legitimate 'twelve *imams*', was ambiguous. Ja'far al-Sadiq, the sixth *imam*, had refused to swear allegiance to Muhammad, not because he considered that his branch of the family had the only valid claim, but because of Muhammad's youth (he told Muhammad's father, 'Abd Allah, 'You are an old man and if you wish I will swear allegiance to you but, by God, I will never swear to him.'),[6] and because he feared that the attempt would end in disaster. In fact, he did not consider himself as a divinely appointed *imam* by strictly hereditary succession, but rather treated the family in a traditional tribal way, holding that the leader should be the most able and experienced. There was also an important difference of policy. Ja'far was developing the view that the *imam* should be a religious leader, who need not necessarily encourage his supporters to overthrow the existing regime, while the Zaydis and Muhammad b.'Abd Allah placed much more emphasis on military action.[7] However, Ja'far's nephew, Husayn, did join the rebels. Then there were the non-Alawi Talibis, especially Hasan b.Mu'awiya, who had been governor of Jibal during his brother's rebellion against the Umayyads,[8] and his cousin, Qasim b.Ishaq, both descended from Ja'far b.Abi Talib. It was, in fact, a wide cross-section of the family and there is no evidence that the descendants of 'Ali had split into different, hostile branches. The Alids maintained a conspiracy of silence, when Mansur was trying to track down Muhammad before his rebellion,[9] and even those Alids most closely connected with the regime, like Hasan b.Zayd, did not betray him. 'Isa b.Zayd probably summed up the feeling of the majority when he asked to be allowed to cut off the heads of any Alids who did not accept Muhammad's leadership.[10] Nonetheless, we do find a few Alids in the Abbasid army which crushed the rebellion, notably, Muhammad b.Zayd b.'Ali, Hasan b.Zayd b.Hasan's son, Qasim, and Muhammad b.'Abd Allah al-Ja'fari: a Hasanid, a Husaynid and a Ja'farid, in fact.[11]

Apart from members of his own family, Muhammad's support came almost entirely from the citizens of Madina. These can be divided into two groups: the *ansar*, and the members of the old Qurashi families which had been prominent in the early days of Islam. The *ansar* were the original inhabitants of the town, who had become the 'helpers' of the Prophet after he had left Makka. They had supported the claims of 'Ali and his descendants since the time of the accession of Abu Bakr and, though they were not an important political force, they remained true to their traditional allegiance. Muhammad placed great emphasis on the people of Madina; he refused to leave the city for Egypt or the desert, as some of his advisers urged him[12] and, after he had declared himself, he preached in the mosque of the Prophet, saying how he had chosen the Madinans to be his supporters.[13] But, reading betweeen the lines, there does not seem to have been mass popular support. The numbers quoted are usually very small (Muhammad had 250 supporters when he declared himself and 300 at the final battle) and all the important offices were held, not by the *ansar*, but by members of the old Qurashi families. Even at this late date, the distinction between *muhajirun* and *ansar* was very much apparent.

The most powerful and influential of the Qurashi families were the Zubayrids.[14] Since 'Abd Allah b.Zubayr had made his bid for the caliphate, some seventy years before, they had been politically quiescent. They had no tradition of loyalty to the Alids, and Zubayr b.'Awwam had been one of 'Ali's leading opponents during his lifetime. They must have joined the revolt because they had been excluded from Mansur's government and considered that they would have more influence under a Madina-based regime of which they were founder members. With the Zubayrids there were a number of 'Umaris,[15] descendants of the second caliph, 'Umar b.al-Khattab, who, again, had no tradition of Alid leanings. Also among his early supporters was Muhammad b.'Abd Allah al-'Uthmani, a direct descendant of that 'Uthman b.'Affan who was so bitterly hated by the early supporters of 'Ali. Muhammad was executed before the start of the rebellion for trying to raise support for the cause in Syria and Khurasan.[16] There was even a member of the Umayyad family who threw in his lot with the rebels.[17] It is interesting to note that, as with the Alids, there were some members of these families, like Khubayb b.Thabit al-Zubayri and Abu Salama al-'Umari, who refused to join.[18] It is impossible to tell whether this represents family differences or, more probably, a sort of family insurance scheme: whichever side won, some members of the family would be among the victors. Finally, Muhammad attracted some support from the *badu* of the surrounding desert, especially from the tribes of Juhayna and Sulaym,[19] with whom he had taken refuge when he was hunted by Mansur's agents, but they do not seem to have contributed to his army in the final battle.

There is no evidence of a Shi'ite party as such in Madina, with a programme and an organisation. Muhammad's support was drawn from a variety of groups which hoped they might have something to gain from its success or which hoped that the rebellion would attract attention to their grievances. The situation in Basra, where Muhammad's brother, Ibrahim, rose in revolt, was very similar in this respect.

The accounts of the rebellion of Ibrahim b.'Abd Allah in Basra make it clear that this was a large-scale affair. His army is said to have numbered 100,000 at one time and, besides the city of Basra itself, he also controlled Fars, Ahwaz and Wasit.[20] It is difficult to decide why so many people in this city should have thrown in their lot, however temporarily, with the Alids. The city, unlike Kufa, had no tradition of loyalty to the Alid cause and had never before been the scene of pro-Alid disturbances. When Ibrahim first arrived in the city, he stayed with the Banu Rasib clan, which did have connections with previous pretenders, notably Ibn Hanafiya and 'Abd Allah b.Mu'awiya, but these were the exception.[21] Nor does it seem to have been, on the whole, a movement of *mawali*, since most of the names that have come down to us are Arab. The Arabs do not seem to have come from any particular tribal group in the city and there was even a Taghlibi from Jazira.[22]

Much of the discontent was probably due to the fact that the Abbasid Revolution had not satisfied the aspirations of large sections of the Muslim community who had hoped the end of the Umayyads would improve their political status. The Arabs of Basra were, with a few exceptions like the Muhallabi family, no more part of the Abbasid political élite than they had been of the Umayyad. The most privileged groups under the new regime were the Khurasanis, for whom Mansur was just then founding the new capital at Baghdad. Perhaps, as well, there was discontent at the survival of Umayyad elements in the new regime, and it must have added insult to injury when Mansur, shortly before the rebellion, sent Syrian troops to keep order in the city. These were commanded by Jabir b.Tuba al-Kilabi, who had actually fought with Ibn Hubayra against the Abbasids at the time of the revolution.[23]

Another irritant was the presence of the Muryaniyin.[24] These were the friends and agents of Abu Ayyub al-Muryani, Mansur's chief secretary, who was a native of Khuzistan and used his position at court to advance their interests in the province. We know that the governor of Ahwaz, Muhammad b.al-Husayn, was a friend of Abu Ayyub and it seems likely that Mughira b.Faz', who drove him out in the name of the Alids, was influential in the area and resented Abu Ayyub's newly acquired importance.[25] We are also told of a family of rich Persian landowners in the area, the Dahjaraniya, who offered Ibrahim financial assistance.[26]

These Basran and, perhaps, Khuzi Arabs seem to have been largely opportunist in their support for the Alids. When it came to a confrontation with the Abbasid forces, many of them melted away and there is no record of any subsequent Alid disturbance in the city. This cannot be said of Ibrahim's other main supporters, the group known as the Zaydiya. After the defeat of Zayd b.'Ali's uprising in Kufa, in 122 (740), there remained in the city a small group of activists, ready to support any Alid who attempted to raise a rebellion. They acknowledged Zayd's son, 'Isa, as their leader but he and his followers were quite prepared to throw their weight behind other members of the family who were prepared to take action.

The Zaydiya seem to have joined Ibrahim in three stages, slipping away as best they could from the heavily policed city of Kufa. Sallam b.Abi Wasil, who had been one of the companions of Zayd b.'Ali, and some of his friends split off from the *hajj* and went to Basra, where Sallam was put in charge of the treasury.[27] A bit later, it seems, 'Isa b.Zayd and his brother Husayn, having escaped after the defeat of Muhammad, for whom they had been fighting, came and joined

Ibrahim's army.[28] Thirdly, Harun b.Sa'd al-'Ijli arrived, with some followers from Kufa. For reasons which are not clear, Ibrahim was, for a while, reluctant to use the services of Harun b.Sa'd at all and when he was accepted he was sent off to Wasit, which he took for the rebels. He is described by Sa'd al-Ash'ari as a leader of a sect of the Zaydiya called the 'Ijliya, and this may point to some differences between him and the rest of the movement.[29]

From the beginning, there was tension between the Zaydiya and the Basrans. This tension developed over two points. First, there was the question of leadership; after the death of Muhammad, some of the Zaydiya were in favour of declaring for 'Isa rather than following Ibrahim.[30] Secondly, the Zaydiya were all Kufans. Kufa was held by Mansur with very strong forces. Ibrahim had never been able to enter it on his travels and Kufans wishing to join the rebels had great difficulty in escaping. The Zaydiya wanted to lead the Alid forces to capture their own city[31] and, presumably, to establish it as the capital, while the Basrans wanted to stay in their city and fortify it against the Abbasid forces. Below the surface, there may have been tension between the *'fityan 'arab'*[32] in Basra and non-Arabs in the Zaydiya. These disagreements were kept under control only by the leaders of the Zaydiya, who insisted that first priority should be given to the war against Mansur and, after that, they could turn their attention to internal matters. In the event, they never had the chance because the rebel forces were decisively defeated.

After the collapse of the great Alid rebellion of 145 (762), there was a twenty-four year gap until the next attempt to overthrow the Abbasids in 169 (786). This was probably due, in part, to the conciliatory attitude of Mahdi to the Alid family and to Ja'far al-Sadiq, who was showing that allegiance to the Alid family did not necessarily mean armed uprising. Indeed, there are very few elements of continuity between the rebellion of 145 (762) and later pro-Alid disturbances.

Of these elements of continuity, the most obvious were the Alid family themselves, many of whom were willing to come out in support of any member of the family who revolted, no matter which branch they came from. But there is no evidence that any of them, except 'Isa b.Zayd, engaged in continuous political activity.

The other element of continuity was provided by 'Isa's followers, the Zaydiya. Some said that Muhammad b.'Abd Allah had made 'Isa heir to his brother Ibrahim, so he automatically took over the leadership of the militant Alids after Ibrahim's death. When the Alid armies were defeated, 'Isa took refuge in Kufa, in the house of Hasan b.Salih b.Hayy, who was a member of the Zaydiya, and he remained concealed there until his death.[33] Around him, there was a small clandestine group, who met in secret and discussed military rebellion. Mansur was worried enough about his activities to declare, shortly before he died, that 'Isa was one of the two men he still feared (the other, ironically, being 'Isa b.Musa, who had led the Abbasid forces against both Muhammad b.Abd Allah and Ibrahim).[34] At one time, a meeting of this group was raided by the authorities in Kufa on the instructions of Mahdi but only one man, Ja'far al-Ahmar, was caught and the rest escaped.[35] Furthermore, 'Isa and his group firmly refused the gifts and pensions with which Mahdi and his adviser, Ya'qub b.Dawud, tried to win them over.[36] But all this planning came to nothing for both 'Isa and Hasan b.Salih died before they could take action. But the group did not disperse. It is true that, after 'Isa's death, his two small sons, Ahmad and Zayd, were taken by a member of the sect and entrusted to the care of Mahdi, so that they grew up in the palace;[37] his other surviving son, Husayn, seems to have taken no part in politics, but every Alid who raised a revolt could count on Zaydiya support. They are found supporting Husayn b.'Ali, Yahya b.'Abd Allah and Abu'l-Saraya. One man, 'Amir b.Kathir, fought for Ibrahim, Husayn b.'Ali and Abu'l-Saraya;[38] another, 'Abd Rabbihi b.'Alqama, was with 'Isa b.Zayd, Yahya b.'Abd Allah and Abu'l-Saray.[39] No other group had a similar involvement in military activity in the Alid cause.

Of all the Alid rebellions in this period, the one led by Husayn b.'Ali in Madina, in 169 (786), is the most curious. It is very difficult to imagine that Husayn, with little preparation and pitifully few supporters, can ever have thought that he stood a chance of success against the might of the Abbasid state. The only information we have about Husayn's activity before this date is that he went to Baghdad and Kufa in the reign of Mahdi. He was given 40,000 *dinars* by the caliph, which he then gave away in the two towns.[40] The story is told to illustrate his generosity, but it may well be that he was giving lavish presents so that he would be accepted as the leader of the Alid family. It is significant that, on this trip, he was accompanied by Hasan b.Hudhayl, a prominent member of the Zaydiya, and he must have sought support in that quarter.

Although he may have had political ambitions before the year of his rebellion, these were given added impetus by the change of government which followed the death of Mahdi. His successor, Hadi, was closely connected with the Khurasani military and immediately changed his father's conciliatory policy to the Alids, withdrawing the gifts and allowances he had made to members of the family.[41] To add to this, Husayn was very heavily in debt. He was borrowing money and selling estates and, when he died in battle, he is said to have left 200,000 *dinar*s in unpaid debts.[42] This financial plight, coupled with the withdrawal of subsidies, may have driven him to rash action.

The immediate cause was the system of mutual surveillance among the Alids, used by the government to keep a check on them. Husayn and Yahya b.'Abd Allah were both accountable to the authorities for Hasan b.Muhammad, son of Nafs al-Zakiya, and, when Hasan disappeared, they were held responsible by the governor of Madina, 'Umar b.'Abd al-'Aziz al-'Umari.[43] As a result of this persecution, Husayn proclaimed himself *amir al-mu'minin,* in the mosque of the Prophet, on 13 Dhu'l-Qa'ada 169 (17 May 786). The response was very small and, with about 300 men, he barricaded himself in the mosque. On 24 May, he was allowed to leave Madina and he headed for Makka.[44] On the way he was intercepted by the Abbasid troops who had accompanied the *hajj* and was defeated and killed.

Given the circumstances and causes of his rebellion, it is not surprising that his main support came from members of his own family. They were mostly Hasanids (Muhammad al-Nafs al-Zakiya's brothers, Yahya, Sulayman and Idris; Ibrahim b.Tabataba, 'Umar b.al-Hasan b.'Ali b.al-Hasan and 'Abd Allah b.Ishaq b.Ibrahim), but there were also Husaynids ('Abd Allah, son of Ja'far al-Sadiq, and 'Abd Allah b.al-Hasan al-Aftas).[45] Apart from the Alids, twenty-six in all, there were some of their *mawali* and some pilgrims, including some of the Zaydiya, who had come from Kufa to join him.[46] The list is very short. There are a number of conspicuous abstentions. Neither the *ansar* nor the old Islamic families joined in, and the people of Madina cursed him as he made his ignominious exit from the town. Mahdi's generosity seems to have won the people over, and it is significant that his governor in the town at the time of the rebellion should have come from the 'Umari family, many of whom had supported Muhammad al-Nafs al-Zakiya. Nor did he have the contacts among the *badu,* which Muhammad had had. There was a last card he tried to play, after he had left Madina; he appealed to the slaves in Makka and said that he would give them their freedom if they joined him. There was some response, but the Abbasid forces were already upon him and it was too late.

Although the rebellion of Husayn had ended so ignominiously, it did have one important consequence. After it was all over, some of the members of the Alid family involved fled to remote corners of the Islamic world in an effort to escape the agents of the caliph. One of these was a brother of Muhammad b.'Abd Allah (The Pure Soul), who escaped, probably with the help of the Zaydiya, to Daylam, a mountainous and still largely independent area at the southeast corner of the Caspian Sea. Six years later, he allowed himself to be persuaded by Fadl b.Yahya, the Barmakid, to accept an *aman* and surrendered himself to the Abbasid forces. Perhaps he had found the hill peoples uncongenial and doubted their loyalty. He was taken to Baghdad, where he subsequently died in mysterious circumstances.[47] However, his brief stay in the area, where he was accompanied by some of the Zaydiya, does seem to have laid the foundations for subsequent Zaydi involvement in Daylam.

After the disaster of 169 (786), Alid activity in the central Islamic lands seems to have come to a virtual halt. Harun's government was powerful and effective and no members of the family seem to have been eager to engage in a trial of strength with it. After the siege of Baghdad and the death of Amin, the position was greatly changed. Ma'mun and his adviser, Fadl b.Sahl, were trying to govern the Muslim world from Marw, the capital of Khurasan, and their hold over Iraq was tenuous. In addition, the government was very unpopular and many Iraqis resented being ruled from distant Khurasan.[48] In these circumstances, it was natural that people would again begin to look to the Alid family for leadership.

The origins of the rebellion of 199 (815) seem to have been very haphazard and there is no suggestion of a carefully worked-out plan. A certain Nasr b.Shabib, hoping to take advantage of the collapse of law and order, left his native Jazira and went to Madina to search for a member of the Alid family who would co-operate with him in raising a rebellion.[49] Muhammad b.Ibrahim b.Tabataba agreed to go with him but, when they reached Jazira, Nasr found that he could not raise much support among the people, who had never shown much interest in the Alid cause before, and he was reduced to paying Muhammad to go away.[50] Thus humiliated, Muhammad was returning to Madina, when he was met by Abu'l-Saraya. Abu'l-Saraya, whose real name was Sarri b.Mas'ud al-Shaybani, had been a soldier in Harthama's army, but had been paid off when his leader was recalled to Marw. He had taken to brigandage, but had not been very successful and was forced to take refuge in the desert with a few followers.[51] He and Muhammad decided to work together. Abu'l-Saraya seems to have been a complete adventurer and there is no record of his involvement in pro-Alid activity before, but he saw it as a wonderful opportunity to win support he had not been able to attract in his own name.

They decided to base their movement on the traditional Alid stronghold of Kufa. Kufa had been quiet during the early Abbasid period, partly, at least, because the caliphs kept it under very strict guard, but the people had not completely lost their enthusiasm for the Alid cause and the rebellion was an immediate success. The governor, Fadl b.al-'Abbas, a member of the Abbasid family and the grandson of 'Isa b.Musa, who had ruled the city for many years after the revolution, was unable to offer any effective resistance and fled the city. Abu'l-Saraya soon defeated Zuhayr b.al-Musayyab, the general sent against him by Hasan b.Sahl, Ma'mun's administrator in Iraq.[52] The success was temporarily interrupted by the sudden death of Muhammad b.Ibrahim. Tabari suggests that he may have been poisoned by Abu'l-Saraya for taking too independent a line, and that his successor, Muhammad b.Muhammad b.Zayd b.'Ali, was an impostor produced by him to fill the gap.[53] There seems no real evidence for this. The pro-Alid Isfahani says that the succession was settled after a public discussion in the mosque at Kufa.[54] Muhammad, although still a young man, was accepted because he was prepared to take the risks involved in leading the rebellion, a classic statement of the Zaydi viewpoint on choosing a leader. Furthermore, he was a grandson of Zayd b.'Ali, who had made a heroic last stand against the troops of the Umayyads in that very mosque, three-quarters of a century before, and this must have made his succession more acceptable.

After this smooth change-over, governors were sent out to all the important cities of southern Iraq and the Hijaz, and coins were minted in the name of Muhammad b.Muhammad.[55] The next year, 200 (815/6), was less successful. Hasan b.Sahl persuaded Harthama to lead his army against Kufa[56] and he seems to have found numerous recruits among the Baghdadis, who would have been very suspicious of a Kufan attempt to take over the leadership of the area. The Kufans proved to have little appetite for a long, hard struggle; with Harthama outside the city walls, Abu'l-Saraya and Muhammad b.Muhammad felt their position in the city getting weaker, and they may even have been given an ultimatum by prominent citizens. They slipped away during the night[57] but, with Kufa gone, their cause was lost and they were defeated near Ahwaz. Then they headed north, hoping to take refuge in Abu'l-Saraya's home territory in Jazira, but they were arrested on the way, Abu'l-Saraya was executed and Muhammad b.Muhammad sent to Ma'mun's court in Marw.[58]

The rebellion attracted widespread support among members of the Alid family, some of whom were appointed as governors to cities which came under rebel control. Muhammad b.Ibrahim, the first leader, was a Hasanid, Muhammad b.Muhammad came from the Zaydi branch of the Husaynids and his brother, Ja'far, was sent as governor to Wasit. Other Husaynids were equally prominent; two sons (Ibrahim and Zayd) of the 'twelver *imam*', Musa al-Kazim, were sent as governors to Yaman and Ahwaz, respectively, while another Husaynid, Hasan al-Aftas, took charge in Makka. Finally, as so often, there was a Ja'fari, 'Abbas b.Muhammad, who was sent to Basra.[59]

Apart from the members of the family, the Zaydiya, of course, played a prominent role. These included Hasan b.Hudhayl, who had been with Husayn b.'Ali and who seems to have been accepted as leader of the group. There was also 'Amir b.Kathir al-Sarraj, who had fought for both Ibrahim b.'Abd Allah, in 145 (762), and Husayn b.'Ali, in 169 (786), 'Abd Rabbihi b.'Alqama, who had been a partisan of 'Isa b.Zayd and Yahya b.'Abd Allah, and others.[60] These were obviously men who had long believed in the Alid cause and in the necessity for armed struggle, and they constituted a hard-core of militant revolutionaries.

The rest of the Kufans were less committed to the cause. Isfahani says[61] that all the people of Kufa joined, except those without wealth or merit, but there are some hints that the *ashraf*, the wealthy leaders of the community, were less enthusiastic than the common people. In the battle against the army of Harthama, the Kufans were spoken of, by their enemies, admittedly, as *ghawgha'* and *ru'a'*, words which mean mob or common people.[62] The *ashraf* were quick to make peace with Harthama when Abu'l-Saraya had been forced to leave the city and one of their number, a member of the family of Ash'ath b.Qays al-Kindi, was appointed as governor. Not all the *ashraf*, however, were hostile to the Alids and some Ash'athis had earlier supported the rebels. Almost all the supporters of whom we have information came from Kufa. Although Abu'l-Saraya boasted that he was the 'lion of Shayban' there is no record of any of his fellow tribesmen joining him. Shaybanis became Kharijis and Shaybanis accepted the leadership of Yazid b.Mazyad and his family but they did not, on the whole, support the Alids.

Isfahani claims that the number of supporters in Kufa was as high as 200,000[63] and, while this figure is probably an exaggeration, it does suggest that it was a widespread popular movement. Besides the traditional enthusiasm of the Kufans for the Alid cause, there were certainly other factors which induced so many Kufans to throw in their lot with Abu'l-Saraya. There was a general dislike of the Abbasid system because of the dominant influence of the military, almost all Khurasani in origin. The people of Kufa, who had played such an important part in the early history of Islam, were reduced to the same frustrating impotence, under Abbasid rule, as they had been under the Umayyads. In Baghdad, during the siege of Amin's reign, there had been a popular uprising, aimed especially at the military and the ruling class in general. It may well be that many Kufans felt these sentiments as well and expressed them in support for the Alids.

Some of the frustration, too, may have been due to difficult economic circumstances and the general decline of Kufa. The growth of Baghdad and its establishment as the leading city of central Iraq must have damaged Kufa's position. Ya'qubi says that the *wujuh* (leading citizens) and richest merchants had left the city for Baghdad.[64] On top of this long-term decline, the civil war and the breakdown of government must have brought more economic problems. The Arab historians provide no information on this, but it seems that trade must have been drastically reduced by the disturbances in all parts of the caliphate and that irrigation and agriculture in Iraq would have suffered from the constant fighting and the depredations of wandering bands of soldiers. Abu'l-Saraya himself, it will be remembered, was an unemployed soldier who was driven, first to brigandage and then to supporting the Alids. For many others in Kufa and the surrounding area, it was a time of considerable hardship and they would be likely to respond to the promise of better things to come, under Alid leadership. The government of Ma'mun was distant and alien, and no Iraqi, either Baghdadi or Kufan, could easily accept the prospect of government from Marw, which would take no account of their needs and hopes.

The rebellion of Abu'l-Saraya, in Kufa, was the most effective of the Alid movements during the civil war, but it was not the only one. There was its offshoot in Makka, which must be briefly considered. Husayn b.al-Hasan al-Aftas was sent to Makka by Abu'l-Saraya, to lead the *hajj* of 199 (815). With the help of Alid sympathisers in the town, and the unwillingness of the Abbasid governor, Dawud b.'Isa, to fight, he easily entered and took control.[65] Makka, unlike neighbouring Madina, had shown very little enthusiasm for the Alid cause before this time, and such support as there was soon began to melt away. According to Tabari, the Alids alienated the local population by persecuting the Abbasids in the city and stripping precious metal from the mosque. After the defeat of Abu'l-Saraya, when it became obvious that the position of the Alids was very weak, Husayn tried to strengthen his position by persuading a much-respected Alid in the city, Muhammad b.Ja'far al-Sadiq, to allow himself to be elected caliph. But this was less successful than he had hoped, for Muhammad was a very old man and his son, 'Ali, scandalised the Makkans by his public immorality.[66] So when, eventually, forces arrived from Iraq, Muhammad was supported only by a mob of water-carriers, black slaves and others, and was easily defeated.[67] Admittedly, this account is based on the hostile narrative in Tabari, but the fact that Isfahani does not go into it may suggest that it was not a very creditable episode. It is interesting, however, to note that, in Makka, as in Kufa, the lower classes seem to have provided much of the Alid support, and it is interesting to recall that Husayn b.'Ali, in 169 (786), had attempted to attract the support of the slaves in Makka, at the end of his rebellion. There were occasions when support for the Alids was an attempt at social revolution.

The end of the rebellion of Abu'l-Saraya marked a turning-point in the history of the Alid movement. It was the last of the large-scale popular uprisings in the central Islamic lands, which had begun with Mukhtar's revolt, a century before. From this point, support for the Alids, which we can begin to call Shi'ism, in the modern sense of the word, began to take different forms. The most important reason for this was probably the attempt made by Ma'mun and his advisers to reach a reconciliation with the Alids. When the revolt in Makka was crushed, many of the leading Alids were taken in captivity to Marw, where Muhammad b.Muhammad, the Kufa leader, was already installed. It was one of these leaders, Muhammad b.Ja'far's nephew, 'Ali b.Musa, who was chosen by Ma'mun to be his heir. The reasons for this move have been discussed elsewhere in this book,[68] but it seems that this winning over of some of the militant Alids must have played a part in the ensuing peace between the two rival families. Even after the death of 'Ali b.Musa, Ma'mun's government maintained much closer links with the Alids than previous Abbasid regimes had done, and the official adoption of the Mu'tazila policy was designed to help such a reconciliation.

This process was certainly helped by the development of the doctrine of the imamate, which meant that the spiritual authority of an Alid leader was distinguished from secular authority. This meant that an Alid could be accepted as *imam* but not as caliph, and his followers would not be expected to come out in armed revolt. Only on the fringes of the Islamic world did militant Shi'ism continue to be influential. In Daylam, Yaman and Morocco the local people, or, at least, sections of them, came to display their separatism by openly adhering to militant support of the Alids.

Notes

1. See, for example, Nawbakhti, *Firaq al-Shi'ah* (Najaf, 1959); Ash'ari, *Maqalat al-Islamiyin*, ed. H. Ritter (Istanbul, 1920-30); 'Abd al-Qahir al-Baghdadi, *Farq bayn al-Firaq*, ed. Kawthari (Cairo, 1948); Shahrastani, *Kitab al-Milal wa'l-Nihal*, ed. M.S. Kaylani (Cairo, 1961). For a discussion of these sources and further bibliography, see Watt, *Formative Period of Islamic Thought*, pp. 1-6, 326.
2. Jafri, *Shi'a Islam*, pp. 289-312.
3. Isfahani, *Maqatil*, pp. 237-54.
4. For the details of the rebellion, see above, pp. 67-8.
5. Tabari, *Ta'rikh*, p. 258; Isfahani, *Maqatil*, pp. 268, 277-8.
6. Isfahani, *Maqatil*, p. 254.
7. See Oman, *Abbasid Husaynid Relations* (Arabica, vol. 22, 1975).
8. Tabari, *Ta'rikh*, vol. 2, p. 1977, vol. 3, p. 202; Isfahani, *Maqatil*, pp. 268, 278.
9. Tabari, *Ta'rikh*, vol. 3, p. 144.
10. Isfahani, *Maqatil*, p. 296.
11. Ibid., p. 268.
12. Tabari, *Ta'rikh*, vol. 3, pp. 227-8; Isfahani, *Maqatil*, p. 268.
13. Tabari, *Ta'rikh*, vol. 3, p. 197.
14. Ibid., vol. 3, pp. 198-9; Isfahani, *Maqatil*, pp. 268, 279, 285, 286.
15. Tabari, *Ta'rikh*, vol. 3, pp. 198, 231, 238-9; Isfahani, *Maqatil*, p. 289.
16. Tabari, *Ta'rikh*, vol. 3, pp. 173-83.
17. Ibid., vol. 3, p. 259.
18. Ibid., vol. 3, p. 199.
19. Ibid., vol. 3, pp. 156, 157, 167, 177, 196, 228, 248; Isfahani, *Maqatil*, p. 286.
20. For details of the rebellion, see above, pp. 68-70.
21. Ash'ari, *Maqalat*, pp. 55-6, 60.
22. Tabari, *Ta'rikh*, vol. 3, p. 290.
23. Ibid., vol. 3, p. 22; Isfahani, *Maqatil*, p. 322.
24. Isfahani, *Maqatil*, pp. 333-4.
25. Ibid., pp. 324-5.
26. Ibid., p. 333.
27. Ibid., pp. 354-5.
28. Ibid., p. 370.
29. Tabari, *Ta'rikh*, vol. 3, pp. 302-4; Isfahani, *Maqatil*, pp. 331-2.
30. Isfahani, *Maqatil*, p. 370.
31. Ibid., p. 344.
32. Ibid., p. 318.
33. Ibid., p. 408.
34. Tabari, *Ta'rikh*, vol. 3, p. 448.
35. Isfahani, *Maqatil*, pp. 416-19.
36. Ibid., p. 411.
37. Ibid., pp. 422-4.
38. Ibid., pp. 362, 457, 552.
39. Ibid., pp. 416, 485, 552.
40. Tabari, *Ta'rikh*, vol. 3, p. 563; Isfahani, *Maqatil*, pp. 441-2.
41. Ya'qubi, *Ta'rikh*, vol. 2, p. 488.
42. Isfahani, *Maqatil*, pp. 442, 483.
43. Tabari, *Ta'rikh*, vol. 3, p. 552.
44. Tabari, *Ta'rikh*, vol. 3, p. 556; Isfahani, *Maqatil*, p. 449.
45. Isfahani, *Maqatil*, p. 446.

46. Ibid., p. 449.
47. See above, pp. 119-20.
48. See above, p. 152.
49. Isfahani, *Maqatil*, p. 518.
50. Tabari, *Ta'rikh*, vol. 3, p. 560.
51. Ibid., vol. 3, pp. 976-7; Isfahani, *Maqatil*, p. 521.
52. Ibid., vol. 3, p. 978; Isfahani, *Maqatil*, p. 526.
53. Tabari, *Ta'rikh*, vol. 3, p. 978.
54. Isfahani, *Maqatil*, p. 532.
55. Tabari, *Ta'rikh*, vol. 3, p. 979; Isfahani, *Maqatil*, pp. 533-4.
56. See above, p. 153.
57. Tabari, *Ta'rikh*, vol. 3, pp. 984-5; Isfahani, *Maqatil*, p. 546.
58. Tabari, *Ta'rikh*, vol. 3, pp. 985-6; Isfahani, *Maqatil*, pp. 548-9.
59. Isfahani, *Maqatil*, pp. 532-3.
60. Ibid., p. 552.
61. Ibid., p. 551.
62. Ibid., p. 544.
63. Ibid., p. 551.
64. Ya'qubi, *Buldan*, p. 235.
65. Tabari, *Ta'rikh*, vol. 3, pp. 981-4.
66. Ibid., vol. 3, p. 990.
67. Ibid., vol. 3, p. 992.
68. See above, pp. 157-8.

A NOTE ON THE SOURCES

The history of the early Abbasid period has to be reconstructed from the literary and historical writings of contemporary and near contemporary authors.[1] Faced by the almost total absence of contemporary administrative documents, except for coins and archaeological evidence which has barely been investigated, we must rely almost exclusively on such accounts. This has its advantages for the modern historian. There is a vast bulk of literary material dealing with this period, much more than for any comparable length of time in classical history or the history of western Europe before the twelfth century. Furthermore, much of this writing is of a very high standard, simple and vivid. We have excellent accounts of the rulers and their courtiers, of the way they behaved and conducted their business. There are, however, problems posed by the nature of the material, which must affect the modern historian's approach. The first is that we have very little information about day-to-day administration. Clearly, there was a large and sophisticated organisation for collecting taxes and paying salaries, but we know almost nothing of its methods of operation. Equally, the literary material tends to be very court-orientated; that is to say that the affairs of the caliph and his counsellors receive very detailed coverage, while the doings of lesser mortals and life in the provinces are comparatively neglected. Finally, there is the problem of bias. The writers on whom we rely were composing their works, for the most part, in areas still ruled by the Abbasid dynasty, and so we must consider the extent to which they suppressed or altered the accounts they had, to suit the political climate they were working in. It is important to recognise these limitations of the sources, because they not only affect our point of view on particular events or personalities, but they also determine the sort of history we can write. The history of the Abbasid caliphate is bound to be vastly different from the history of, say, early mediaeval Catalonia or later mediaeval England, where there is an abundance of administrative documents but a comparative dearth of chronicle sources. We cannot make up for the deficiency, but we can at least be aware of it and acknowledge that we have a fascinating but rather one-sided view of politics in the period.

214

Naturally, it is to the writers of history that we turn first for an account of the early Abbasid period. The histories of this period can be divided into two types; the universal histories, which attempt to cover the affairs of the whole Islamic world, and the local or town histories which are less ambitious but often just as interesting.

Of the universal historians, the greatest is Tabari. He was born in 225 (839), in the city of Amul, in Tabaristan, but soon left his native city to pursue his education at the centres of Islamic learning. After visiting Syria and Egypt, he settled in Baghdad, in about 258 (871/2) and that city was his permanent residence until his death in 310 (923). He was greatly respected by his contemporaries for his scholarship, and his *Ta'rikh al-Rusul wa'l-Muluk* is the most comprehensive account we have of the early Islamic state.[2] It begins with an account of the patriarchs and prophets, culminating in Muhammad, and then goes on to give a detailed account of the Rashidun, Umayyads and Abbasids, up to 302 (915). His account of the Abbasids is composed of two different sorts of information. The first sort is bare mentions of events, appointments of governors and other officials, the travels of the caliph and the names of the leaders of the *hajj* and the *sa'ifa*, which must be taken from official records now lost. On to this framework, he attaches narratives and detailed circumstantial accounts of events he considered important. For the Umayyad period and the early years of the Abbasid caliphate, the author was heavily dependent on previous historians, like Mada'ini and Abu Mikhnaf, but from the reign of Mansur onwards, he makes less use of these. Much of his information is anonymous, but he also uses the accounts of contemporary observers. Some of these were members of the Abbasid family, others were court officials or members of their families; much of the information we have about the events connected with the death of Hadi and the accession of Harun, for example, comes from Yahya b.al-Hasan b.'Abd al-Khaliq, who was the uncle of Fadl b.al-Rabi' and whose own father played a minor role in the events himself. Equally, much of the information about the battle of Rayy, in 195 (811), comes from Ahmad b.Hisham, who was Tahir's *sahib al-shurta* at the time. Whether these accounts were written down in the form of memoirs, or simply passed on by word of mouth, is not clear. Nonetheless, Tabari's account rests heavily on eyewitness reports, which make it both vivid and, perhaps, unreliable.

The first point to note, when assessing his reliability, is that the sources we can identify almost all come from a fairly small group of courtiers and government officials. This means that he is one-sided, in the sense that he reflects the views of the governing élite, he largely ignores the provinces (with the exception of Khurasan) and he has little to say about the lives of those outside the charmed circle. The second point to consider is whether he should be regarded as a propagandist for the Abbasid dynasty. There is some evidence which would support this point of view; Tabari makes almost no mention of the massacre of the Mawsilis by Abbasid troops, in 133 (750/1), and fails to note the terms of the *aman* given by Mansur to his uncle, 'Abd Allah b.'Ali, but subsequently dishonoured by the caliph. The second omission is especially significant, since Azdi quotes the full text from Mada'ini, whom Tabari himself used as a source; in fact, Tabari must have seen the text but neglected to use it. But there are many other indications which make it seem unlikely that this was part of a systematic propaganda work. Tabari gives considerable space to the unedifying manœuvres by which Mansur sought to dispose of his uncle, he recounts the betrayal and execution of Yahya b.'Abd Allah, the Alid, by Harun, and the brutal treatment of the Barmakids; above all, the bulk of his account of the Alid rising of 145 (762/3) is taken directly from the account of the pro-Alid 'Umar b.Shabba and no attempt is made to denigrate the Alid pretender. Tabari, in fact, may be guilty of sins of omission, but not, it would seem, of systematic distortion.

None of the other general histories is as full and complex as Tabari's. Ya'qubi – died, 284 (897) – wrote a generation before Tabari.[3] Although he was himself sympathetic to the Alids, this does not seriously affect his narrative, which ranges widely over affairs at court but also includes details of governors in such provinces as Armenia and Sind, which Tabari does not always notice. Ya'qubi seems to have worked mostly at the Tahirid court in Khurasan and this gives his work a rather different slant from the very Baghdad-centred approach of Tabari. Baladhuri – died, *c.* 279 (892/3) – on the other hand, was a courtier to the caliph Mutawwakil and was therefore close to the Abbasid dynasty. But here, again, his political leanings did not seriously affect his discussion of the early Abbasid period. His *Ansab al-Ashraf* does not follow the chronological pattern of Tabari and Ya'qubi, but is, rather, a vast series of biographies.[4] Most of the subjects he deals with lived before the period covered in this book, but his account of the Abbasid Revolution, especially the Abbasid take-over of Basra, the reign of Saffah and the rebellion of 'Abd Allah b.'Ali, are vital contributions to our understanding. He, like Tabari, is heavily dependent on courtiers and members of the ruling family for his material and, again, this leads to a certain neglect of provincial affairs. Rather different is his other surviving work, the *Futuh al-Buldan.*[5] This is an account of the Arab conquest of the provinces of the Islamic world. Naturally, most of the events he describes took place in the early years of Islam, but he does discuss the subsequent history of disturbed provinces like Sind and Ifriqiya, on which he gives us much new information.

Where Baladhuri is fairly remote and dispassionate, the next source to be considered is strongly and obviously partisan. The *Maqatil al-Talibiyin* of Abu'l-Faraj al-Isfahani — died, 365 (975) — is an account of the martyrdoms of the various Alid claimants to the caliphate.[6] He gives accounts of the various rebellions and, most valuably, detailed lists of those who participated, so enabling the historian to have some idea of the composition of the Alid movement at this time. On questions of fact, he and Tabari rarely disagree, but their interpretations and opinions are often different. This does not in any way detract from the usefulness of the *Maqatil*, which is vital for an understanding of the most important opposition movement within the Muslim world.

Jahshiyari — died, 306 (912) — was a leading member of the Abbasid bureaucracy in the late third (tenth) century. It is not surprising, therefore, that his *Kitab al-Wuzara'* (Book of Wazirs) is full of praise for bureaucrats of a previous generation.[7] The Barmakids and their followers are the heroes of the book, and their opponents, like Fadl b.al-Rabi', are severely treated. The book is also very limited in its concentration on affairs at court and the historian should be careful before accepting all his judgement at face value; for Jahshiyari, the political events of the first Abbasid century were no more than a series of court intrigues, and friendship, hatred and jealousy were the main motive forces of his characters.

To find an antidote to the excessively metropolitan concerns of most of the general historians, it is necessary to turn to provincial writers. Naturally, these vary greatly in scope and usefulness. Some large and prosperous areas, like Khurasan or Basra, have left no detailed accounts of local affairs in this period at all. In others, the local history is only a bare outline of events, like the anonymous *Ta'rikh-i Sistan*[8] or Ibn al-'Adim's — died, 660 (1261) — work on Aleppo[9] (although both these, it should be noted, are much fuller for later periods). Two provinces have left us local histories of real distinction. In Egypt, political affairs are covered, in a dry but meticulous fashion, by Muhammed b.Yusuf al-Kindi — died, 350 (961).[10] While he allows himself few digressions, he is always careful to give precise details of the comings and goings of the governors and their subordinates. His perspective is confined to the Arab ruling class in Fustat and

Alexandria, the vast Coptic population of the country being no more than an occasional nuisance, but, within these limitations, his work is invaluable. Abu Zakariyya al-Azdi's − died, 334 (946) − *Ta'rikh al-Mawsil* is a much broader work.[11] While concentrating on the affairs of his native city, he tries, as Kindi does not, to integrate them into the general history of the caliphate. He is less methodical than the Egyptian but makes much fuller use of vivid eye-witness accounts and contemporary documents. Both these works introduce us to local historical traditions which are quite separate from the one used by the court historians, and provide a useful check on them. They also show that provincial political life had its own personalities and interest and was not simply a branch of the Baghdad administration.

In the third (ninth) century, the Arabs began to develop a tradition of geographical writing.[12] This originated in the form of guide-books for those wishing to use the *barid* (official post) to travel around the Muslim world. Almost all the early geographers devote considerable space to detailing the various staging posts on the *barid* and the distance betwen them. In addition, some of them mention the revenue which should be derived from each of the provinces, a useful source for estimating the relative importance and prosperity of different areas. To enliven this rather austere formula, geographers took to adding short accounts of different places and of marvels or historical events connected with them. Some of these additions are entirely fanciful, but others provide information of real value. Ibn Khurdadhbih − died, 300 (912) − the earliest writer in this genre whose work has come down to us, describes the political geography of both Khurasan and North Africa in some detail.[13] The historian, Ya'qubi, also wrote a geography, the *Buldan*, which, besides the usual accounts of routes to be followed, gives us the earliest and fullest accounts of the foundation and population of Baghdad and Samarra, accounts which are a major contribution to our understanding of the period.[14] Slightly later was Qudama b.Ja'far − died, 337 (948/9). Only part of Qudama's work is available in print, but in that, besides the itineraries, the author gives us the most complete account of the taxation system, especially as it operated in the all-important provinces of the Sawad.[15] Finally Ibn al-Faqih, known as Hamadhani − died, 365 (975) − after his native town, produced a geography which is much more literary and anecdotal in character than the others.[16] Most of this information is of little direct benefit to the political historian, but, in two important areas, he makes a real contribution. The first of these is in the account of the Arab conquest and settlement of Tabaristan and the second is the discussion of the origins of the Barmakid family. Of course, these writers only represent the beginning of the great Arab tradition of geographical writing, but their successors have little new to add about the early Abbasid period, and accounts dating from later centuries must be used with some caution when trying to assess conditions at that time.

Finally, mention must be made of the Christian writers of the period.[17] Although they were writing within the Muslim world and some of them wrote in Arabic, they belong to a completely different historiographical tradition. They use previous Christian chronicles but never refer to contemporary Muslim ones. Their work is of great value because it provides a check on the Muslim sources and because it expresses a view different from that of the Muslim élite. The *Kitab al-'Unwan* is an Arabic chronicle, written in a matter-of-fact style by Agapius, a tenth-century bishop of Manbij, in northern Syria.[18] Unlike most of his co-religionists, he has little interest in church affairs and devotes most of his work to political events. As might be expected, he is well informed on events in his own area, like the revolt of 'Abd Allah b.'Ali, but also provides useful details about events as far away as Khurasan. Unfortunately, the history breaks off at the beginning of Mahdi's reign and the rest of the manuscript is lost. Also in Arabic is the *History of the Coptic Patriarchs of Alexandria*[19] but it has none of the range of Agapius' work, being largely a catalogue of the persecution and trials which his church suffered at the hands of the Muslims and other Christian sects. Although he lived many years after the events, Michael the Syrian's Syriac *Chronicle* is clearly based on good early sources.[20] This is especially true of his account of Jazira and northern Syria during the civil war which followed the death of Harun, a subject on which he is more interesting than any of the Muslim authorities. Important for different reasons is the Syriac *Chronicle* ascribed (wrongly) to Dionysius of Tell-Mahré. As Cahen has pointed out, this provides very important information about the tax system which both Christian and Muslims in the area found very oppressive.[21] The Christian sources are nothing like as comprehensive as the Muslim, but they do provide information on certain areas which we cannot neglect.

The different classes of source material each have their own strengths and weaknesses and it is important that the latter be borne in mind. Nevertheless, the general standard of writing is very high. Not only is the level of historical understanding impressive and the command of detail good, but the writing is often very vivid and immediate. One of the chief pleasures in studying the early Abbasid period is to be able to do so through the eyes of such intelligent and articulate observers.

Notes

1. This chapter is intended as an introduction to the sources for the general reader and does not pretend to be comprehensive. The specialist wanting further details should refer to H. Kennedy, 'Politics and the Political Elite in the Early Abbasid Caliphate', unpublished PhD thesis, Cambridge, 1977, pp. i-xlvii.

2. Tabari, *Ta'rikh al-Rusul wa'l Muluk*, ed. M.J. de Goeje *et al.* (Leiden, 1879-1901). For details of his life, see Ibn al-Nadim, *Fihrist*, pp. 234-5; Yaqut, *Irshad*, vol. 6, pp. 423-62; Margoliouth, *Arabic Historians*, pp. 101-11; Petersen, *'Ali and Mu'awiyah*, pp. 149-58; 'Tabari' in EI (1).

3. Ya'qubi, *Ta'rikh*, ed. M. Houtsma (Leiden, 1883). For further details, see Yaqut, *Irshad*, vol. 2, pp. 156-7; Petersen, *'Ali and Mu'awiyah*, pp. 169-74; Y. Marquet, 'Le Si'isme au IXe Siècle' in *Arabica*, vol. 19 (1972).

4. Baladhuri, *Ansab al-Ashraf*, Instanbul Manuscript Suleymaniye Kutuphanesi, Reisulkuttap, no. 597. For further details, see Ibn al-Nadim, *Fihrist*, p. 113; Yaqut, *Irshad*, vol. 2, pp. 127-32; Margoliouth, *Arabic Historians*, pp. 116-19; Petersen, *'Ali and Mu'awiyah*, pp. 136-48; 'Baladhuri' in EI (2); see also the introduction by Goitein to his edition of vol. 5 of the *Ansab al-Ashraf*.

5. Baladhuri, *Futuh al-Buldan*, ed. S. Munajjid (Cairo, 1957).

6. Isfahani, *Maqatil al-Talibiyin*, ed. D.S. Saqr (Cairo, 1949). For the details of his life, see Ibn al-Nadim, *Fihrist*, p. 155, and Yaqut, *Irshad*, vol. 5, pp. 149-68, both of which give most attention to the author's other work, the famous *Kitab al-Aghani*.

7. Jahshiyari, *Kitab al-Wuzara'*, ed. M. al-Saqqa *et al.* (Cairo, 1938) and Jahshiyari, *Lost Fragments of the Kitab al-Wuzara'*, ed. M. Awwad (Damascus, 1943). See Sourdel, 'Le Valeur litteraire et documentaire du "Livre des Vizirs" d'al-Gahsiyari' in *Arabica*, vol. 2 (1955).

8. Anon, *Ta'rikh-i Sistan*, ed. Malik al-Shu'ara Bahar (Tehran, 1935).

9. Ibn al-'Adim, *Zubdat al-halab min ta'rikh Halab*, ed. S. Dahhan (Damascus, 1951).

10. Kindi, *Kitab al-Wulat*, ed. R. Guest (London, 1912).

11. Azdi, *Ta'rikh al-Mawsil*, ed. A. Habibah (Cairo, 1967).

12. For the early development of Arabic geographical writing, see 'Djughrafiya' in EI (2), and A. Miquel, *La geographie humaine du Monde Musulmane* (Paris, 1967).

13. Ibn Khurdadhbih, *Kitab al-Masalik wa'l-Mamalik*, ed. M. de Goeje (Leiden, 1889).

14. Ya'qubi, *Kitab al-Buldan*, ed. M. de Goeje (Leiden, 1892).

15. Qudama b.Ja'far, *Kitab al-Kharaj*, ed. M. de Goeje (Leiden, 1889).

16. Ibn al-Faqih, *Kitab al-Buldan*, ed. M. de Goeje (Leiden, 1885).

17. For Christian historians who wrote in Syriac, see J.B. Segal, 'Syriac Chronicles as source material for the History of Islamic Peoples' in *Historians of the Middle East*, ed. B. Lewis and P.M. Holt (London, 1962). For Christian writers in Arabic, see the basic biographical and bibliographical data in G. Graf, *Geschichte der Christlichen Arabischen Literatur*, vol. 2 (Rome, 1947).

18. Agapius of Manbij, *Kitab al-'Unwan*, ed. with French translation by A. Vasiliev in *Patrologia Orientalis*, vol. 8 (Paris, 1911). See Graf, *Geschichte*, vol. 2, pp. 39-40.

19. Severus b.al-Muqaffa', *History of the Patriarchs of the Coptic Church of Alexandria*, ed. with English translation by B. Evetts in *Patrologia Orientalis*, vols. 1, 5, 10 (Paris, 1904-15).

20. Michael the Syrian, *Chronique*, ed. with French translation by J. Chabot

(Paris, 1899-1900).

    21. Dionysius of Tell-Mahré, *Chronique*, in French translation by J. Chabot (Paris, 1895). See C. Cahen, 'Antagonisms Sociaux en Haute-Mesopotamie au temps des premiers Abbasides d'après Denys de Tell-Mahré' in *Arabica*, vol. 1 (1954).

SOME SUGGESTIONS FOR FURTHER READING

The political history of the early Abbasid period is comparatively little explored by modern authors, and western Orientalists, especially, have tended to concentrate on cultural and intellectual history. Although it deals only with the period to the accession of Harun, *The Abbasid Caliphate*, by F. Omar, is detailed and sound on the revolution and its aftermath. The bizarre misprints in the text should not obscure the fact that this is an important work of scholarship and essential reading for anyone who wishes to understand the period. In addition, Omar has written useful articles on the *Composition of Abbasid Support*, the *Reign of al-Mahdi* and the article *Harun al-Rashid* in the new edition of the *Encyclopaedia of Islam*. The works of M.A. Shaban provide an interesting interpretation of the period. *The Abbasid Revolution* is a detailed examination of the Khurasani background to the movement, laying stress on its Arab character, while the second volume of his *Islamic History* offers a more general discussion of the caliphate and its decline. While the present author would not accept all of Shaban's hypotheses, they are always stimulating. Mention should also be made of E. Ashtor, *Social and Economic History of the Near East*. This is an ambitious attempt to provide a summary of developments. Written by an acknowledged expert in the field, it is nonetheless easy for the general reader to approach and, while some parts may have to be revised in the light of subsequent research, it is still very valuable.

In addition to these general works, there are also a number of more specialised articles. Much of the political history of the period has been examined by what might be called 'the Italian school', that is, Francesco Gabrieli and Sabatino Moscati, details of whose works can be found in the bibliography. These articles are essentially works of source criticism, providing an outline narrative of events, with an analysis of the original accounts, useful for those wishing to study the period in more detail. The revolution has been the subject of much discussion, on which see C. Cahen, *Points de Vue sur la Revolution Abbaside*. Recently, the connection between the *Da'wa*, in Khurasan, and the Abbasid family has been re-examined by T. Nagel and M. Sharon, both of whom have challenged the traditional account.

Relations within the Abbasid family during the reign of Mansur have been examined by J. Lassner and we are promised a more general work on the politics of the period. Further details on the reigns of Mahdi, Hadi, Harun and Amin can be found in N. Abbott, *Two Queens of Baghdad*, which discusses the roles of Khayzuran and Zubayda and the family lives of the caliph. The period has also been examined from a different point of view in D. Sourdel's masterly work, *Le Vizirat Abbaside*. Full of detail, supported by meticulous scholarship, this work throws light on many aspects of Abbasid history.

Regional histories are very unevenly distributed. Iran is the best served. Both volume 4 of the *Cambridge History of Iran* and the rather more interpretive *Golden Age of Persia*, by R. Frye, are important. For the fringes of the Iranian plateau, we have C.E. Bosworth on Sistan, V. Barthold on Transoxania and M. Rekaya on the areas to the south of the Caspian, all excellent accounts. For Sind, Y. Friedmann has recently discussed the evidence and shown how very little we do know. Baghdad has been examined by G. Le Strange, who produced the maps we still rely on today, Creswell, who looks at the architecture of the Round City and, more recently, by Lassner and El-Ali. Lassner, *Topography of Baghdad*, is especially useful for the reasons for the foundation of the city, while El-Ali considers the different groups who settled there. On Iraq outside Baghdad and Syria there is virtually nothing, Egypt is covered by the dry narrative of G. Wiet, while Ifriqiya has been commented on by M. Talbi, whose main interests, however, lie outside our period.

Religious and religio-political history have received considerable attention. The best introductions are probably W.M. Watt, *The Formative Period of Islamic Thought*, and S.H.M. Jafri's *Origins and Early Development of Shi'a Islam*, but the more specialised articles by M.G.S. Hodgson and W.M. Watt should also be consulted. The religious policy of Ma'mun has been scrutinised with important results in D. Sourdel, *La Politique Religieuse*.

Finally, for those not already acquainted with it, mention must be made of the *Encyclopaedia of Islam*. This is in two editions, the old one, which is complete, and the new one, which has at present reached the letter K. This contains articles by many distinguished scholars and the student should become used to referring to it, not only for names of people and sects or groups, but also for the geographical articles, which are often the most detailed accounts available of a given area.

BIBLIOGRAPHY

Sources

'Adīm, Kamāl al-Dīn Ibn al-. *Zubdat al-halab min ta'rīkh Ḥalab*, ed.
   S. Dahhān. Damascus, 1951
Agapius of Manbij. *Kitāb al-'Unwān*, ed., with French translation,
   by A. Vasiliev in *Patrologia Orientalis*, vol. VIII. Paris, 1911
Akhbār al-'Abbas wa waladihi, ed. A.A. Dūrī and A.J.M. al-Muṭṭalibī.
   Beirut, 1971
Athīr, 'Izz al-Dīn Ibn al-. *al-Kāmil fi'l-Ta'rīkh*, ed. C.J. Tornberg.
   Leiden, 1866-71
Azdī, Abū Zakarīyā. *Ta'rīkh al-Mawṣil*, ed. A. Habibah. Cairo, 1967
Azraqī, Muhammad b.'Abd Allah. *Akhbār Makka*, ed. F. Wüstenfeld.
   Leipzig, 1858
Balādhurī, Ahmad b.Yahyā. *Ansāb al-Ashrāf*. Istanbul Manuscript
   Suleymaniye Kutuphanesi, Reisulkuttap, no. 597, vol. 1
Balādhurī, Ahmad b.Yahyā. *Futūh al-Buldān*, ed. S. Munajjid. Cairo,
   1957
Bal'amī, Abū 'Alī Muhammad. *Chronique*, trans. H. Zotenberg. Paris,
   1867-74
Bīrunī, Muhammad b. Ahmad. *Athār al-Bāqiya*, trans. H. Sachau.
   London, 1879
Dhahabī, Muhammad b.Ahmad. *Ta'rīkh al-Islām*. Cairo, 1967-9
Dīnawarī, Abū Ḥanīfa. *Akhbār al-Ṭiwal*, ed. V. Guirgass and I.I.
   Krachkovskii. Leiden, 1912
Dionysius of Tell-Mahré. *Chronique*, trans. J. Chabot. Paris, 1895
Faqīh al-Hamadhānī, Ibn al-. *Kitāb al-Buldān*, ed. M.J. de Goeje.
   Leiden, 1885
Gardīzī, 'Abd al-Ḥayy b.Daḥḥāk. *Zayn al-Akhbār*. Cambridge
   Manuscript, 213, King's College, Cambridge
Ḥamza b.Ḥasan al-Iṣfahānī. *Ta'rīkh Sinī Mulūk al-Ard*. Beirut, 1961
Idhārī, Ahmad b.Muhammad Ibn. *Bayān al-Mughrib*, vol. 1, ed. G.S.
   Colin and E. Lévi-Provençal. Leiden, 1948
Iṣfahānī, Abū'l-Faraj. *Maqātil al-Ṭalibīyīn*, ed. D.S. Saqr. Cairo, 1949

Iṣfahānī, Abū'l-Faraj. *Kitāb al-Aghānī*. Cairo, 1963

Isfandiyār, Ibn. *History of Tabaristan*, trans. E.G. Browne. London, 1905

Jāḥiz, 'Amr b.Baḥr. *Kitāb al-'Uthmānīya*, ed. A. Harun. Cairo, 1955

Jāḥiz, 'Amr b.Baḥr.'Fī Manāqib al-Turk wa 'Āmmat Jund al-Khilāfa' in *Tria Opuscula auctore Abu Othman Amr b.Baḥr al-Djahiz Basrensi'*, ed. G. van Vloten. Leiden, 1903

Jāḥiz, 'Amr b.Baḥr.'Bayān Madhāhib al-Shi'a' in *Iḥdā 'Ashrata Risāla*. Cairo, 1906

Jāḥiz, 'Amr b.Baḥr.'Faḍl Hāshim 'alā 'Abd Shams' in *Rasā'il al-Jāḥiz*, ed. H. al-Sandūbī. Cairo, 1933

Jahshiyārī, Muḥammad b.'Abdūs. *Kitāb al-Wuzarā*, ed. M. al-Saqqa *et al*. Cairo, 1938

Jahshiyārī, Muḥammad b.'Abdūs. Lost fragments of the *Kitāb al-Wuzarā*, ed. M. 'Awwād. Damascus, 1943

Khallikān, Aḥmad b.Muḥammad Ibn. *Wafayat al-A'yan*, ed. I. 'Abbās. Beirut, 1968

Khayyāt, Khalīfa Ibn. *Ta'rīkh*, ed. A. al-'Umari. Najaf, 1967

Khurdādhbih, 'Abd Allah Ibn. *Kitāb al-Mamālik wa'l-Masālik*, ed. M. de Goeje. Leiden 1889

Kindī, Muḥammad b.Yūsuf. *Kitāb al-Wulāt*, ed. R. Guest. London, 1912

Mas'ūdī, 'Alī b.al-Husayn. *Murūj al-Dhahab*, ed. C. Pellat. Beirut, 1973

Michael the Syrian. *Chronicle*, ed., with French translation, J. Chabot. Paris, 1899-1910

Muḥammad b.Habīb. *Kitāb al-Muhabbar*, ed. I. Lichtenstädter. Hyderabad, 1949

Nadīm, Muḥammad b.Isḥāq Ibn al-. *Kitāb al-Fihrist*, ed. G. Flügel. Leipzig, 1871-2

Narshakhī, Muḥammad b.Ja'far. *The History of Bukhara*, trans. R. Frye. Cambridge, Mass., 1954

Nawbakhtī, Ḥasan b. Mūsā. *Kitāb Firāq al-Shī'a*. Najaf, 1959

Nizām al-Mulk. *Siyāsatnāmeh*, ed. H. Darke. Tehran, 1962

Qudāma b.Ja'far. *Kitāb al-Kharāj*, ed. M. de Goeje. Leiden, 1889

Qutayba, 'Abd Allah b.Muslim Ibn. *Kitāb al-Ma'ārif*, ed. T. Ukasha. Cairo, 1950

Rabbihi, Aḥmad b.Muḥammad Ibn 'Abd. *'Iqd al-Farīd*, ed. A. Amīn *et al*. Cairo, 1940

Rusta, Aḥmad b.'Umar Ibn. *Kitāb al-A'lāq al-Nāfisa*, ed. M. de Goeje. Leiden, 1892

Sam'ānī, 'Abd al-Karīm b.Muḥammad. *Kitāb al-Ansāb*, ed. D.S.

Margoliouth. London, 1912

Severus b.al-Muqaffa'. *History of the Patriarchs of the Coptic Church of Alexandria*, ed. and trans. B. Evetts in *Patrologia Orientalis*, vols. I, V, X. Paris, 1904-15

Shābushtī, 'Alī b. Muḥammad, *Kitāb al-Diyārāt*, ed. G. Awād. Baghdad, 1966

Ṭabarī, Muḥammad b.Jarīr. *Ta'rīkh al-Rusul wa'l-Mulūk*, ed. M.J. de Goeje *et al.* Leiden, 1879-1901

Ta'rīkh-i Sīstān, ed. Malik al-Shu'arā Bahār. Tehran, 1935

Ṭayfūr, Ibn Abī Ṭāhir. *Kitāb Baghdad*, ed. H. Keller. Leipzig, 1908

'Uyūn wa'l Ḥadā'iq, ed. M. de Goeje. Leiden, 1869

Ya'qūbī, Aḥmad b.Abī Ya'qūb. *Ta'rīkh*, ed. M. Houtsma. Leiden, 1883

Ya'qūbī, Aḥmad b.Abī Ya'qūb. *Kitāb al-Buldān*, ed. M. de Goeje. Leiden, 1892

Yāqūt, Ya'qūb b.'Abd Allah. *Mu'jam al-Buldān*, ed. F. Wüstenfeld. Leipzig, 1886

Yāqūt, Ya'qūb b.'Abd Allah. *Irshād al-'Arīb*, ed. D.S. Margoliouth. London, 1907-27

Secondary Works

Abbott, N. *Two Queens of Baghdad.* Chicago, 1946

Adams, R. McC. *The Land behind Baghdad.* Chicago, 1965

Arendonk, C. van. *Les Debuts de l'Imamat Zaidite au Yemen.* Leiden, 1960

Arioli, A. 'La Rivolta di Abū Sarayā', *Ann. Fac. Ling. Lett. Stran. Ca' Foscari*, vol. 5, 1974

Ashtor, E. *Histoire des Prix et des Salaires dans l'Orient Medievale.* Paris, 1969

Ashtor, E. *Social and Economic History of the Near East.* London, 1976

Ayalon, D. 'The Military Reforms of al-Mu'tasim: their Background and Consequences'. Unpublished paper in the library of the School of Oriental and African Studies, London

Barthold, V. *Turkestan down to the Mongol Invasion.* London, 1928

Bosworth, C.E. *Sistan under the Arabs.* Rome, 1968

Bosworth, C.E. 'The Tahirids and Arabic Culture', *Journal of Semitic Studies*, vol. 14, 1969

Bosworth, C.E. 'The Tahirids and Persian Literature', *Iran*, vol. 7, 1969

Browne, E.G. *A Literary History of Persia*. Cambridge, 1928

Bulliet, R. *The Patricians of Nishapur*. Cambridge, Mass., 1972

Bulliet, R. *The Camel and the Wheel*. Cambridge, Mass., 1975

Cahen, C. 'Fiscalité, Antagonisms Sociaux en Haute-Mesopotamie au Temps des Premiers Abbasides d'après Denys de Tell-Mahré', *Arabica*, vol. 1, 1954

Cahen, C. 'Points de Vue sur la Revolution Abbaside', *Revue Historique*, vol. 230, 1963

Cahen, C. *Jean Sauvaget's Introduction to the History of the Muslim East: A Bibliographical Guide*. Berkeley and Los Angeles, 1965

Cambridge History of Iran, vol. 4, ed. R.N. Frye, *The Arab Invasion to the Saljuqs*. Cambridge, 1975

Caskel, W. 'Al-Uhaidir', *Der Islam*, vol. 39, 1964

Creswell, K.A.C. *Early Muslim Architecture*. Oxford, 1932-40

Crone, P. 'The Mawālī during the Umayyad Period'. Unpublished PhD thesis at the School of Oriental and African Studies, London, 1973

Dahhan, S. 'The Origin and Development of the Local Histories of Syria', in B. Lewis and P.M. Holt (eds.), *Historians of the Middle East*. London, 1962

Dennett, D.C. *Conversion and Poll-Tax in Early Islam*. Cambridge, Mass., 1950

Dunlop, D.M. *The History of the Jewish Khazars*. Princeton, 1954

Dunlop, D.M. 'Arab Relations with Tibet', *Islam Tetkikleri Enstitusu Dergisi*, 1973

Duri, A.A. *'Asr al-'Abbasi al-Awwal*. Baghdad, 1945

Duri, A.A. 'The Iraq School of History', in B. Lewis and P.M. Holt (eds.), *Historians of the Middle East*. London, 1962

El-Ali. 'The Foundation of Baghdad', in A. Hourani and S.M. Stern (eds.), *The Islamic City*. Oxford, 1970

Friedmann, Y. 'A Contribution to the Early History of Islam in India', in M. Rosen-Ayalon (ed.), *Studies in Memory of Gaston Wiet*. Jerusalem, 1977

Frye, R. 'The Role of Abu Muslim in the Abbasid Revolution', *Muslim World*, vol. 37, 1947

Frye, R. *The Golden Age of Persia*. London, 1975

Frye R. and Sayili, A.M. 'The Turks in the Middle East before the Saljuks', *Journal of the American Oriental Society*, vol. 63, 1943

Gabrieli, F. 'La Successione di Hārūn Al-Rasid e la Guerra fra Al-Amīn e Al-Ma'mun', RSO, vol. 11, 1928

Gabrieli, F. 'Al-Ma'mun e Gli Alidi', *Morgenländische Texte und Forschungen*, vol. 2, 1929

Goitein, S. 'Introduction' to vol. 5 of the *Ansāb al-Ashraf* of
Balādhurī. Jerusalem, 1938

Goitein, S. 'The Origin of the Vizirate', *Islamic Culture*, vol. 16, 1942

Graf, G. *Geschichte der Christlichen Arabischen Literatur*, vol. 2;
published as vol. 133 of *Studi e Testi*. Rome, 1947

Hodgson, M.G.S. 'How did the early Shi'a become Sectarian?' *Journal
of the American Oriental Society*, vol. 75, 1955

Ismail, O. 'Mu'tasim and the Turks', *Bulletin of the School of Oriental
and African Studies*, vol. 29, 1966

Jafri, S.M. *Origins and Early Development of Shi'a Islam*. London,
1979

Jawad, M. and Sousa, A. *Kharītah Baghdad*. Baghdad, 1958

Kaabi, M. 'Les Origines Ṭāhirides dans la Da'wa 'Abbaside', *Arabica*,
vol. 19, 1972

Lambton, A.K.S. *Landlord and Peasant in Persia*. Oxford, 1953

Lapidus, I. 'The Separation of State and Religion in the Development
of Early Islamic Society', *International Journal of Middle East
Studies*, vol. 6, 1975

Lassner, J. *The Topography of Baghdad in the Early Middle Ages*.
Wayne State, 1970

Lassner, J. 'Did the Caliph Abu Ja'far al-Manṣūr Murder his Uncle
'Abdallah b.'Ali? And Other Problems Within the Ruling House of
the Abbasids', in M. Rosen-Ayalon (ed.), *Studies in Memory of
Gaston Wiet*. Jerusalem, 1977

Le Strange, G. *Palestine under the Moslems*. London, 1890

Le Strange, G. *Lands of the Eastern Caliphate*. Cambridge, 1905

Le Strange, G. *Baghdad during the Abbasid Caliphate*. London, 1909

Lewicki, T. 'The Ibadites in Arabia and Africa', *Cahiers d'Histoire
Mondiale*, vol. 13, 1971

Margoliouth, D. *Lectures on Arabic Historians*. Calcutta, 1930

Marquet, Y. 'Le Si'isme au IXe Siècle à travers l'Histoire de
Ya'qubi', *Arabica*, vol. 19, 1972

Melikoff, I. *Abu Muslim le 'Porte-Hache' de Khorāsān*. Paris, 1962

Miguel, A. *La Geographie Humaine de Monde Musulman*. Paris, 1967

Miles, G.C. *The Numismatic History of Rayy*. New York, 1938

Minorsky, V. *A History of Sharvan and Darband*. Cambridge, 1958

Moscati, S. 'La Rivolta di 'Abd al-Gabbar contra il Califfo al-Manṣūr',
RANL, Series 8, vol. 2, 1945

Moscati, S. 'Studi sul Califatto di al-Mahdī', *Orientalia*, vol. 14, 1945

Moscati, S. 'Nuovi Studi sul Califatto di al-Mahdī', *Orientalia*, vol. 15,
1946

Moscati, S. 'Le Califat d'al-Hādī', *Studia Orientalia*, vol. 13, 1946

Moscati, S. 'Studi su Abu Muslim', RANL, Series 8, vols. 4 and 5, 1949-1950

Moscati, S. 'Il Testament di Abū Hāsim', RSO, vol. 27, 1952

Nagel, T. *Untersuchungen zur Entstehung des Abbasidischen Kalifates.* Bonn, 1972

Oates, D. *Studies in the Ancient History of Northern Iraq.* Oxford, 1968

Omar, F. 'The Composition of Abbasid Support', *Bulletin of the College of Arts, Baghdad*, vol. 2, 1968

Omar, F. *The Abbasid Caliphate.* Baghdad, 1969

Omar, F. 'Some Observations on the Reign of al-Mahdī', *Arabica*, vol. 21, 1974

Omar, F. 'Some Aspects of Abbasid-Husaynid Relations during the Early Abbasid Period', *Arabica*, vol. 22, 1975

Pellat, C. *Le Milieu Basrien et la Formation de Djahiz.* Paris, 1953

Pellat, C. *The Life and Works of Jahiz.* London, 1969

Petersen, E.L. *'Alī and Mu'awiya in Early Arabic Tradition.* Copenhagen, 1964

de Planhol, X. *Les Fondaments Geographiques de l'Histoire de l'Islam.* Paris, 1968

Rekaya, M. 'La Place des Provinces sud-Caspiennes dans l'Histoire de l'Iran', RSO, vol. 48, 1973-4

Rekaya, M. 'Mise au point sur Theophobe et l'Alliance de Babak avec Theophile', *Byzantion*, vol. 44, 1974

Rosenthal, F. *A History of Muslim Historiography.* Leiden, 1968

Sadighi, G. *Les Mouvements Religieux Iraniens au IIe et à IIIe Siècles de l'Hegire.* Paris, 1938

Sauvaget, J. *La Poste aux Chevaux dans l'Empire des Mamelouks.* Paris, 1941

Segal, J.B. 'Syriac Chronicles as Source Material for the History of Islamic Peoples', in B. Lewis and P.M. Holt (eds.), *Historians of the Middle East.* London, 1962

Shaban, M.A. *The Abbasid Revolution.* Cambridge, 1970

Shaban, M.A. *Islamic History 600-750.* Cambridge, 1971

Shaban, M.A. 'The Political Geography of Khurāsān and the East at the time of the Arab Conquest' in *Iran and Islam*, ed. C.E. Bosworth. Edinburgh, 1971

Shaban, M.A. *Islamic History 750-1050.* Cambridge, 1976

Sharon, M. 'The Abbasid Da'wa Re-examined' in *Arabic and Islamic Studies*, vol. 1. Bar-Ilan University, 1973

Sourdel, D. 'La valeur litteraire et documentaire du *Livre des Vizirs* d'al-Gahsiyari', *Arabica*, vol. 2, 1955

Sourdel, D. 'Les Circonstances du mort de Ṭāhir Ier en Khurāsan', *Arabica*, vol. 5, 1958

Sourdel, D. *Le Vizirat Abbaside*. Damascus, 1959

Sourdel, D. 'La Politique Religieuse du Calife 'Abbaside al-Ma'mūn', *Revue des Études Islamiques*, vol. 30, 1962

Sousa, A. *Faydanat Baghdad*. Baghdad, 1963

Spuler B. *Iran in Fruh-Islamischer Zeit*. Wiesbaden, 1953

Talbi, M. *L'Emirat Aghlabide*. Paris, 1966

Vajda, G. 'Les Zindiqs en Pays d'Islam au début de la periode Abbaside', RSO, vol. 17, 1938

Vanly, I.C. 'Le Deplacement du Pays Kurde vers l'Ouest', RSO, vol. 50, 1976

Vasmer R. 'Die Eroberung Ṭabaristan durch die Araber zur Zeit des Chalifen al-Manṣūr', *Islamica*, vol. 3, 1927

Veccia Vaglriei, L. 'Le Vicende del Harigismo in Epoca Abbaside', RSO, vol. 24, 1949

Waines, D. 'The Third Century Internal Crisis of the Abbasids', *Journal of the Economic and Social History of the Orient*, vol. 20, 1977

Watt, W.M. 'Shi'ism under the Umayyads', *Journal of the Royal Asiatic Society*, 1960

Watt, W.M. 'The Rafidites', *Oriens*, vol. 16, 1961

Watt, W.M. 'The Political Attitudes of the Mu'tazilah', *Journal of the Royal Asiatic Society*, 1963

Watt, W.M. 'The Re-appraisal of Abbasid Shi'ism' in *Arabic and Islamic Studies in Honour of H.A.R. Gibb*. Leiden, 1965

Watt, W.M. *The Formative Period of Islamic Thought*. Edinburgh, 1973

Wellhausen, J. *The Religio-Political Factions in Early Islam*, R.C. Ostle (ed.). Oxford, 1975

Wiet, G. *L'Egypte Arabe 642-1517*. Paris, 1937

INDEX

For the purposes of deciding alphabetical order, the definite article *al* and the words Abū (father of) and Ibn (son of) are discounted.

The system of transliteration used is essentially that of the Cambridge History of Islam.